T0327437

Elgar Research Agendas outline the future of research in a given area. Leading scholars are given the space to explore their subject in provocative ways, and map out the potential directions of travel. They are relevant but also visionary.

Forward-looking and innovative, Elgar Research Agendas are an essential resource for PhD students, scholars and anybody who wants to be at the forefront of research.

Titles in the series include:

A Research Agenda for Place Branding
Edited by Dominic Medway, Gary Warnaby and John Byrom

A Research Agenda for Social Finance
Edited by Othmar M. Lehner

A Research Agenda for Regional and Local Government
Edited by Mark Callanan and John Loughlin

A Research Agenda for Geographies of Slow Violence Making Social and Environmental Injustice Visible
Edited by Shannon O'Lear

A Research Agenda for Evaluation
Edited by Peter Dahler-Larsen

A Research Agenda for Animal Geographies
Edited by Alice Hovorka, Sandra McCubbin and Lauren Van Patter

A Research Agenda for Experimental Economics
Edited by Ananish Chaudhuri

A Research Agenda for International Business and Management
Edited by Ödül Bozkurt and Mike Geppert

A Research Agenda for International Business and Management

Edited by

ÖDÜL BOZKURT

Senior Lecturer in International Human Resource Management, Department of Management, University of Sussex Business School, UK

MIKE GEPPERT

Professor of Strategic and International Management, Friedrich Schiller University Jena, Germany

Elgar Research Agendas

Cheltenham, UK • Northampton, MA, USA

Published by
Edward Elgar Publishing Limited
The Lypiatts
15 Lansdown Road
Cheltenham
Glos GL50 2JA
UK

Edward Elgar Publishing, Inc.
William Pratt House
9 Dewey Court
Northampton
Massachusetts 01060
USA

Paperback edition 2022

A catalogue record for this book
is available from the British Library

Library of Congress Control Number: 2021935908

This book is available electronically in the **Elgar**online
Business subject collection
http://dx.doi.org/10.4337/9781789902044

ISBN 978 1 78990 203 7 (cased)
ISBN 978 1 78990 204 4 (eBook)
ISBN 978 1 0353 0902 3 (paperback)

Printed and bound by CPI Group (UK) Ltd, Croydon, CR0 4YY

Contents

Figures

Tables

Contributors

Suma Athreye (FRSA, FAcSS) is Professor of Technology Strategy at Essex Business School. Her main research interests lie in the fields of Economics of Innovation/Technology Management and International Economics/International Management. Suma has published extensively on these subjects and won several research grants for work in these areas. She currently serves as Area Editor of the *Journal of International Business and Policy* and on the Editorial Board of the academic journals *Research Policy, Industrial and Corporate Change, International Journal of Technological Learning, Innovation and Development* and *Multinational Business Review*.

Florian Becker-Ritterspach is a Professor of Economic and Organisational Sociology at the Hochschule für Technik und Wirtschaft Berlin (HTW) and acts as a founding Dean at the German International University in Cairo (GIU). He received his PhD from the University of Groningen and completed his habilitation in 2014 at the University of Potsdam. Prior to joining the HTW, he worked as a tenured Professor of International Business at the German University in Cairo (GUC) and as a tenured Assistant Professor of International Business and Management at the University of Groningen. He has also held visiting positions at the Social Science Research Centre Berlin (WZB), the Copenhagen Business School (CBS) and the Berlin School of Economics and Law (HWR). He has continually acted as convenor and organiser at international conferences and holds different editorial roles at international business journals. Next to questions of power, politics and conflict, his research focuses on multinationals in and from emerging markets. Florian has published his work in *British Journal of Management, critical perspectives on international business (cpoib), European Management Journal, International Journal of Human Resource Management, Journal of International Management, Management Learning, Management International Review* and *Organization Studies*, among others.

Ödül Bozkurt is Senior Lecturer in International Human Resource Management at the University of Sussex Business School, where she is also the Director of the Future of Work Research Hub and the Director of International Affairs. Since her PhD in Sociology at the University of California, Los Angeles, where she studied the organisation and experience of work for high-skilled professionals at the national/transnational interface in mobile telecommunications multinationals, Ödül has worked in business/management schools in the United Kingdom. She has prior degrees in Political Science and International Relations and History. She has published, with a range of co-authors, on the mobility and diffusion of staff and practices in MNEs in journals including the *Human Resource Management Journal, International Journal of HRM, Journal of World Business* and *Human Resource Management.* She is Book Reviews Editor of *Journal of International Management* and she teaches a class on Comparative Business Systems. Other teaching and research Ödül is involved in on the contemporary world of work extensively relates to the impact of international business in the broader economic, political and social spheres, and she is particularly excited about the prospects of the IB/M domain recognising its greater societal significance.

Brent Burmester studied law at New Zealand's Victoria University of Wellington and later at the University of Auckland, from which he also received a PhD in International Business. He is currently based at the University of Auckland Business School's Department of Management and International Business, and is Director of its Centre for Research on Modern Slavery. Brent's primary interest is the political character and capability of multinational enterprises, and he researches at the intersection of multiple "internationals", including business, economics, law, and politics. He is an Associate Editor of *critical perspectives on international business (cpoib).*

Jonathan P. Doh is Associate Dean of Research and Global Engagement, Rammrath Chair in International Business, Co-Faculty Director of the Moran Center for Global Leadership, and Professor of Management at the Villanova School of Business. He teaches and does research at the intersection of international business, strategic management, and corporate responsibility. Previously, he was on the faculty of American and Georgetown Universities and a trade official with the US Department of Commerce. Jonathan is author or co-author of more than 85 refereed articles, 35 chapters, a dozen teaching cases and simulations, and eight books. His articles have appeared in *AMR, AMP, BEQ, JIBS, JOM, JMS, JWB, MISQ, OS* and *SMJ,* among others. His most recent co-authored books are *Aligning for Advantage: Competitive Strategies for the Political and Social Arenas* (Oxford University Press, 2014), and *International Management: Culture, Strategy, and Behavior* (McGraw-Hill/

Irwin), which is in its 11th edition. Jonathan has presented more than 100 papers and organised or chaired for more than 35 panels at AOM, AIB, and SMS and has served these organisations in numerous leadership capacities and is an elected fellow of the Academy of International Business. He has been Associate or Consulting Editor of numerous journals and was Editor-in-Chief of *Journal of World Business* from 2014 to 2018. In January of 2020, he assumed the position of General Editor for *Journal of Management Studies*. He holds a PhD in Strategic and International Management from George Washington University.

Christoph Dörrenbächer is a Professor of Organisational Design and Behaviour in International Business at the Berlin School of Economics and Law (Department of Business and Economics), Berlin/Germany since 2010. Previously he worked as a consultant and research fellow at various organisations in Germany and abroad, including the Social Science Research Centre, Berlin and the University of Groningen, the Netherlands. Visiting appointments were with the United Nations Centre on Transnational Corporations (New York), the Central European University (Budapest) and the Manchester Metropolitan University. He holds a PhD from the Faculty of Social Sciences of the Free University, Berlin. His research focus is on critical international business, power and politics in multinational corporations as well as on industrial relations, headquarters–subsidiary relationships and careers in multinational corporations. He has published widely in renowned international academic journals including *The British Journal of Management, International Business Review, International Journal of Management Reviews, Journal of World Business, Organization Studies, Management International Review* and *Journal of International Management*. He currently serves as co-editor-in-chief of the journal *critical perspectives on international business (cpoib)*.

Lukas Ellermann received a BA in the company-linked (dual) Bachelor Program "Business Administration" at the Berlin School of Economics and Law. Major research interests comprise supply chain management and modern slavery. He is currently working as a Commercial Project Manager at Siemens AG, handling projects for the water, food and beverage, and automobile industries.

Khaled Fourati is an academic practitioner with over ten years' experience in the design and implementation of multi-country projects aiming at fostering inclusive digital economies in emerging markets. He is a Research Associate at the Gordon Institute of Business Science, University of Pretoria. He is actively participating in the development of a sustainable food system with a particular interest in plant-based, foodtech, and cellular agriculture. He is the Founder and Managing Director of Joyvigo, a plant-based cultured dairy alternative start-up focusing on digestive health and dietary lifestyles. Khaled received his DBA, International Business, from the Gordon Institute of Business Science, University of Pretoria.

Mike Geppert received his PhD in Sociology from the Humboldt University of Berlin in 2000, followed by about fourteen years' work at business schools of British universities at Swansea, Queen Mary and Surrey. He has also been a visiting professor at several universities in Australia, Brazil, Denmark, Finland, Ireland, Israel, the Netherlands, Russia and the USA. Currently Mike works as Professor of Strategic and International Management at the Friedrich Schiller University in Jena (Germany). His main research focus is on socio-political issues and sensemaking within multinational companies, and on cross-national comparisons of management, organisation and employment and industrial relations of firms situated in various industrial sectors. Mike serves at the editorial boards of several journals. His work has been published in journals such as *British Journal of Management, critical perspectives on international business (cpoib), European Journal of Industrial Relations, German Journal of Industrial Relations, Human Relations, International Journal of Human Resource Management, International Journal of Management Reviews, Journal of East European Management Studies, Journal of International Management, Journal of Management Studies, Management International Review* and *Organization Studies.*

Verena Girschik is Assistant Professor of CSR, Communication, and Organisation at Copenhagen Business School. Her research focuses on the responsibilities of multinational companies in the contexts of complex societal problems and humanitarian crises. Zooming in on the relations between companies, governments, NGOs, and other societal actors, she explores how companies negotiate their roles and responsibilities, how they perform them, and with what consequences. Her research has been published in *Journal of Management Studies, Human Relations, Business & Society,* and *critical perspectives on international business (cpoib).*

Edward Granter is a Senior Lecturer (Associate Professor) in Organisational Behaviour at the University of Birmingham, UK. His research focuses on the sociology of work (both as a discipline and empirically), and the Critical Theory of Adorno, Horkheimer and Marcuse. On the former he has published books including *The SAGE Handbook of the Sociology of Work and Employment* (with Edgell and Gottfried) and the textbook *The Sociology of Work and Employment* (with Edgell, also SAGE). On the latter, he has written various book chapters on Critical Theory at the request of editors such as Paul Adler and Stewart Clegg. He has written on extreme work for *Organization* and *Work, Employment & Society,* on totalitarianism and Critical Theory for

Management Learning, on the theory of the society of rackets for *Competition & Change*, and on digital nomads for *New Technology Work & Employment*. He is the author of *Critical Social Theory and the End of Work* (Routledge, 2009) which anticipated current debates around automation and the future of work.

Jasper Hotho is Associate Professor of International Business at the Department of International Economics, Government and Business at Copenhagen Business School, and a Senior Editor for the journal *Organization Studies*. His research focuses on the opportunities and complications that arise from private sector involvement in the delivery of humanitarian assistance.

Leo McCann is Professor of Management at the University of York. His research and teaching focuses on globalisation, the sociology of professional work, and on management and organisational history. He is the author of *Managing in the Modern Corporation* (Cambridge University Press), *International and Comparative Business* (Sage) and *A Very Short, Fairly Interesting, and Reasonably Cheap Book about Globalization* (Sage). He is the co-editor in chief of *Competition and Change*, the critical journal of political economy, globalisation and financialisation. Research articles by Leo and his co-authors have appeared in journals such as *Journal of Management Studies, Work, Employment & Society, Organization Studies* and *Human Relations*. He is currently working on an archival history project about management and managerialism in major US and global organisations during the Kennedy-Johnson era.

Ursula Mense-Petermann is Professor of Economic Sociology and the Sociology of Work at Bielefeld University, Germany. Formerly, she held a Chair in Sociology at the Business and Management Department of Klagenfurt University, Austria. Her research interests include micro-politics, sensemaking and inter-cultural encounters in MNCs, and she has published the respective research in journals such as *Journal of International Management* and *Competition & Change*. A particular focus of her recent MNC-related projects was on China as a host country for German MNCs, and on Chinese MNCs investing in Germany. A second research focus is on transnational labour markets, and she has investigated highly-skilled as well as low-skill mobility for work. She is a co-author of *Expatriate Managers: The Paradoxes of Working and Living Abroad* (Routledge), and has published articles on Eastern European meatpackers working in the German meat industry in *Global Networks* and the *Journal of Industrial Relations*.

Giulio Nardella is a Lecturer in Strategy and Responsible Business at Loughborough University, School of Business and Economics, UK. Dr

Nardella's main research interests lie in the study of corporate irresponsibility and organisational reputation. His research uses behavioural perspectives to explore the mechanisms by which corporate social irresponsibility behaviour is socially regulated, as well as the subsequent financial impacts of irresponsible corporate conduct. To date, his research has been published in journals such as the *Journal of World Business* and *British Journal of Management*. His research has won multiple awards at conferences such as Academy of Management and British Academy of Management.

Rajneesh Narula is the John H. Dunning Chair of International Business Regulation at the Henley Business School, University of Reading, UK. His research and consulting have focused on the role of multinational firms in development, innovation and industrial policy, R&D alliances and outsourcing. He has published over 100 articles and chapters in books on these themes. He is an editor of *Journal of International Business Studies*. He holds honorary appointments at United Nations University-MERIT, Norwegian School of Business, Oxford University and the University of Urbino.

Niina Nummela is a Professor of International Business at the Turku School of Economics at the University of Turku, Finland and holds a Visiting Professorship at the University of Tartu, Estonia. Her areas of expertise include international entrepreneurship, cross-border acquisitions, and research methods. She has published widely in academic journals (including *Journal of International Business Studies*, *Journal of World Business*, *International Business Review* and *Management International Review*) and contributed to several internationally published books, also as an editor. She has also co-edited special issues for journals and she has several years of editorial experience (*International Small Business Journal*, *Journal of International Business Studies*, for example). In a recent bibliometric analysis, she was ranked among the 30 most impactful scholars in the international entrepreneurship field.

Roger Strange is Professor of International Business at the University of Sussex Business School, UK. His current research focuses on four main areas of international business: the reasons for, and the implications of, the growing trend towards the externalisation of production in global value chains; the effects of corporate governance factors on foreign direct investment decisions; the determinants of MNE subsidiary location, and the effects of location on firm competitiveness; and the impact of new digital technologies on international business theory and practice. He is a former President of the European International Business Academy (EIBA). He is the author/editor of 14 books, and over 90 journal articles and book chapters. His work has been published in journals such as *Journal of International Business Studies*, *Journal of World*

Business, International Business Review, Management International Review and *Journal of Management Studies.*

Irina Surdu is an Associate Professor of International Business Strategy at Warwick Business School, University of Warwick, UK. Her current research agenda focuses on the international growth and subsequent investment strategies of multinational enterprises, with a particular interest in the exit and re-entry behaviours of these firms. Her research has appeared in journals such as *Journal of International Business Studies, Journal of World Business, International Business Review, Journal of International Management* and *British Journal of Management.* Over the last few years, this research has won multiple awards at conferences such as Academy of Management, Academy of International Business UK-I, British Academy of Management and European International Business Academy. She has previously worked as a Lecturer at Henley Business School, University of Reading and remains a member of the John H. Dunning Centre for International Business. She is currently an Associate Editor of *Multinational Business Review* and part of the Editorial Board of *Journal of International Business Studies.*

Brian Wierman is an independent scholar, consultant and US Marine. His current scholarship investigates "alternative" organisational structures, and their influence on culture and management. He is pursuing his doctorate through the University of Manchester (UK). Brian consults with organisations in Utah and Europe, and teaches MBA and undergraduate business courses at Westminster College in Salt Lake City, and Kent State, in Kent, Ohio. In his military capacity, he is a strategic planner for the US Joint Staff at the Pentagon.

Peter Zettinig, DSc, is University Research Fellow and adjunct Professor in International Business at the University of Turku, Finland. He has previously worked as Senior Lecturer and International Business Program Director at Victoria University of Wellington in New Zealand. Peter's research focuses on phenomena related to international business strategies, their organisational and inter-organisational consequences and the management thereof. His research has been published in peer-reviewed journals such as *Organizational Dynamics, Foresight, Thunderbird International Business Review, European Management Journal, Journal of Cross-Cultural Management, critical perspectives on international business (cpoib), European Journal of Innovation Management, Journal of Teaching International Business* and *Competitiveness Review.* Peter has been leading a number of industry projects, most recently related to ecosystem level strategising in shipbuilding and maritime firms and for the Finnish State's Export Credit Agency.

Acknowledgements

The present book was made possible by the nineteen academics from seven countries in four continents who joined us in the endeavour to "think out of the box" about how we can re-energise and revive the research agenda in International Business and Management. Thus, our first and foremost thanks go to all of our authors, who saw this project come to fruition.

Secondly, we are grateful to all the participants – Suma Athreye, Jonathan P. Doh, Ans Kolk and Roger Strange – who took part in the panel "International Business Studies at a crossroads?", which we organised at the Academy of International Business – UK & Ireland Chapter Conference at the University of Sussex in April 2019. The panel and the conversations it generated proved to be the kick start for our book project. Thirdly, we extend sincere thanks to the Ernst Abbe Foundation in Jena, which kindly supported us to get together at the Friedrich Schiller University Jena in March 2020, where we discussed the first chapter drafts. Fourthly, we would like to express our appreciation of the kind gesture by Jeff Desjardins of the Visual Capitalist website for giving us the permission to use one of their impactful visuals in Chapter 4. Finally, we would like to acknowledge Rachel Downie and Francine O'Sullivan at Edward Elgar Publishing, who provided us with the opportunity to engage in this important debate by inviting us to pursue this exciting book project, and who were always there when we needed support and guidance.

We cannot name everyone who supported us in our project journey. However, we owe a particular debt of gratitude to Sarah Bützler, whose meticulous attention to detail and superb professionalism made the often frustrating processes of nitty gritty format-editing and proof-reading in the final preparation of a manuscript one of the smoothest experiences of this kind we have ever had and also to Christoph Dörrenbächer, who provided very helpful comments on an early draft of our introductory chapter.

1. A Research Agenda for International Business and Management: the promises and prospects of thinking outside the box

Mike Geppert and Ödül Bozkurt

1.1 Introduction

Over the past two decades there has been no shortage of reflective commentary on the state of research in International Business and Management (IB/M)[1] or of efforts to identify what needs to be studied next and which avenues of research are most promising. Meta-analyses of popular themes in extant academic literature and suggestions for future IB/M research agendas are not new or uncommon (see e.g. Buckley, 1996). However, especially in the last ten years articles taking stock of the preoccupations and output of the field have become more overtly critical. From fundamentally descriptive and lightly speculative discussions about what lies ahead for IB/M in terms of focal topics and themes, reflections have moved on to pointing at a state of "crisis" in the discipline; a dead end for research and thinking. Increasingly serious, indeed disconcerted appraisals even from mainstream scholars have taken on a tone of "wake-up" calls, like that by Delios (2017), advocating not just reform but a far more comprehensive "rebirth" of the field. Leading scholars have conjoined their demands to "revitalise" the whole discipline by demanding a rethink of core theories, topics and methods, and in particular a redefinition of IB/M's remit to include the "big questions" (Buckley et al., 2017). IB/M scholars are increasingly implored to think out of the box in their future research and collectively invigorate their shared intellectual domain. These deliberations have been taking place against a backdrop of both persistence on established ways of thinking and rising concerns about disciplinary distinctiveness. On the one

1

hand, an institutional infrastructure of IB/M comprising disciplinary associations, conferences and journals of prestige remains formative of the scholarly community and indeed its internal power dynamics and hierarchies. On the other hand, it is argued that "IB scholars' disciplinary identity is on the block" (Michailova and Tienari, 2014: 52). Old friends of the field in economics and strategy have for some time been seen as "major competitors" (Shenkar, 2004) increasingly encroaching or even usurping the disciplinary domain.

Here our volume comes into play. We are interested in what such out of the box type of research could be, what it might look like and what it will involve doing. When starting the journey of our book project, we asked all contributors and our commentator to draw on their specific expertise and recent research to reflect more broadly on which directions they felt future IB/M research needs to move in. We invited authors from among the most established names in IB/M, and also scholars who probe a range of issues directly linked to international business and management activity in related disciplines including strategy, sociology and political science. By bringing together scholars of varying levels of embeddedness in the academic field of IB/M in this small sandpit, we responded to the repeated calls for bringing diverse voices into the discussion and avoiding identikit thinking. The book shares our authors' thoughts on how they see IB/M as a discipline moving in the future and their suggestions for how that path may best be charted.

In this introductory chapter we provide an overview of the context for the ensuing discussion. First, we summarise what mainstream IB/M scholars have identified as the key problems of the field, why some of them have seen it to be in crisis and the kind of research agendas they have proposed for future studies. Next, we consider the overtures for closer engagement with research from the growing sphere of "critical perspectives on IB" and the suggestions generated from this perspective towards making the whole field more critically reflective and relevant (again). Having set the background scene, we turn to the ten substantive contributions and the subsequent commentary chapter of this volume. We introduce each chapter by briefly characterising the contents and drawing out the recommendations they put forth for a future research agenda in IB/M.

1.2   The perpetual crisis of IB/M and proposals from the mainstream

International Business (IB) emerged as a distinct academic field in the post-war era, particularly coming into its own amidst the boom of advanced Western economies and the international business activity linked with that context, in the mid-1950s (Engwall et al., 2018: 1080). Research from this initial self-consolidation period has focused on and still largely concentrates on economics-based accounts aiming to explain a rather limited number of key issues and foremost international trade, foreign direct investment (FDI) and, with the most emphasis, the emergence, role and function of the multinational enterprise (MNE) as a tool for internationalisation. Later on a big "M" for "Management" has been added to studies in IB after the field started to open up to research from management and organisation studies. This stream of research developed largely parallel to mainstream IB, with a strong functionalist bias in the study of the MNE (Ghoshal and Westney, 1993). The field also began to engage in the study and comparison of small and medium-sized international businesses, in addition to the large MNEs that had in earlier years been the rather exclusive organisational form in focus. More recently IB/M scholars have discovered the usefulness of mainstream sociological theories, and in particular comparative and neo-institutionalism as conceptual lenses for making new sense of old problems, such as home and host country-specific influences on MNEs (see e.g. Buckley, 2002; Engwall et al., 2018; Meyer and Peng, 2016).

Notwithstanding the changing contours and scope of IB/M, however, the opening up to neighbouring disciplines did not quite trigger the kind of revitalisation and engagement with new and critical conceptual ideas that figurehead scholars called and hoped for (Dörrenbächer and Geppert, 2017). Wider societal and ecological issues have hardly been considered and if so, rather reluctantly and peripherally, and just in the last decade. Whether this was due to a general disregard for the call and (international) "business as usual" being the path of least resistance for most scholars, or if there were shortcomings in the execution of attempts to truly engage with interdisciplinary insights can be debated. Regardless, from the 1990s onwards there has been a rise of depictions of the discipline in crisis. The most important problem raised has been the almost indignant persistence of the narrow focus of most IB/M studies on a limited number of issues and especially the internationalisation processes of MNEs, i.e. their strategies and structures, often through increasingly complex measures of performance based on quantitative research methods and data, the latter increasingly from third-party databases. Arguably the buckling down on the MNE may also have been aggravated by IB/M's simultaneous efforts to retain and highlight its distinctiveness as a discipline – some influential scholars explicitly making the case that sticking to what it does best constitutes the field's "comparative advantage" and that IB/M's best path forward would be to home in on its primordial question, "What determines the international success and failure of firms?" (Peng, 2004: 105).

Another – and in the field highly recognised – call by Buckley (2002) sought to strike both a self-appreciative tone by asking to reflect on the field's past achievements and a self-transformative tone by noting it was "running out of steam" and proposing major reforms. The crisis discourse in IB/M has not abated since, with many arguing that what academics are producing has increasingly become irrelevant for the real-life problems of policymakers, practitioners and citizens (see e.g. Cheng et al., 2009). Warnings follow from these observations that the outcome of the crisis may well see IB/M "decline further in impact, insight and status" (Cheng et al., 2009: 1073). In this sense, the aforementioned claim by Delios (2017) that IB/M requires nothing less than a "rebirth" is more an emphatic re-statement of long-standing views rather than an idiosyncratic intervention. He delivers the message with dramatic flair, but the concern that the field has become detached from new phenomena in the globalising world and fails to explain anything new is shared by many. The position taken here, that radical change instead of incremental reforms is needed to revitalise the field, may not be as widely shared, however. Most mainstream debates on the crisis, if they agree with the term, focus on decidedly more incremental reforms. Let's concentrate therefore on the reformist views and have a closer look at what leading scholars suggest.

First, there is an ongoing demand that IB/M studies need to go beyond the classical topics like FDI or the MNE. Accordingly, review articles in core IB/M journals propose that the work within the field needs to open up and propose a series of novel topics that a future research agenda should include. These recommendations range from focusing on security issues and risks of terrorism (see e.g. Griffith et al., 2008; Henisz et al., 2010) to the study of the impact of new technological developments and the role of Information and Communication Technologies (ICT) on internationalisation processes (see e.g. Aharoni and Brock, 2010; Engwall et al., 2018). However, the suggested novel topics for the IB/M research agenda often look random, mostly presenting the research interests of the authors of the review articles and an expression of the *zeitgeist* of popular themes, with little coherent justification establishing links to the discipline. They often seem like lists of topics seen as pressing, even "hot" at a certain moment in time, and consequently often end up without lasting effects on the research agenda.

Second, there is an ongoing call for interdisciplinarity. Classical IB/M theories and conceptual constructs are depicted as having made important contributions, but also as being too narrow for expanding the research agenda and insufficient for opening up conceptually to address "topics that matter", i.e. for contributing to an understanding of issues of immediate relevance for the world of practice. IB/M scholars are repeatedly implored to engage with research and researchers in neighbouring fields of the social sciences. Accordingly, to make sense of a complex world research has to be multidisciplinary so that multiple phenomena like cultural factors, technological advances, political, economic, organisational and managerial issues can be taken into account simultaneously (Aharoni and Brock, 2010). Interdisciplinarity is demanded not just for new theory-building and discovering new methodological approaches but also for leveraging greater research impact in the wider academic community (Buckley et al., 2017; Seno-Alday, 2010). There seems to be no shortage of ideas as to why interdisciplinarity might help revitalise theorising, research philosophy and methods. In practice, though, multidisciplinary research is rather rare in IB/M and if it takes place at all it does not necessarily lead to the outcomes that the authors advocating them may have wished for.

Third, it has also been suggested that IB/M scholars should leave their comfort zones and ask "big questions" and engage with "grand challenges" (Buckley et al., 2017) in a world becoming ever-more globalised and nationally contextualised at the same time (Witt, 2019). These demands go beyond the call for incorporating novel topics into the research agenda and for more interdisciplinarity. Rather, these other acts of reform are to follow from the recalibration of the overall ambition of the discipline and up the ante. Buckley, for so many the bellwether of the field, together with Doh and Benischke, sees the resetting of the field's horizons as a key condition for its future:

> Only if IB scholars take grand challenges seriously, accept that these phenomena are distinct, develop innovative research designs, and concede to the sometimes-equivocal nature of their findings, will they develop novel and interesting theoretical insights that are also relevant to society at large. (Buckley et al., 2017: 1061)

The "grand challenges" in question are wide and varied, aligned with urgent societal concerns, including with the gamut of "broader issues such as climate change, poverty, migration, terrorism, and infectious disease" (Buckley et al., 2017: 1046). These are far reaching aims for reforming the classical IB/M research agenda, and certainly highly ambitious. Notably, these calls for such major reforms and change have been made mainly by some of the field's most prominent figures. Many of these influential voices have been prolific contributors to the consolidation and continuity of the classical IB/M research agenda, which they now see in desperate need of reform. Leaving aside the question as to whether their omnipresence on both sides of the self-satisfaction vs. desperately-requiring-reform fence may blur the message, it remains to be seen if and how the so-far still rather structural-conservative IB/M academic community will – or can – take the advice on board and fill it with life. In our view most mainstream IB/M studies remain as they were, anchored in the economics tradition and, if going beyond, hardly questioning the rationalistic bias of core theoretical constructs and established methodological techniques. Scholars who are truly interested in reforming, revitalising and thus making their discipline more relevant again may need to think about why this does not happen despite the many highly concerned calls plus the suggestions for ways forward. There are other voices in this conversation, too, and we note some of those next.

1.3   Critical perspectives in IB/M

The rise over the past twenty years of the broader body of scholarship under the banner of "Critical Management Studies" (CMS) (Alvesson et al., 2009), characterised by an attempt to offer "a range of alternatives to mainstream management theory with a view to radically transforming management practice" (Adler et al., 2007: 1), has had little intersection with and impact on IB/M on the whole. Nonetheless, along with the calls for a revitalisation and recalibration of focus for the field by mainstream scholars, there has been a slow but clear growth of thinking, theorising and research that has come to be consolidated as "critical perspectives" in IB/M. Like all such challenger perspectives that seek to redefine a domain, this body of work includes offshoots in terms of topics and themes, as well as direct critiques of the mainstream. The matter for critical scholars seems not so much the often tiring academic debates of whether modest reforms versus radical changes in the research agenda are needed. The discontent is much more foundational and the demand for change is more central in the critical perspective. For some, critical IB/M research is in fact an overt "political project" that aims to study and, in the tradition of action research, actively address and deal with the problematic socio-economic and environmental consequences of contemporary international business activities (see e.g. Cairns, 2019).

Specific platforms, fora and outlets matter for anchoring, supporting, and legitimising bodies of research that embody certain perspectives, especially if these are shifting the disciplinary ground, and in this effort the launch of the journal *critical perspectives on international business* (*cpoib*) in 2005 merits attention. This is not to say that *cpoib* is the exhaustive manifestation of a critical approach in IB, as many critical studies on classical IB/M themes appear in high impact publications in general management or neighbouring subfields, such as *Human Relations, Journal of Management Studies* and *Organization Studies*.[2] The journal's existence, endurance, and recognition, however, clearly marks the vitality of a "critical" lens in IB/M, as it continues to evolve as new contributors come in, helping to shape the outlet's collective voice. Reflective of its position and mission, *cpoib* has repeatedly dedicated time to debates on what that might mean, from initial ambitions to offer a "new paradigm" (Cairns and Roberts, 2011: 289) on the heels of the decades that saw globalisation as ever-ascendant to directly targeting discussions in the mainstream about the shortcomings of the discipline (Roberts and Dörrenbächer, 2012: 4). Most recently the editors depict "critical IB studies" as being "concerned with the discussion of the nature and impact of international business activities" (Dörrenbächer and Gammelgaard, 2019: 239), and "objecting to the one-sidedness of managerialist research", situating the field firmly within the CMS mission and agenda. The "critical" is not conceived as an add-on or a complementary sideshow to the mainstream in this vision, *cpoib* having been developed as a direct "counter-reaction to mainstream IB" by addressing omitted themes and missing theoretical perspectives (Dörrenbächer and Gammelgaard, 2019: 241).

A systematic review of the body of research that has been consolidated in critical IB/M around the specific platform of the *cpoib* has revealed five salient thematic areas: positioning critical international business research, postcolonial international business studies, effects of international business activities, financialisation and the global financial crisis, and "black international business" and corporate social responsibility (Dörrenbächer and Gammelgaard, 2019: 243). Both in terms of authorship and thematic foci, the journal's endeavour of "challenging the orthodox" (Roberts and Dörrenbächer, 2014, 2016) has yielded a body of research that spends a fair amount of effort on self-reflection, but also one which offers both studies of topics neglected by the mainstream and framing widely studied topics in new, different ways.

Beyond the reshuffling of research topics and themes and the reframing of questions and priorities, the critical perspective offers a fundamental sensibility that diverges from the recent reincarnations of the mainstream in the field. In Cairns' words, this pertains to a foundational recognition that "international business is a political project, with important social and economic implications" (Cairns, 2019: 269) and an aspiration for the field to be "a political and social project for change to what can be, not an academic exercise in observing, measuring and reporting what is" (Cairns, 2019: 269). Such an orientation had indeed been integral to some of the earliest examples of the IB/M canon. Most notably Hymer (1979) applied Marxist theory to his depiction of the MNE, which mainstream IB/M drew on extensively. The gap between the approaches appears to have become harder to bridge, with most efforts from the mainstream remaining largely reformist and incremental whilst the critical IB/M perspective demands a radical, systematic overhaul of the research agenda of the field. In our view the latter does not involve a wholescale abandonment of established mainstream IB research themes, but rather more openness for critical approaches and reflective forms of theorising in the tradition of critical thinking. Indeed, one wonders why critical perspectives have so far had only limited impact on IB/M generally, since many of the disciplinary reorientation prompts offered up by the critical agenda in fact align closely with the more intramural misgivings of the mainstream. We next look at several obstacles that stymie the fruitful and, as agreed by all sides, needed, transformation of the field and the opening up of an invigorated future research agenda.

1.4   Obstacles to overcome and thinking outside the box

As academics whose research in the IB/M domain draws on organisation studies, economic sociology, and the sociology of work, the merits of cross-disciplinary curiosity are obvious to us and the failure of mainstream and critical IB/M communities to speak to each other striking. This is especially so given the extent of overlap in the calls for attention to themes by scholars from both orientations (Dörrenbächer and Gammelgaard, 2019: 253). Indeed, a small number of scholars have been able to claim space and voice their views in journals and platforms visible and attended by others from both critical and mainstream approaches, but by all measures cross-fertilisation remains difficult and extremely limited. Cairns (2019: 264) even ponders whether IB/M "deserves" the dismissal by critical management studies scholars who see more potential for transforming the core debates in other subfields such as organisation studies, human resource management, or even strategy, but think the critical project in IB/M is hopeless in terms of having a real impact.

The mainstream does not bear the title without a reason: it is the dominant, indeed often the hegemonic framing of IB/M and it has institutional, social and intellectual consolidation, legitimacy and momentum. It also claims a far greater segment of the "workforce" that produces the IB/M scholarship, working according to its principles and rules. With these inevitably come entrenched hierarchies of knowledge and methodologies, reflected in the unease with which even IB and IM relate to one another as disciplinary fields and groups of scholars, with the former typically claiming more weight and status even if implicitly. A degree of alignment in any disciplinary community propels collective knowledge generation by providing a critical mass of curiosity and scholarship around certain key themes and research agendas, but too much closure renders the collective unable to renew itself. In particular, we find that three key obstacles limit the promise of most of the reformist, mainstream calls for dealing with the crisis in the field.

Firstly, we observe that the specific treatment of proposals for "theory development" take a certain approach to what is meant by "theory", one which continues to take as the main referent the delimited version of IB/M predicated on the centrality of the MNE, its internationalisation and an economistic explanation of everything entailed therein. While this theory may offer avenues of exploration yielding novel insights, we would argue that any significant theoretical reinvigoration of the field will need to think of Theory with a capital T, and dare to seek more substantial breaks from "establishment IB/M".[3]

Secondly, theoretical calcification is closely intertwined with epistemological and hence also methodological single-mindedness, all the way to the tipping point into solipsism. A brief glance over key conferences and journals in the field will confirm that there is more than a faint suggestion that IB/M may be encroaching on such intellectual territory. It is widely known and curiously just as widely accepted that methodologically the field has become increasingly more quantitative, at the expense especially of in-depth qualitative research which, even though it has produced some of the most significant milestones of the discipline, remains at the periphery. The quantitative techniques applied in the field have become more sophisticated than ever before, fed and fuelled as they are by the availability and promises of large data sets, almost exclusively compiled and offered for purchase through software packages and subscriptions by third parties. Anecdotally, it is increasingly less common to find the IB/M scholar who collects their own primary, customised data. Methodologies help us generate insights not in terms of their pure qualities but by how appropriately they are used and applied to the relevant research questions. We take the risk of research becoming data-driven, as opposed to generating the data its questions demand. The latter has become a particularly important problem in the field.

Thirdly, we note the implications of the calls for reform or for revolution for expectations that scholars will rise to the challenge of being reformers and revolutionaries. Who, specifically, are we counting on to overhaul, reimagine and revamp the IB/M agenda, rendering it exciting, insightful and perhaps most importantly, relevant beyond the confines of academia and to a wide range of external stakeholders? Where will they come from? Why will they have chosen IB/M as the home for their intellectual efforts? Most calls for change currently come from established scholars, especially senior professors. They are, at least in the case of the UK, just as likely to have had their undergraduate and postgraduate training in a range of disciplines other than IB/M, including economics, sociology and other social sciences. This has presumably equipped them with broader awareness of disciplinary strengths (and limitations) on the whole. For the younger generations of scholars that have come of age in the era of the ever-ascendant Business School, it is much harder to imagine where the exposure to, let alone engagement with, some of the core paradigms, debates and theoretical frameworks of relevant related disciplines would have been possible. As the calls for multidisciplinarity, methodological pluralism and theoretical agility mount, it may ironically, if not sadly, be the case that the community of scholars expected to deliver on these are rather ill-equipped and poorly socialised to do so. Many young IB/M scholars' careers are further streamlined by the strict and increasingly standardised reward systems of Business Schools and departments, pressuring them to publish in the "top ranked" IB/M journals, which remain largely conservative in their openness for novel critical themes and methods, especially if these are not delivered with the mastery of highly experienced academics. Only this approach enables junior scholars to move up in the hierarchy of the field. The institutionalised occupational sanctions of the field go a long way in explaining why even modest calls for reforms in the field's research agenda, which largely come from senior scholars, might fall on deaf ears in the less established cohorts.

We make no mistake and note that current IB/M research is exceedingly "rigorous", but would further add that it is mainly so in its own terms. Such "rigour" is often invoked in the dismissal of the critical agenda as digressive, imprecise, even irrelevant; i.e. outside the scope of IB/M. On the other hand, some of the empirical ambition, conceptual precision and analytical leverage offered by best examples of mainstream IB/M remain underappreciated and underutilised by those adopting a critical approach. The wealth of insights the field has produced on the organisational form of the MNE and its internal workings, both theoretically and empirically, open up rather than block some of the lines of inquiry espoused by the critical perspective. Many insights generated by mainstream IB/M can be effectively utilised to tackle new questions from outside the proverbial canonical box, helping a critical understanding of a broad range of issues such as green washing, slave work in global value chains, international crime (Enderwick, 2019) and others. Whilst we cherish the value of divergent perspectives for intellectual growth, and are not proponents of the "why can't we all get along" school of anodyne, non-committal commentary, we do think there is extremely fruitful terrain to cover in IB/M by those who share the will and ability to "think outside the box" and who can remain open-minded about at least some of their theoretical convictions.

1.5   This book: looking ahead and thinking outside the box

This book aims to engage with calls from both mainstream and critical voices for a renewal and revitalisation of IB/M research by offering the space to contemplate to a diverse group of scholars. Our contributors come from various walks of IB/M life, from different persuasions, subfields of interest, disciplinary backgrounds and geographical locations – the diversity was very much intentional, though of course as always, still partial. We invited them to reflect on the state of the field and its future in an open-ended way, but did encourage them to be at their imaginative, even provocative best. After several months of gestation of initial ideas and the development of full contributions, the group had the bitter-sweet fortune of holding one of the last face-to-face meetings in March 2020 in Jena before COVID-19 stopped such academic forums. Debate was multi-directional with contributors having envisioned the research agenda for IB/M in different ways, but what they all had in common was an effort to draw on their various expertise to "think out of the box".

The eleven chapters that follow provide a range of new directions, correctives, suggestions, nudges, invitations and road maps for the future of IB/M. They have many points of intersection and could have been interwoven in myriad ways, but taken together we found them chiselling the research agenda for the field in four broad ways: revisiting core IB/M theories; contemplating the changing relationship between nation-states and MNEs; drawing attention to power and ideology in international management; and studying and theorising new phenomena. The volume is not an exhaustive grand statement prescribing a particular research agenda, but rather through these chapters we highlight and offer some of the most promising openings and opportunities for the re-energising of the field urged by all.

The three chapters of Part I revisit classical concepts of mainstream IB/M and suggest novel ways of looking at and dealing with them. The authors offer new ways of thinking out of the classical IB "toolbox" when looking at "factoryless good producers" (FGPs), which resist accurate capture within the common conceptual model of internalisation theory (Chapter 2). They also question whether core rationalistic ideas about objectivity and rationality of managerial decisions in regard of international expansions can capture the heterogeneity of observed managerial and firm behaviour (Chapter 3). Additionally, mainstream "canonical" models of internationalisation and outward FDI of emerging market MNEs are revisited and criticised for overlooking and failing to explain novel developments (Chapter 4).

Roger Strange's chapter raises the question as to whether "we need a theory of externalisation" in future studies on MNEs, and argues that this is needed because novel forms of coordination in lately evolving forms of contemporary MNEs can hardly be understood when applying some core concepts out of the IB/M toolbox. Classic IB/M theories are presented as being historically-bound. The internalisation approach is seen as having been suitable for the study of direct ownership and hierarchical MNEs in the post-war era but not when it comes to the study of evolving FGPs. FGPs are portrayed as an empirical puzzle, managing and controlling their business activities in different ways than the classic transaction-cost efficient MNE, in ways that can hardly be captured in internalisation theory-based models. In FGPs we are confronted with the ineffectiveness both of direct ownership and strict forms of hierarchical integration and this, it is argued, requires alternative ways of theorising. Accordingly, a theory of externalisation is outlined in order to shed light on newly emerging asymmetric power relations, which play an even more crucial role when it comes to the control of contract manufacturers and external suppliers. Future studies, it is concluded, need to go beyond the current focus on FGPs which originate from advanced economies though and study novel FGPs that pop up in emerging economies. In such home country contexts scholars need to be especially aware, it is further argued, of the distinct "institutional, economic and/or other characteristics of their home countries".

The next chapter by *Giulio Nardella, Rajneesh Narula and Irina Surdu* starts with a critique of the rationalistic bias in mainstream IB/M theorising. The authors point to the limits of the micro-foundations in the field which often presents the strategic choices of international managers as being objective and unilateral, without paying adequate attention to context-specific and multi-faceted aspects of real-life decision-making processes. The contributors suggest looking into the potential of behavioural concepts, such as cognitive biases, heuristics and reference points and how applying these ideas might be fruitful to enrich and complement future IB/M theorising. These critical reflections on non-rational and ex-post rationalisation of internalisation decisions lead to the authors' proposing various routes for future studies that would pursue the outlined behavioural perspective of international management. The suggested research questions focus consequently on behavioural aspects of MNE strategic choices, managerial biases and organisational behaviour, behavioural aspects of firm governance, and new methodologies. Especially the latter issue is seen as essential for "making these micro-foundational concepts actionable in international business management research". This is a focal quest which has been brought up in many chapters of our volume, and most pronounced in Chapter 11.

The final chapter in this section by *Suma Athreye* revisits established theories on internationalisation in the field and focuses especially on the conceptual limitations of the FSA/CSA (firm specific advances/country specific advances) framework. The model has been developed and tested for the study of internationalisation activities of Western MNEs. The author first shows how and why the FSA/CAS framework is ill-equipped to conceptually capture and properly explain internationalisation processes of emerging multinational enterprises (EMNEs). Based on her own and other empirical studies the author shows that EMNEs' outward investment strategies differ significantly from what established internationalisation theories would predict. Three important observations are highlighted: (a) that EMNEs were able to raise money for overseas foreign investment when it was not available in the home country, (b) that EMNEs' high growth in export volumes is closely linked with major advances in terms of trade, as illustrated by the way four BRIC country governments became major net foreign (currency) creditors, and (c) that data on millionaire migration can be linked with the role of corruption legacies in home countries, which has significantly determined the direction of outward FDI flows. Given the problems with established models the author proposes a "real option framework" which is understood as being "capable of incorporating the realities of EMNE expansion far better than the FSA/CSA framework". Finally, the crucial role of interdisciplinarity is highlighted which in the author's view needs to be on top of a future research agenda.

Chapters 5 and 6 in Part II focus on the central object of many studies in IB/M and indeed the field itself: the MNE. Both reflect on the changing relationship between the MNE and the nation-state. In the centre of interest is the question of how MNEs are linked with nation-states and other internationally operating key actors when dealing with national and transnational institutional constraints in order to enable and support thriving internationalisation activities. Chapter 5 revisits established IB/M research on the role of home country institutions and points to an important research gap when it comes to the role of specific home country measures (HCMs) provided by governments and associated actors in order to support firm internationalisation. Chapter 6 looks into the increased importance of close interactions between states and MNEs with a special interest in the role of MNE diplomacy, which has hardly been acknowledged and studied in contemporary IB/M research.

Florian Becker-Ritterspach and Khaled Fourati look anew at home country influences on internationalisation of MNEs. First, they review four established mainstream IB/M frameworks and how these have dealt with the role of the home country in firm internationalisation. Additionally, they review insights from culturalist and institutionalist, so-called country-of-origin effects studies and conclude that most of the former research has hardly paid attention to how national governments support internationalisation with concrete HCMs. For the latter, however, they especially find the growing body of studies on EMNEs relevant because this stream of research pays not just more but also more detailed attention to how home country institutions prove both enabling and constraining for the "capacity of the MNEs to access needed resources externally". They then look closer into an emerging field of study, focusing on HCMs that national governments employ to promote and support their MNEs. Accordingly, a key point of reference in the outlined research agenda is the quest for shedding more light on the antecedents, patterns and consequences of HCMs. Becker-Ritterspach and Fourati further want future researchers on HCMs to concentrate their research efforts on crucial questions like (a) how countries differ in their firm internationalisation measures, (b) how imprinting of home country institutions influences the success and failure in certain host country contexts, and (c) how the extent and willingness of home countries to provide distinct support measures abroad matter when it comes to developing the lasting competitive advantages of the MNE.

In his chapter *Brent Burmester* argues that MNEs need to continuously mediate all kinds of divides, be it social, cultural, institutional and geopolitical, which emerge between the MNE itself and other key international actors. The role of MNEs in the newly emerging international arena is seen as diplomatic because they are political actors that need to interact with other powerful international players when dealing with those increasingly complex divides, here described as "estrangements", in order to produce and reproduce a thriving "international society". The author criticises IB/M for not paying sufficient attention to these socio-political developments, despite having the MNE in the centre of interest of research since the field was established. The main reason for this neglect is seen in the narrowing of theoretical and empirical research on the economic functioning of the MNE, which has downplayed its important diplomatic role in the economy and society. The diplomatic role of MNEs is described as essential because "they, more than any other international actor, enact the totality of practices that characterise the contemporary global political economy". It is emphasised that early IB research, before the economistic turn, actually dealt with the many non-economic roles of international firms but then abandoned these interests, and thus never developed an agenda for the study of the diplomatic role of MNEs. Accordingly, the development of a research agenda for the study of MNE diplomacy is seen as overdue in IB/M, as Burmester stresses that such an endeavour would provide the opportunity to revisit insights from earlier work and combine these ideas with deep insights, developed in neighbouring subfields in the wider social sciences which have never neglected the important non-economic roles that MNEs play as international actors.

While the first two sections thereby prompt rethinking some of the best trodden ground of IB/M, the contributions in Part III are joined in calling attention to themes that the field has only sporadically engaged with, and almost always at the margins: the role and importance of power relations and ideology in international management.

In Chapter 7, *Leo McCann, Brian Wierman and Edward Granter* invite the field to "treat ideology seriously". Through a discussion of the empirical cases of two management fads, "Holacracy" and "Evolutionary Teal Organizations", they highlight how "hypermediated, 'faddish' products" like these constitute a part of international management knowledge that has so far gone under-recognised and under-researched. Their empirical examples would appear "not like IB/M" to mainstream researchers but provide astute and highly recognisable examples of management principles and aspirations that are disseminated internationally, beyond the boundaries of individual MNEs. This probe into the global circulation of business ideologies leads the team to a number of proposals for a future research agenda: a linking of IB/M with the rich knowledge on the "promotion, circulation and translation of management knowledge", the exploration of the "nature of discourses that constitute business ideology" (including in comparative perspective), the study of such ideology and knowledge production as big and growing global business itself, and attending to the "need to better understand the real-world impacts of business ideology". This is a contribution that not only challenges the hardened disciplinary boundaries of IB/M as embodied in the field's key outlets, curriculum and institutions, but which also directly confronts the national-culturalist paradigm that, in its many revised guises, still dominates international management (and especially international human resource management).

Ursula Mense-Petermann also sees power relations and the importance of conceptual repertoires in which actors understand business and management as necessary and important main arteries in the future IB/M research agenda, but draws us back into the MNE to discuss how these matter to the central

institution of the field. In particular, she notes that despite the growing literature on emerging economy multinationals (EMNEs), we still understand too
little about their internal workings, their geopolitical embeddedness, and how
these are tightly intertwined. For Mense-Petermann, research on these themes
should sidestep the mere replication of the hitherto dominant modes of inquiry
and needs to focus on the real-life practices over abstract strategy by firms,
and on the micro-political negotiations around these by actors. Specifically,
she advocates the adoption of a sensemaking approach for the recommended
integration of an understanding of actors' agency and the organisational
context. Incorporating insights from post-colonial scholarship on domination
effects, this lens could prove highly revelatory in understanding how socially
constructed hierarchical orders between cultures' identities are negotiated
and enacted inside the EMNE. Without contending with such power relations
and sensemaking, IB/M's treatment of EMNE internationalisation will remain
seriously compromised. Ethnographic research in particular promises to be
the best suited methodological tool for the task at hand. Chapter 8 concludes
with confidence that despite challenges, the scholarly community will find
ways to carry out in-depth qualitative fieldwork, as efforts will be well worth
the empirical rewards.

Finally, in Part IV our volume has three chapters that honour the calls for
revision and relevance in IB/M by engaging in the study of novel phenomena
and developing new theory to enable us to do so. Chapters 9, 10 and 11 all contribute to the revision effort by highlighting topics that are increasingly more
salient in the empirical world of IB/M, as well as offering concrete theoretical
and methodological proposals for how we can go about engaging with them.

Verena Girschik and Jasper Hotho's contribution, Chapter 9, is on the pro-
gressively more prominent roles MNEs play in societal crises today, across
a wide spectrum of situations ranging from armed conflict to humanitarian
emergencies. As we were starkly reminded in the days of the COVID-19
pandemic during which we have put this volume together, societal crises and
the need for humanitarian action they create involve not only public and third
sector organisations but also businesses, including multinationals. Girschik
and Hotho's review of extant IB/M scholarship on MNE activity in relation to
/ at times of crises highlights the complexity of this relationship and the need
to approach it with great contextual sensitivity. Drawing particularly on the
case of the shipping industry and the migration crisis in the Mediterranean
over recent years, they highlight three observations about MNE involvement
in societal crises. Taken together these observations challenge the dominant
approach in extant scholarship which reduces the explanation of MNE behaviour in face of crises to cost minimisation and/or risk avoidance, following

economistic theories of the firm. According to the authors, MNEs have other motivations in engaging or disengaging with crises beyond risk minimisation; the "conventional dependent variables" of IB research – location, investment and exit – cannot capture the highly variable ways in which MNEs (have to) respond to crises in their daily operations. Furthermore, rather than being generated solely by the external environment, societal crises are influenced and shaped by MNE activity. These are important, immediate phenomena that rightfully deserve attention in the research agenda for the field.

In Chapter 10, *Christoph Dörrenbächer and Lukas Ellermann* turn to one of "the most evil phenomena in International Business", modern slavery. Besides being an excellent example of how IB/M scholars can incorporate new empirical developments into the disciplinary domain, this contribution also demonstrates how they can do this by engaging with, rather than dismissing, previous treatments of the subject matter. Dörrenbächer and Ellermann explore the conditions that enable modern slavery first through a multidisciplinary literature review, then engaging closely with the most influential work on the topic from within business and management studies, that of Crane. Taking up the five macro-institutional contextual variables that this theory posits define the incidence of modern slavery across different economies, the authors discuss how these can be operationalised for empirical analysis that would allow comparisons. Walking us through this effort for the variables of regulatory, socio-economic, industry and geographic contexts, the chapter elaborates further on the fifth variable in Crane's theory of modern slavery – cultural context. The authors draw on the extensive, if potentially contentious, data accumulated in IB/M scholarship on the cultural context using Hofstede's theory of the six dimensions to probe cross-correlations with data on modern slavery. The conclusions are not definitive, but the chapter illustrates how the reiterative inquiry into new topics would draw on and develop data and theory from established debates in the field, and how the research agenda of the field can involve empirical studies utilising the accumulated insights of the discipline.

Novel phenomena by definition are constantly changing and the final substantive contribution in the volume, Chapter 11, offers a proposition for how IB/M can theorise unfolding empirical realities in a complex, dynamic world. *Peter Zettinig and Niina Nummela* begin by celebrating the heritage of the discipline of finding inspiration and theoretical puzzles in empirical observations, and go on to advocate a futures-oriented perspective for IB/M research to enhance its relevance and practical utility. The emphasis on the plural is intentional, indeed critical, since the authors see an alertness to emerging phenomena and to the multiple possible trajectories and outcomes in time as the lynchpin of an approach to IB/M research that will render it relevant to a variety of audiences. Recognising that "relevance" is contingent rather than fixed and self-evident, they propose theorising through "envelope" frameworks, as these can be utilised to address the issues different stakeholder groups prioritise and care about in an agile, dynamic way. For IB/M scholarship of the future, such theorising, coupled with a critical realist approach to empirical research, can afford a proactive role and legitimacy beyond the academic community, letting the field regain influence on important stakeholders. Zettinig and Nummela contend we must accept that "there is no theory of everything", but as "an integrative field of investigation dealing with complex phenomena", IB/M has a great deal to offer and a rich research agenda.

Last but not least, we invited *Jonathan P. Doh*, who has prominently contributed to calls for reform in IB/M to offer a concluding commentary on our volume's contributions. His reflections in Chapter 12 on the previous chapters, which all offer different ways of "thinking outside the box", provide an illustration of how the disciplinary conversation can be taken forward.

Notes

1. In putting together this volume we debated at length which abbreviation would be the appropriate one to use for International Business and Management, as our contributors as well as the wide range of literature we read in relation to the state of the "field" opted for different wording. In the end we decided, in line with the title of the volume, itself the outcome of an initial negotiation with our publishers, to use IB/M. All variations referring to the discipline throughout the book have been replaced by this abbreviation.
2. There have been a number of mainstream IB/M scholars who have become actively involved in the exploration of critical IB/M themes in their research in recent years and they offer important examplars. However, the impact of this kind of publication has to date remained rather limited in the core of the field.
3. Theoretical disputes between mainstream and critical scholars may therefore be not so much purely theoretically driven as fundamentally about different political understandings, triggered by a deeper discord between the two IB/M camps about whether "global capitalism" as we know it can be reformed at all or requires a radical or even revolutionary overhaul.

References

Adler, P.S., Forbes, L.C. and Willmott, H. (2007). Critical management studies. *Academy of Management Annals*, 1(1): 119–179.

Aharoni, Y. and Brock, D. (2010). International business research: Looking back and looking forward. *Journal of International Management*, 16(1): 5–15.

Alvesson, M., Bridgman, T. and Willmott, H. (Eds) (2009). *The Oxford Handbook of Critical Management Studies*. Oxford: Oxford University Press.

Buckley, P. (1996). The role of management in international business theory: A meta-analysis and integration of the literature on international business and international management. *Management International Review*, 36: 7–54.

Buckley, P. (2002). Is the international business research agenda running out of steam? *Journal of International Business Studies*, 33: 365–373.

Buckley, P., Doh, J. and Benischke, M. (2017). Towards a renaissance in international business research? Big questions, grand challenges, and the future of IB scholarship. *Journal of International Business Studies*, 48(9): 1045–1064.

Cairns, G.M. (2019). Critical engagement in international business: Creating meaning for a broad constituency. *critical perspectives on international business*, 15(2/3): 262–272.

Cairns, G. and Roberts, J. (2011). Reflections on seven years of critical perspectives on international business. *critical perspectives on international business*, 7(4): 289–296.

Cheng, J.L.C., Henisz, W.J., Roth, K. and Swaminathan, A. (2009). Advancing interdisciplinary research in the field of international business: Prospects, issues and challenges. *Journal of International Business Studies*, 40(707): 1070–1074.

Delios, A. (2017). The death and rebirth (?) of international business research. *Journal of Management Studies*, 54(3): 391–397.

Dörrenbächer, C. and Gammelgaard, J. (2019). Critical and mainstream international business research. *critical perspectives on international business*, 15(2/3): 239–261.

Dörrenbächer, C. and Geppert, M. (2017). Multinational corporations and organization theory: An introduction to post-millennium perspectives. In C. Dörrenbächer and M. Geppert (Eds), *Multinational Corporations and Organization Theory: Post Millennium Perspectives* (Vol. 49). Bingley: Emerald Publishing, 3–42.

Enderwick, P. (2019). Understanding cross-border crime: The value of international business research. *critical perspectives on international business*, 15(2/3): 119–138.

Engwall, L., Pahlberg, C. and Persson, O. (2018). The development of IB as a scientific field. *International Business Review*, 27(5): 1080–1088.

Ghoshal, S. and Westney, D.E. (1993). *Organization Theory and the Multinational*. New York: St. Martin's Press.

Griffith, D., Tamer Cavusgil, S. and Xu, S. (2008). Emerging themes in international business research. *Journal of International Business Studies*, 39(7): 1220–1235.

Henisz, W., Mansfield, E. and Von Glinow, M. (2010). Conflict, security, and political risk: International business in challenging times. *Journal of International Business Studies*, 41(5): 759–764.

Hymer, S.H. (1979). *The Multinational Enterprise: A Radical Approach*. Cambridge: Cambridge University Press.

Meyer, K. and Peng, M. (2016). Theoretical foundations of emerging economy business research. *Journal of International Business Studies*, 47(1): 3–22.

Michailova, S. and Tienari, J. (2014). What's happening to international business? University structural changes and identification with a discipline. *critical perspectives on international business*, 10(1/2): 51–64.

Peng, M.W. (2004). Identifying the big question in international business research. *Journal of International Business Studies*, 35(2): 99–108.

Roberts, J. and Dörrenbächer, C. (2012). The futures of critical perspectives on international business. *critical perspectives on international business*, 8(1): 4–13.

Roberts, J. and Dörrenbächer, C. (2014). Challenging the orthodox: A decade of critical perspectives on international business. *critical perspectives on international business*, 10(1/2): 2–20.

Roberts, J. and Dörrenbächer, C. (2016). Renewing the call for critical perspectives on international business: Towards a second decade of challenging the orthodox. *critical perspectives on international business*, 12(1): 2–21.

Seno-Alday, S. (2010). International business thought: A 50-year footprint. *Journal of International Management*, 16(1): 16–31.

Shenkar, O. (2004). One more time: International business in a global economy. *Journal of International Business Studies*, 35(2): 161–171.

Witt, M.A. (2019). De-globalization: Theories, predictions, and opportunities for international business research. *Journal of International Business Studies*, 60: 1053–1077.

PART I

Revisiting core IB/M theories

2. Do we need a theory of externalisation?

Roger Strange

2.1   Introduction

Recent years have witnessed the proliferation of *factoryless goods producers* (FGPs) in the contemporary global economy (Bayard et al., 2015; Bernard and Fort, 2015; Coyle and Nguyen, 2019; Fontagné and Harrison, 2017; Kamal, 2018; Morikawa, 2016). Such FGPs have externalised (outsourced) the production activities within their global value chains (GVCs) to independent contract manufacturers.[1] Typically, such FGPs only undertake selected pre-production (e.g. design, R&D, engineering) and/or post-production (e.g. sales, marketing, distribution) activities. Notable examples include Apple (Dedrick et al., 2010; Denicolai et al., 2015), Dyson (Bernard and Fort, 2015), Nike (Donaghu and Barff, 1990), Nokia (Ali-Yrkkö et al., 2011) and Uniqlo (Usui et al., 2017), but there is evidence of the substantial externalisation of production activities to contract manufacturers worldwide across a range of industrial sectors including garments, footwear, toys, electronics, pharmaceuticals, and automotive components. UNCTAD (2011: 133) estimated that contract manufacturing activities employed more than 13 million workers worldwide in 2010, mostly in emerging and developing economies. These activities generated more than $750 billion sales.[2]

Aggregate data on the scale of the FGP phenomenon are piecemeal, for reasons which will be discussed later in this chapter. Some authors have attempted to provide estimates for individual countries, though these are typically partial and dated. Bernard and Fort (2015: 521) estimated that the number of FGPs in the United States was 13,500 in 2007, and that these FGPs employed over 672,000 workers. Important sectors were pharmaceuticals, apparel and electronics. Furthermore, the importance of FGPs had risen substantially since 1992 when the corresponding figures were 4,900 firms and 285,000 workers.

The number of FGPs rose further to 16,500 by 2016 (Kamal, 2018). Morikawa (2016) reports that there were 2,688 FGPs in Japan in 2013, employing over 1.1 million workers. Coyle and Nguyen (2019) estimate that 1 million people were employed by FGPs in the UK in 2016. Important sectors were chemicals and pharmaceuticals, biotechnology, and electronics.

The aggregate data above focus on employment within FGPs, but the influence of FGPs is much broader and more geographically dispersed. The scope and nature of the FGP business model is well illustrated by the case of the US footwear and apparel firm, Nike. In November 2019, Nike employed 76,700 employees worldwide mostly in product design and development, marketing, distribution and sales. Nike has for many years outsourced the production of its footwear and other goods to contract manufacturers: this production was undertaken in 533 factories located in 41 countries and employing 1.16 million, with materials provided by another 78 facilities in 11 countries.[3] Many of the factories are located in Vietnam, China and Indonesia, and no single factory accounts for more than 10 per cent of total Nike output. The finished products are shipped to 6 US and 67 overseas distribution centres worldwide, and thence to retailers. Three points are worth emphasising at this stage: many more people are employed in the Nike GVC than are employed directly by Nike itself; the raw material and labour costs involved in the production of Nike footwear typically account for less than 50 per cent of the retail price (Bissell-Linsk, 2017); and Nike's major suppliers also do business with other shoe and apparel makers, including New Balance, Adidas, and Puma.

The objective of this chapter is to provide a theoretical explanation for the existence of FGPs as organisational forms where lead firms (Apple, Dyson, Nike, Nokia, etc.) have externalised the production activities within their GVCs,[4] yet are still able to exert control over these production activities without direct ownership. Control is the key issue. Internalisation theory provides a compelling explanation for the conditions under which it will be optimal for lead firms to bring geographically dispersed GVC activities under common ownership (and hence control), and hence for the existence of the integrated multinational enterprise (MNE). Internalisation theory would predict that FGPs will exist when it is more efficient for lead firms to outsource the production activities to contract manufacturers and to coordinate these activities through arm's length contractual arrangements which specify the obligations of each party. Such legal contracts do provide a degree of control, but also suffer from a number of well-recognised shortcomings that limit their efficacy. First, contracts are, by nature, incomplete (Grossman and Hart, 1986) and cannot cover all possible future contingencies, including the contract manufacturer developing and selling "similar" products to other buyers. Second, contracts for know-how and other intangible assets suffer from moral hazard in that, once provided by the FGP, the know-how cannot be "unlearned" by the contract manufacturer. Contract manufacturers may only respect and renew the contracts with their FGPs if the ongoing benefits arising from the relationship outweigh the potential benefits of selling their output to alternative customers. Third, many contract manufacturers are hosted by countries where the legal enforceability of contracts is weak (World Bank, 2020; World Justice Project, 2019; Zhou and Poppo, 2010). A contract is only as effective as the legal institutions that support the effective implementation of contract law.

In this chapter, we advance a theory of externalisation that explains how FGPs are able to reap the efficiency benefits of outsourcing their production activities whilst at the same time maintaining tight control over their organisationally fragmented GVCs through the possession of key isolating mechanisms (Rumelt, 1984, 1987). Such mechanisms may take many forms including *inter alia* formal property rights, firm-specific technical and/or marketing capabilities, and multinationality. We outline this theory of externalisation in the next section, before going on to consider some of the conceptual and practical implications of the growing FGP phenomenon.

2.2   A theory of externalisation

Any production process may be depicted schematically as a value chain linking the inputs to the delivery of the final output to the customer (see Figure 2.1). The lead firms typically purchase raw materials, parts and components from independent suppliers, which they combine with their own distinctive intangible assets in product design, process engineering, R&D, and technological know-how. These pre-production activities feed into a range of production activities that generate a series of intermediate goods and/or services that are subsequently assembled into the finished manufactured products. These products are then branded, promoted, sold and distributed to the final customers as part of the post-production activities, after which firms often provide a range of after-sales services (e.g. systems integration, maintenance, training, accessory sales) as part of what has been termed the servitisation of business (Vandermerwe and Rada, 1988). Value is created at each stage in this process, though how much value is created by each activity and by whom it is captured are issues to which we return below. These activities may all be located in one country, but often the activities are located in different countries hence the value chains are GVCs.

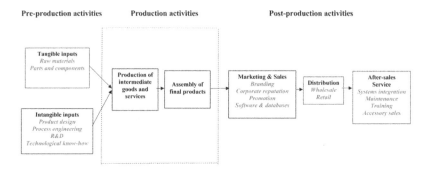

Figure 2.1   A typical global value chain

Now there are many good reasons why firms might choose to integrate these pre-production, production, and post-production activities under common ownership. Vertical integration may *inter alia* improve scheduling and coordination; eliminate imperfect competition in upstream markets; facilitate investments in specialised assets, so protecting product quality and proprietary technology and avoiding opportunistic recontracting; allow price discrimination; and increase bargaining power vis-à-vis buyers and suppliers (Strange and Magnani, 2018). The benefits of the cross-border integration of GVCs have typically been explored though the lens of internalisation theory (Buckley and Casson, 1976; Hennart, 1982; Rugman, 1981). Internalisation theory highlights the relative costs and benefits of coordinating geographically dispersed activities within GVCs internally by the management of a firm rather than externally through the market, and provides a parsimonious explanation for the existence of MNEs as the most efficient governance solution.[5]

The internalisation of GVC activities also provides direct control not only over the activities, but also over the associated flows of knowledge. But the GVCs of many manufactured products are not fully integrated.[6] In the case of FGPs, all the production activities are externalised to one or more contract manufacturers (see Figure 2.2) who may be located in the same country, or overseas. The contract manufacturers purchase raw materials, parts and components from independent suppliers, and transform them into finished products using proprietorial designs, specifications and possibly technological know-how provided by their FGP. In return, the FGP pays a processing fee[7] to their contract manufacturers to compensate them for their purchases of tangible inputs and the remuneration of their employees, and takes ownership of the finished goods. The FGP then brands, promotes, sells and distributes the product to the final customers. The GVCs thus involve intra-firm flows not only of physical products, but also flows of finance and of intellectual property embodied in intangible assets.

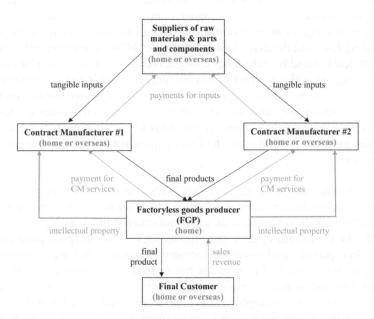

Figure 2.2   The global value chain of a factoryless goods producer

An internalisation theory of FGPs might simply conclude that conditions must now be such that a market-based mechanism (i.e. the externalisation of the production activities) is more efficient than a hierarchical solution (the MNE). The extant literature has highlighted various explanations for why and how FGPs may favour outsourcing to reduce production costs relative to the costs of undertaking activities in-house (Strange and Magnani, 2018). One popular explanation is that FGPs externalise activities in order to focus on their core competencies, and thus economise on their scarce financial and managerial resources. Such core competencies represent the collective learning in the FGP, especially how to integrate multiple streams of technological and managerial competencies to enable individual firms to adapt quickly to changing opportunities, and form the basis of competitive advantage. There are, however, both conceptual and practical difficulties in actually specifying which activities are core (and thus should be internalised) and which activities are non-core (and thus may be usefully externalised). A second popular argument highlights the exploitation of learning opportunities and knowledge complementarities resulting from integration with independent agents in intermediate markets, in what has been termed strategic outsourcing. The emphasis is on the maximisation of value generated in the value chain, instead of on the minimisation of transaction costs. The FGPs not only seek direct cost benefits but also explore alternative solutions for securing higher value and innovative outcomes. In addition, a range of other rationales have been advanced for outsourcing, including *inter alia* the FGPs having greater flexibility in response to volatile output demand and/or technology changes; reduced investment in plant and equipment; being able to benefit from the specialised skills and/or economies of scale enjoyed by outside suppliers; suppliers having lower labour and/or other production costs; and access to better quality inputs due to competition between outside suppliers. These explanations all hint at potential efficiency benefits from the externalisation by FGPs of productive activities to contract manufacturers.

But internalisation theory suggests that FGPs also relinquish control when they externalise their production activities. The FGPs will clearly have negotiated legal contracts with their contract manufacturers, and these contracts will specify the obligations of each party (including required outputs, payments, etc.), time periods, and sanctions for non-compliance. But legal contracts only provide a degree of control, for the reasons cited above: contracts are incomplete and do not cover all possible future contingencies; contracts for know-how and other intangible assets suffer from moral hazard; and the legal enforceability of contracts is weak in many countries. Thus, legal contracts are unlikely to provide FGPs with a sufficient level of control over their contract manufacturers. Hence, we argue that a theory of externalisation is required which explains how FGPs are simultaneously able to externalise their production activities whilst maintaining direct behaviour control over their contract manufacturers (Strange and Humphrey, 2019). This theory has two elements. The first element explains how and why FGPs possess power asymmetries over their contract manufacturers, and are able to leverage this power both to exert control over the externalised activities and to determine the distribution of the value created within the entire GVC. Such power asymmetries are a necessary condition for the existence of FGPs, but will only sustain a competitive advantage if there are *ex post* limits on their acquisition and/or imitation by the contract manufacturers and potential competitors (Ghemawat, 1986; Mansfield et al., 1981). These limits are provided by the possession of isolating mechanisms (Rumelt, 1984, 1987).[8] The second element of the theory of externalisation thus considers various possible isolating mechanisms that FGPs can employ to assure their long-term dominance over their contract manufacturers.

We first consider how and why FGPs possess power asymmetries over their contract manufacturers.[9] Drawing upon resource dependency theory (Cook, 1977; Cook and Emerson, 1984; Pfeffer, 1981; Pfeffer and Salancik, 1978; Ulrich and Barney, 1984), we suggest that limitations on the availability of resources and capabilities foster specialisation and necessitate organisational interdependence, and thus create resource dependencies, between lead firms and their GVC partners. Power derives from these dependencies: the more power enjoyed by one party, the more influence it has to determine the nature of the exchange relationship. Each party will try to alter the balance in its dependence relationships by acquiring control over resources and capabilities that either maximises the other party's dependence on itself, and/or minimises its own dependence on the other party. When a lead firm and its partners all possess scarce resources and capabilities, there is a power balance and the parties are interdependent. Alternatively, if neither the lead firm nor its partners possess scarce resources and capabilities then neither party enjoys a power advantage. In the typical FGP–contract manufacturer relationship (see Figure 2.2), however, the FGP is providing scarce and valuable intangible assets in the form of product designs, process engineering, R&D and/or technological know-how whilst the contract manufacturers are offering routine and widely available manufacturing and assembly operations. The FGPs possess scarce resources and capabilities not enjoyed by their contract manufacturers, the contract manufacturers are in the position of dependence, and the FGPs are able to leverage their power to exert control over the externalised production activities within their GVCs even in the absence of direct ownership.

Why do the contract manufacturers not circumvent their subordinate relationships with their FGPs by selling the final products direct to the customers? After all, they have been provided with all the requisite designs, specifications and technological know-how to manufacture the products by their FGPs, and they themselves clearly have the necessary manufacturing resources and capabilities. The second element of our theory of externalisation thus considers possible isolating mechanisms that FGPs can employ to hinder imitation of their valuable resources and capabilities, and hence sustain over time their positions of power over their contract manufacturers.[10]

The extant literature has identified several potential isolating mechanisms. Lawson et al. (2012) provide a helpful categorisation. Their first category relates to firm-specific technical knowledge, particularly when such knowledge is tacit and/or complex and/or developed though cumulative experience and learning, and is hence difficult for potential competitors to imitate. The second category relates to mechanisms to protect the knowledge embodied in products and/or processes, either by a reduction in the likelihood of knowledge leakage or through formal property rights allocated by the state (e.g. patents, trademarks, licences). The third category relates to the first-mover advantages (Lieberman and Montgomery, 1998) associated with being first to the market and thus in a position, as Lawson et al. (2012: 422) emphasise, to "gain pre-emptive access to geographic space, technological space, and customer perceptual space". And the fourth category stresses the roles of market-based firm-specific assets such as corporate reputations and brand names, marketing capabilities, and distribution channels. Strong brand names and corporate reputations differentiate the firm's products from those of competitors, enhance customer switching costs and promote consumer lock-in (Farrell and Klemperer, 2007), and act as proxies for quality, making it more difficult and expensive for potential competitors to imitate. Marketing capabilities allow firms to anticipate market trends and to offer benefits to consumers that are hard for competitors to imitate (Srivastava et al., 1998). Effective distribution channels are a vital channel for managing the seller–buyer interface (Day, 1994).

We would add three other potential isolating mechanisms. A fifth category should highlight the capability to collect and evaluate "big data" about emerging trends and opportunities in multiple markets in real-time (Strange and Zucchella, 2017). The possession of such a capability will require considerable investment in a range of technical, analytical and governance skills to realise the potential benefits in terms of value creation: large FGPs should have the financial wherewithal to develop such a capability, but the outlay will typically be beyond small contract manufacturers. A sixth category would focus on the geographic scope of the FGP (Kim, 2013, 2016). FGPs are typically multinational enterprises that undertake activities, including knowledge creation and market research activities, in many different countries. These different national environments drive FGPs to develop a range of heterogeneous resources and capabilities, which are not directly available to contract manufacturers confined to single countries. Furthermore, these heterogeneous resources and capabilities may result from firm-specific combinations of activities undertaken in different countries (Kafouros et al., 2018). Contract manufacturers may find it difficult even to acquire these resources and capabilities indirectly because of uncertainty and causal ambiguity. A seventh and final category focuses on the range of activities provided to the customers as part of the servitised offering that accompanies the manufactured products of many firms (Sánchez-Montesinos et al., 2018; Vandermerwe and Rada, 1988). Providing such services to customers in multiple markets is a complex undertaking, made more difficult by cultural, geographic and other dimensions of distance.

Our suggested theory of externalisation thus highlights that FGPs need to enjoy power asymmetries over their contract manufacturers if they are to maintain control over the production activities in their GVCs in the absence of direct ownership (internalisation), that those asymmetries are founded on the FGPs' possession of valuable and scarce resources and/or capabilities, and that the scarcity of these resources and capabilities depends upon the FGPs developing effective isolating mechanisms. The greater the potency of the protection provided to FGPs by possession of some/all of these various isolating mechanisms, and the less their contract manufacturers enjoy such mechanisms, the more able will FGPs be to externalise activities and yet capture the rents within their GVCs. FGPs exist because they meet these conditions and are thus able both to externalise production activities and, moreover, to determine the distribution of the value created throughout their entire GVCs. Table 2.1 provides a succinct comparison of internalisation theory and externalisation theory.

Table 2.1   A comparison of internalisation theory and externalisation theory (as applied to the production of goods)

	Internalisation theory	Externalisation theory
Main focus	Why do lead firms internalise GVC activities?	How do lead firms coordinate externalised GVC activities?
Lead firms	Multinational enterprises (MNEs)	Factoryless goods producers (FGPs)
Who carries out the productive activities?	Integrated MNEs and affiliates	Contract manufacturers (CMs)
What is internalised?	Internalisation of operations and knowledge	Externalisation of operations + internalisation of knowledge
Source of control by lead firms	Control through ownership	Control through asymmetric power relations
Mechanisms of control	Hierarchical control	Isolating mechanisms
Main source of competitive advantage	Efficient cross-border governance arrangement	Exploitation of power asymmetries
Industry classification of lead firms	Manufacturing (ISIC Section D)	Wholesale and retail trade (ISIC Section G)

2.3   Implications of the growth of factoryless goods producers

The proliferation of FGPs worldwide is more than just a matter requiring theoretical explanation: it has a number of important conceptual, statistical, and policy implications. The first issue concerns the definition of the "firm". A legal definition would focus on the ownership of assets. However, given the degree of control that FGPs have over their contract manufacturers, perhaps a more meaningful definition might also embrace the latter's activities. Similar views have previously been expressed by Stephen Hymer (Strange and Newton, 2006), by John Dunning and Sarianna Lundan (2008), and by Keith Cowling and Roger Sugden (1998: 67) who conceived the modern corporation as "the means of coordinating production from one centre of decision-making". It is also feasible that some FGPs may undertake all their pre-production and post-production activities in their domestic economies, whilst their contract manufacturers and their suppliers are all located overseas. In such cases, should the FGPs be defined as MNEs or simply as domestic firms?

A second issue is the definition of a "manufacturing firm". According to Revision 4 of the International Standard Industrial Classification (ISIC), a lead firm should be classified as a manufacturer only if it purchased some of the raw materials, parts and components (the tangible inputs) from the suppliers and provided them to the contract manufacturers. But the FGPs (as depicted in Figure 2.2) do not purchase any of these tangible inputs, hence should be classified as traders of goods under ISIC Section G (wholesale and retail trade) (UNECE, 2015). Yet FGPs sell manufactured products that typically they have designed and marketed under their brand names, and there have been ongoing discussions in various fora about the appropriate industrial classification of FGPs.[11] If FGPs are classified as manufacturing firms, then domestic manufacturing output (and employment) will appear higher than if they are classified as traders – and politicians and policy-makers may draw different conclusions about the health of domestic manufacturing industry – whilst the recorded output (and employment) in domestic services would fall. The issue is more than just semantics, as various commentators have acknowledged. For instance, Coyle and Nguyen (2019) comment that "factoryless manufacturing is an increasingly significant phenomenon. It is important to start collecting relevant statistics if the dynamics of production in modern economies are to be understood, and for sector-based policies to be appropriately designed and targeted". Whitefoot et al. (2015) suggest that policies and initiatives to promote manufacturing should take a value-chain perspective that also embraces pre-production and post-production activities. Levinson (2017) notes that "changes in the structure of manufacturing make it difficult to design government policies that support manufacturing-related value added and employment".

The third issue relates to the recording and interpretation of the inputs and outputs of FGPs in international trade statistics (Linsi and Mügge, 2019; UNECE, 2015). FGPs, and more generally the growth of production organised in GVCs, have stimulated international trade in intermediate goods and services to the extent that it accounts for more than 60 per cent of total trade. This has led the OECD and the WTO to undertake work on measuring trade in value-added (TiVA), and to the publication of the World Input-Output Database (UNECE, 2015). The basic issues are neatly illustrated in the celebrated analysis of the trade implications of 2010 Apple iPhone 3G production (Xing and Detert, 2010).[12] Apple is a typical FGP which has externalised the production activities for most of its electronic products, including the iPhone. It is a US firm, which undertakes most of its product design, R&D and branding activities in the United States. The parts and components for the iPhone 3G were sourced from various suppliers (including Toshiba, Samsung, Infineon, Broadcom, etc.) located primarily in Japan, Korea, Germany, and the United States and shipped to the Taiwanese contract manufacturer, Foxconn, for assembly in the People's Republic of China (PRC). Foxconn exported 11.3 million finished iPhones to the United States in 2009 for subsequent distribution and sale at a retail price of $500. The unit ex-factory cost of these iPhone was $179, of which $60.60 was paid to Japanese suppliers, $30.15 to German suppliers, £22.96 to Korean suppliers, $10.75 to US suppliers, and $48.04 to suppliers elsewhere (see Figure 2.3). The unit assembly cost in the PRC was a mere $6.50. The total value of the iPhones exported to the United States in 2009 was thus $2022.7 million, and the recorded net US bilateral deficit with China was $1901.2 million.[13] But this substantial trade deficit on finished iPhones included imported parts and components from Japan and other countries worth $1827.8 million. In value-added trade statistics, the bilateral US trade deficit with China falls to just $73.4 million (i.e. the cost of assembly of the 11.3 million iPhones). The iPhone is just one product, but the example provides a clear example of how conventional international trade statistics can be misleading when FGPs have externalised their production activities to contract manufacturers located overseas. One suggested alternative treatment (Bayard et al., 2015) would be to register the final products of FGPs as outputs in their domestic economies (i.e. Apple products would be registered as US products) using services provided by their (overseas) contract manufacturers. This would result in lower recorded imports of goods, a concomitant rise in the recorded imports of services, but no change in the overall balance on trade. Some commentators see this as preferable to the existing treatment in conventional trade statistics, but critics point out that it would overstate the health of domestic manufacturing industry. Furthermore, and more perversely, goods produced overseas by contract manufacturers and sold directly to customers in third countries would be recorded as exports from the FGP's domestic economy even if they had never physically entered the domestic economy.[14]

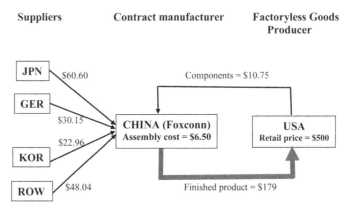

Note: The monetary amounts shown are the unit costs for one iPhone. Apple sold 11.3 million iPhones in the USA in 2009. The profit margin on one iPhone was 64 per cent.

Figure 2.3   The global value chain for the Apple iPhone 3G, 2009

The fourth issue concerns the extent to which FGPs not only externalise their production activities, but are able to externalise responsibility for employee remuneration and working conditions at their contract manufacturers (Balcet and Ietto-Gillies, 2020; Burmester et al., 2019; Strange, 2011; see Chapter 10) and for environmental problems (e.g. pollution, carbon emissions) within their GVCs. Thankfully, there are signs that FGPs (and other MNEs) are increasingly being held to account for the activities undertaken on their behalf by suppliers and contract manufacturers. As Strange and Humphrey (2019: 1406) note, consumer and NGO pressures have obliged lead firms

> to take responsibility for the labour and environmental impacts of their value chains, as discussed by van Tulder, van Wijk & Kolk (2009) and many others. Campaigners for labour rights make the link between brand name companies such as Apple and the labour policies used by subcontractors, often pointing to how these conditions arise (directly or indirectly) from the way in which buyers pressure their suppliers to reduce costs and make rapid adjustments in production volumes. Therefore, the externalisation of activities may leave a lead firm in the position where it does not

have direct control over its suppliers' factories, but it is still held responsible to some extent for its suppliers' behaviour.

The fifth and final issue relates to the implications for the distribution of income worldwide over the past thirty years as a result of the global shifts in the location of production activities from the advanced economies to the emerging economies (Buckley and Strange, 2015). These global shifts have arisen due to a combination of the growth of indigenous firms from the emerging economies, increased FDI by MNEs from the advanced economies, and the offshore outsourcing strategies of FGPs. In the latter case, many FGPs have externalised productive activities to contract manufacturers in offshore locations but have – as described above – still retained control over their geographically dispersed and organisationally fragmented GVCs. As a result, most of the value created in the GVCs is captured by the FGPs in advanced economies whilst the contract manufacturers in the emerging economies receive only a small proportion. This is clearly seen in the iPhone case provided above, where the income accruing to the manufacturers undertaking the assembly operations in PRC was only 1.3 per cent ($6.50 / $500) of the retail price. The majority of the income ($500 - $179) accrues to Apple, and is dispersed to its employees and other stakeholders who are likely to be resident in the United States and other advanced economies.

2.4   Final comments

In this chapter we have outlined a theory of externalisation to explain not only the existence of factoryless goods producers, but also their ability to exert effective control over the activities throughout their organisationally fragmented GVCs. We have stressed the key role played by isolating mechanisms both in providing this control and in conferring upon the FGPs the power to determine the distribution of the value created within their GVCs. Various potential isolating mechanisms have been identified, including the capability for big data analytics, multinationality, and the provision of associated services.

We have also highlighted the empirical importance of FGPs in many countries, and the need to measure their activities so as to properly attribute them across sectors and countries and thus help countries formulate appropriate economic policies. These measurement efforts are ongoing in many national and international statistical organisations. In the meantime, attention might usefully be devoted to providing detailed in-depth case studies of the operations of FGPs and the evolution of their relationships with their contract manufacturers.

A final comment relates to the fact that most FGPs have clearly originated in more advanced economies, which raises the question of whether their genesis might depend upon particular institutional, economic, and/or other characteristics of their home countries. Following Richard Langlois (2003), we suggest that the optimal balance between internalisation and externalisation depends upon the interplay between technology, institutions and organisation – and this balance depends on historical circumstances (Jones and Khanna, 2006). Langlois notes that Adam Smith had predicted a finer division of labour between firms as markets grew, as a result of increases in population and per capita incomes coupled with reductions in barriers to trade and transportation costs. Smith suggested that this process would *ceteris paribus* lead to increased coordination through markets. But Langlois noted that the coordination needs of high-throughput technologies in the early decades of the twentieth century outweighed the abilities of contemporary institutions and markets to meet those needs, with the result that firms became (on average) more vertically integrated. The visible hand – to echo Alfred Chandler's famous work – of managerial coordination came to replace, at least in part, the invisible hand of the market. It is also worth noting that this was also the period during which large vertically integrated MNEs came to dominate the global economy (Chandler and Mazlish, 2005; Jones, 1993; Wilkins, 2001), and also the period that spawned the original contributions to internalisation theory. More recently, the global markets for many goods and services have developed apace as new (emerging) countries have experienced high rates of economic growth and as institutions (both those within these countries, and those guiding the global trading system) have evolved to support market exchange. It is in this historical context that Langlois (2003) advanced his vanishing hand hypothesis to explain the growth of externalisation. Such a perspective would also suggest that FGPs may soon become common in the more developed emerging economies.

Acknowledgement

I would like to thank Ödül Bozkurt, Mike Geppert, Irina Surdu and the participants at the March 2020 Paper Development Workshop in Jena for helpful comments on an earlier draft of this chapter. The usual disclaimer applies.

Notes

1. See Coyle and Nguyen (2019: 5–7) for a discussion of alternative definitions of FGPs.
2. Aggregate data on contract manufacturing are not readily available, and UNCTAD (2011) provides the most recent estimates for 2010. It should be stressed that the data are estimates – see UNCTAD (2011: 131) for the methodology – but are likely to underestimate the size of the contract manufacturing phenomenon.
3. This information is provided by Nike at https://www.manufacturingmap.nikeinc .com and related to November 2019. The information on direct employment at Nike is from https://www.statista.com/statistics/243199/number-of-employees-of -nike-worldwide/.
4. We use the term "lead firm" to refer to firms which have outsourced significant activities within their GVCs to independent partners. Various synonymous terms are used in the literature, including *inter alia* flagship firm, hub firm, focal firm, orchestrator, network orchestrator, joint value orchestrator, strategic centre, strategic nexus, meta-integrator, and principal.
5. See Chapter 3 for a further perspective on the strengths and weaknesses of internalisation theory, and its underpinning assumptions.
6. The United Nations Economic Commission for Europe (UNECE) identifies a number of "alternative production arrangements" that contrast with the vertically integrated model of the MNE. First, there are "factoryless goods producers" (FGPs), which are discussed at length below. Second, there is the "transformation of goods owned by a domestic principal" in which the principal (lead firm) purchases (some of) the raw materials, parts and components, and sends these inputs to a contractor (often overseas) to be transformed into a final product. The lead firm maintains ownership of the raw materials etc. throughout the transformation process and has ownership of the final product after processing. In contrast, FGPs do not buy or have ownership of the raw materials etc., and simply take ownership of the final product received from the contract manufacturer. Third, a "goods under merchanting" arrangement involves the supplier not only providing the raw materials etc., but also the intangible assets. The lead firm is simply a trader who takes ownership of the final product, and handles the marketing and distribution. See UNECE (2015) for further details.
7. This processing fee will exclude the value of the intangible inputs provided by the FGP.
8. Isolating mechanisms at the firm-level are analogous to barriers to entry at the industry-level. Barney (1991) notes that effective isolating mechanisms rely on path dependence, causal ambiguity and/or social complexity.
9. See Strange (2011) for a more extensive discussion.
10. The efficacy of many isolating mechanisms may also tend to dissipate over time as rivals emerge to imitate successful products and strategies, and as capability and resource asymmetries erode (Denicolai et al., 2015). A similar view is expressed by Le Breton-Miller and Miller (2015: 397) who comment that "scholars have focused on the properties of resources and the isolating mechanisms that sustain their rents in the face of competition. Unfortunately, they have devoted far less attention to the sources of vulnerability of many of these resources."
11. Factoryless goods manufacturing was first identified as a significant phenomenon in 2008. In 2010, the Economic Classification Policy Committee (ECPC) of the

US Office of Management and Budget (OMB) recommended that from 2017 all FGPs should be re-classified to the manufacturing sector. This proposal was later withdrawn pending further research work. See Coyle and Nguyen (2019) and UNECE (2015) for further details. UNECE (2015) note that FGPs have quite different production functions and cost structures to traditional vertically integrated manufacturing firms, and hence recommend that they be treated and analysed separately in the national accounts and in input-output tables.

12. Professor Xing has since updated the analysis to examine the trade implications of iPhone X production in 2018 (Xing, 2019).
13. This trade deficit related to iPhone production, together with the aggregate US bilateral trade deficit with the PRC, has been the subject of considerable disquiet for successive US presidents including Barack Obama and Donald Trump.
14. See Chapter 7 of UNECE (2015) and Loungani et al. (2017) for further discussion.

References

Ali-Yrkkö, J., Rouvinen, P., Seppälä, T. and Ylä-Antilla, P. (2011). Who captures value in global supply chains? Case of Nokia N95 smartphone. *Journal of Industry, Competition, and Trade*, 11(3): 263–278.

Balcet, G. and Ietto-Gillies, G. (2020). Internationalization, outsourcing and labour fragmentation: The case of FIAT. *Cambridge Journal of Economics*, 44(1): 105–128.

Barney, J. (1991). Firm resources and sustained competitive advantage. *Journal of Management*, 17(1): 99–120.

Bayard, K., Byrne, D. and Smith, D. (2015). The scope of US "factoryless manufacturing". In S.N. Houseman and M.J. Mandel (Eds), *Measuring Globalization: Better Trade Statistics for Better Policy*, Volume 2. Kalamazoo, MI: WE Upjohn Institute for Employment Research, 81–120.

Bernard, A.B. and Fort, T.C. (2015). Factoryless goods producing firms. *American Economic Review: Papers & Proceedings*, 105(5): 518–523.

Bissell-Linsk, J. (2017). Nike's focus on robotics threatens Asia's low-cost workforce: Developing countries at risk of losing cheap manufacturing if leisurewear companies accelerate automation. *Financial Times*, 22 October.

Buckley, P.J. and Casson, M. (1976). *The Future of the Multinational Enterprise*. London: Macmillan.

Buckley, P.J. and Strange, R. (2015). The governance of the global factory: Location and control of world economic activity. *Academy of Management Perspectives*, 29(2): 237–249.

Burmester, B., Michailova, S. and Stringer, C. (2019). Modern slavery and international business scholarship: The governance nexus. *critical perspectives on international business*, 15(2/3): 139–157.

Chandler Jr, A.D. and Mazlish, B. (Eds) (2005). *Leviathans: Multinational Corporations and the New Global History*. Cambridge: Cambridge University Press.

Cook, K.S. (1977). Exchange and power in networks of interorganizational relations. *Sociological Quarterly*, 18(1): 62–82.

Cook, K.S. and Emerson, R. (1984). Exchange networks and the analysis of complex organizations. *Sociology of Organizations*, 3: 1–30.

Cowling, K. and Sugden, R. (1998). The essence of the modern corporation: Markets, strategic decision-making and the theory of the firm. *The Manchester School*, 66(1): 59–86.

Coyle, D. and Nguyen, D. (2019). No plant, no problem? Factoryless manufacturing and economic measurement. National Institute of Economic and Social Research, Economic Statistics Centre of Excellence, ESCoE Discussion paper, no. 2019-15.

Day, G.S. (1994). The capabilities of market-driven organizations. *Journal of Marketing*, 58(4): 37–52.

Dedrick, J., Kraemer, K.L. and Linden, G. (2010). Who profits from innovation in global value chains? A study of the iPod and notebook PCs. *Industrial and Corporate Change*, 19(1): 81–116.

Denicolai, S., Strange, R. and Zucchella, A. (2015). The dynamics of the outsourcing relationship. In R. van Tulder, A. Verbeke and R. Drogendijk (Eds), *Multinational Enterprises and Their Organizational Challenges*. Progress in International Business Research, Volume 10. Bingley: Emerald, 341–364.

Donaghu, M.T. and Barff, R. (1990). Nike just did it: International subcontracting and flexibility in athletic footwear production. *Regional Studies*, 24(6): 537–552.

Dunning, J.H. and Lundan, S.M. (2008). *Multinational Enterprises and the Global Economy*, 2nd edition. Cheltenham, UK and Northampton, MA, USA: Edward Elgar Publishing.

Farrell, J. and Klemperer, P. (2007). Coordination and lock-in: Competition with switching costs and network effects. In M. Armstrong and R. Porter (Eds), *Handbook of Industrial Organization*. Amsterdam: Elsevier, 1967–2002.

Fontagné, L. and Harrison, A. (Eds) (2017) *The Factory-Free Economy: Outsourcing, Servitization, and the Future of Industry*. Oxford: Oxford University Press.

Ghemawat, P. (1986). Sustainable advantage. *Harvard Business Review*, 64(5): 53–58.

Grossman, S.J. and Hart, O.D. (1986). The costs and benefits of ownership: A theory of vertical and lateral integration. *Journal of Political Economy*, 94(4): 691–719.

Hennart, J.-F. (1982). *A Theory of Multinational Enterprise*. Ann Arbor: University of Michigan Press.

Jones, G. (1993). *Transnational Corporations: A Historical Perspective*. London: Routledge.

Jones, G. and Khanna, T. (2006). Bringing history (back) into international business. *Journal of International Business Studies*, 37(4): 453–468.

Kafouros, M., Wang, C., Mavroudi, E., Hong, J. and Katsikeas, C.S. (2018). Geographic dispersion and co-location in global R&D portfolios: Consequences for firm performance. *Research Policy*, 47(7): 1243–1255.

Kamal, F. (2018). *A Portrait of US Factoryless Goods Producers* (Working paper no. 25193). National Bureau of Economic Research.

Kim, M. (2013). Many roads lead to Rome: Implications of geographic scope as a source of isolating mechanisms. *Journal of International Business Studies*, 44(9): 898–921.

Kim, M. (2016). Geographic scope, isolating mechanisms, and value appropriation. *Strategic Management Journal*, 37(4): 695–713.

Langlois, R.N. (2003). The vanishing hand: The changing dynamics of industrial capitalism. *Industrial and Corporate Change*, 12(2): 351–385.

Lawson, B., Samson, D. and Roden, S. (2012). Appropriating the value from innovation: Inimitability and the effectiveness of isolating mechanisms. *R&D Management*, 42(5): 420–434.

Le Breton-Miller, I. and Miller, D. (2015). The paradox of resource vulnerability: Considerations for organizational curatorship. *Strategic Management Journal*, 36(3): 397–415.

Levinson, M. (2017). *What Is Manufacturing? Why Does the Definition Matter?* (CRS Report R44755). Washington, DC: Congressional Research Service.

Lieberman, M.B. and Montgomery, D.B. (1998). First-mover (dis)advantages: Retrospective and link with the resource-based view. *Strategic Management Journal*, 19(12): 1111–1125.

Linsi, L. and Mügge, D.K. (2019). Globalization and the growing defects of international economic statistics. *Review of International Political Economy*, 26(3): 361–383.

Loungani, P., Mishra, S., Papageorgiou, C. and Wang, K. (2017). *World Trade in Services: Evidence from a New Dataset*. Washington, DC: IMF.

Mansfield, E., Schwartz, M. and Wagner, S. (1981). Imitation costs and patents: An empirical study. *Economic Journal*, 91(364): 907–918.

Morikawa, M. (2016). Factoryless goods producers in Japan. *Japan and the World Economy*, 40: 9–15.

Pfeffer, J. (1981). *Power in Organizations*. Marshfield, MA: Pitman.

Pfeffer, J. and Salancik, G. (1978). *The External Control of Organizations: A Resource Dependence Perspective*. New York: Harper & Row.

Rugman, A.M. (1981). *Inside the Multinationals: The Economics of the Multinational Enterprise*. New York: Columbia University Press.

Rumelt, R.P. (1984). Towards a strategic theory of the firm. In R. Lamb (Ed.), *Competitive Strategic Management*. Englewood Cliffs, NJ: Prentice Hall, 566–570.

Rumelt, R.P. (1987). Theory, strategy and entrepreneurship. In D.J. Teece (Ed.), *The Competitive Challenge: Strategies for Industrial Innovation and Renewal*. Cambridge, MA: Ballinger, 137–158.

Sánchez-Montesinos, F., Opazo Basàez, M., Arias Aranda, D. and Bustinza, O.F. (2018). Creating isolating mechanisms through digital servitization: The case of Covirán. *Strategic Change*, 27(2): 121–128.

Srivastava, R.K., Shervani, T.A. and Fahey, L. (1998). Market-based assets and shareholder value: A framework for analysis. *Journal of Marketing*, 62(1): 2–18.

Strange, R. (2011). The outsourcing of primary activities: Theoretical analysis and propositions. *Journal of Management & Governance*, 15(2): 249–269.

Strange, R. and Humphrey, J. (2019). What lies between market and hierarchy? Insights from internalization theory and global value chain theory. *Journal of International Business Studies*, 50(8): 1401–1413.

Strange, R. and Magnani, G. (2018). Outsourcing, offshoring and the global factory. In G. Cook and F. McDonald (Eds), *The Routledge Companion to the Geography of International Business*. Abingdon: Routledge, 60–77.

Strange, R. and Newton, J. (2006). Stephen Hymer and the externalization of production. *International Business Review*, 15(2): 180–193.

Strange, R. and Zucchella, A. (2017). Industry 4.0, global value chains and international business. *Multinational Business Review*, 25(3): 174–184.

Ulrich, D. and Barney, J.B. (1984). Perspectives in organizations: Resource dependence, efficiency, and population. *Academy of Management Review*, 9(3): 471–481.

UNCTAD (2011). *World Investment Report 2011: Non-Equity Modes of International Production and Development*. New York and Geneva: UNCTAD.

UNECE (2015). *Guide to Measuring Global Production*. New York and Geneva: United Nations.

Usui, T., Kotabe, M. and Murray, J.Y. (2017). A dynamic process of building global supply chain competence by new ventures: The case of Uniqlo. *Journal of International Marketing*, 25(3): 1–20.

van Tulder, R., van Wijk, J. and Kolk, A. (2009). From chain liability to chain responsibility. *Journal of Business Ethics*, 85(2 Supplement): 399–412.

Vandermerwe, S. and Rada, J. (1988). Servitization of business: Adding value by adding services. *European Management Journal*, 6(4): 314–324.

Whitefoot, K.S., Valdivia, W.D. and Adam, G.C. (2015). *Innovation and Manufacturing Labour: A Value-Chain Perspective*. Washington, DC: Brookings Center for Technology Innovation.

Wilkins, M. (2001). The history of multinational enterprise. In A.M. Rugman and T.L Brewer (Eds), *The Oxford Handbook of International Business*. Oxford: Oxford University Press, 3–35.

World Bank (2020). *Doing Business 2020: Comparing Business Regulations in 190 Economies*. Washington, DC: World Bank Group.

World Justice Project (2019). *Rule of Law Index 2019*. Washington, DC: World Justice Project.

Xing, Y. (2019). How the iPhone widens the US trade deficit with China: The case of the iPhone X. *VOXEU*. https://voxeu.org/article/how-iphone-widens-us-trade-deficit -china-0.

Xing, Y. and Detert, N. (2010). How the iPhone widens the United States trade deficit with the People's Republic of China (Working Paper no. 257). Asian Development Bank Institute.

Zhou, K.Z. and Poppo, L. (2010). Exchange hazards, relational reliability, and contracts in China: The contingent role of legal enforceability. *Journal of International Business Studies*, 41(5): 861–881.

3. Behavioural theory and MNE decision-making: changing the narrative in international business management

Giulio Nardella, Rajneesh Narula and Irina Surdu

If we are uncritical we shall always find what we want: we shall look for, and find, confirmations, and we shall look away from, and not see, whatever might be dangerous to our pet theories. (Popper, 1957: 124)

3.1 Introduction

Scholars of international business management point out that the research agenda is "running out of steam" (Buckley, 2002: 365; see also Buckley et al., 2017; Doh, 2015), noting that we need to extend current theories to tackle topics which better reflect developments in the international business environment such as the outcomes of globalisation, new technologies, the role of stakeholders on firm strategy, the emergence of emerging market multinational enterprises (EMNEs) and the impact of our field on related disciplines (Mudambi et al., 2018; Narula, 2017, 2018; Narula and Verbeke, 2015). Some scholars have gone further and argued that international management requires a "shift" whereby "old" theories/perspectives on multinational enterprise (MNE) growth can and should be "replaced" with "new" theories, although this view remains controversial. Perhaps we experience a failure to see beyond dominant assumptions associated with MNE growth (as such, it may be possible that there has, in fact, not been a shift). Although there is now greater theoretical diversity, recent literature reviews (Mudambi et al., 2018; Surdu and Mellahi, 2016; Surdu et al., 2018a; Teagarden et al., 2018) confirm that international management-related choices continue to be studied primarily through an organisational economics lens whose underlying assumptions remain deeply rooted in either the Simonian view of bounded rationality, or the neo-classical view of the rational actor. The focus remains on finding "new" (and presumably, better) theories, rather than gaining a better understanding of the micro-foundations of theories used, their relevance, as well as inherent limitations.

In light of the growing empirical evidence on the heterogeneity with which MNEs strategise (e.g. Benito et al., 2009; Buckley et al., 2007; Elia et al., 2019; Kano and Verbeke, 2015; Surdu et al., 2019), theories which use (bounded) rationality as a micro-foundation are gradually making room for complementary, behavioural perspectives. This is because managers do not always behave rationally (Aharoni et al., 2011; Buckley et al., 2007; Dörrenbächer and Geppert, 2017; Elia et al., 2019; Schubert et al., 2018; Strange, 2018; Surdu et al., 2019). Behavioural economics, allied with recent psychological discoveries (Ardalan, 2018; Muradoglu and Harvey, 2012) provides relevant insight into the nature of business decisions, with particular relevance for international business. For instance, behavioural scholars argue that cognitive biases and judgement heuristics often influence economic decision-making, and they tend to be stronger in circumstances where decision-makers are faced with a specific threat, e.g. the uncertainty associated with entering unstable and distant international markets.

The objective of this chapter is to propose a revitalisation of core arguments to diversify and hopefully, improve the manner in which we analyse decisions about international expansion. Our focus is to convince the reader that not all MNE decisions can be adequately explained by using predominantly rational models of decision-making. For instance, once a firm has decided to internationalise, it is left with a multitude of choices, including those related to whether to escalate its commitment into that market, adapt its organisational practices, and at the other end of the spectrum, to de-escalate commitment, or exit the market completely. Further, it is not useful to take a static, single-period view. Over time, attitudes towards that market and perceptions associated with its attractiveness, may have changed and some firms may return to previously exited markets; whilst others may opt to change the locations of their international operations. Many international expansion-related choices are therefore decided in dynamic and uncertain host environments, and in situations of imperfect information about the alternatives available. In other cases, the choices we observe may, in fact, be ex-post justifications for decisions made with little forethought or significant prior deliberative rationalisation (Weick, 1995; Weick et al., 2005).

Mainstream international business management research does not discuss what may bound a manager's ability to act as a rational economic actor. For us, taking a simplistic view of bounded rationality (which underpins many of our "pet" theories) makes it difficult to explain differences in managerial choices and understand why, in the same contexts, two managers would behave differently. A narrow focus on (bounded) rationality holds us back from understanding the behaviour of managers.

This chapter starts with an overview of dominant ideas in international business management and their limited potential to explain, on their own, the dynamic behaviour of the MNE. We explain the concept of bounded rationality as a complex and multi-faceted micro-foundation, which goes beyond the idea that managers make decisions bounded only by their information processing capabilities. We provide examples of notable studies published in international business (IB) and management journals and which incorporate complementary ideas about managerial cognitive limitations, biases and other related behavioural concepts, and propose directions for future research. Overall, this chapter aims at building intellectual bridges and a common language between IB, strategic management, economics and social psychology, starting with how behavioural perspectives can enrich our knowledge of the modern MNE.

3.2   Dominant assumptions in international business management

Most IB and management theoretical perspectives recognise that decisions are made under unavoidable constraints. In conditions of considerable uncertainty often associated with internationalisation choices, managers may be unable to specify strategic outcomes and their associated probabilities. Transaction cost economics (TCE) based theories such as earlier versions of internalisation theory (Buckley and Casson, 1976; Hennart, 1982; Rugman, 1980) focused on opportunism as a primary constraint. Broadly speaking, this early work posited that, in order to avoid the risk of opportunistic behaviour when internationalising, managers might opt for high control governance choices that help them reduce transaction costs associated with incomplete market contracts (Buckley and Casson, 1976; Verbeke and Greidanus, 2009). In this manner, firm resources with a high level of specificity are protected from opportunistic behaviour, and knowledge transfer between the international subsidiary and its parent MNE is more likely to take place (Delios and Beamish, 1999). Thus, the expectation was to reduce opportunism-based transaction costs through higher investment. Brouthers and Hennart's (2007) review concluded that many internalisation predictions have been validated in empirical work at the time.

Building on TCE thinking, internalisation studies assumed the existence of bounded rationality by recognising that economic actors are indeed rational but only boundedly so (Simon, 1955). When decision-makers are boundedly rational and as market/contracts tend to be incomplete, opportunistic behaviour was expected to arise primarily because decision-makers are limited in their ability to process information. Later versions of internalisation theory integrate TCE, entrepreneurial and resource-based view (RBV) logics, recognising that firms make decisions based on resources whose utilisation depends on the experience and capabilities of the manager (Narula and Verbeke, 2015, Narula et al., 2019). MNEs are therefore likely to incur bounded rationality-based transaction costs associated with international expansion. While new internalisation theory emphasises that managers are boundedly rational, the few empirical studies which draw on new internalisation theory do not specify what the boundaries of rationality are, thus limiting theoretical advancement; e.g. drawing on new internalisation theory, Nguyen and Almodóvar (2018) explain the export intensity of foreign subsidiaries as a function of funding access and overall financial resources, significantly underplaying the role of management.

Other notable international management perspectives (Johanson and Vahlne, 1977) have placed emphasis on the characteristics and patterns of internationalisation, linking them to firm-level knowledge acquired in time through experience and learning. From a learning perspective, knowledge acquired through experience leads to more hierarchical modes of operation such as wholly owned subsidiaries (Vahlne and Johanson, 2017). Further, knowledge acquired in one market can be transferred to other markets, leading to MNEs increasing their location scope by entering more institutionally and culturally distant host countries. Recent studies examine how experience accumulated by the MNE over time will lead to favourable attitudes towards risk, faster market entries and increased market commitment (e.g. Casillas and Moreno-Menendez, 2014; Casillas et al., 2015). Such an approach makes a series of (often unsupported) assumptions. First that managerial preferences, and thus their behaviours, do not change over time; second that the external environment of the firm remains stable; third that irrespective of corporate governance all firms have the same risk attitudes and decision-making horizons; and fourth, there is the implied assumption that after an extensive period of experiential knowledge acquisition, MNE behaviour will increasingly resemble rational behaviour.

However, experiences also create biases, which in turn, may significantly influence MNE choices. The considerable heterogeneity observed in firm behaviour (Buckley et al., 2007; Strange, 2018; Surdu et al., 2019) suggests that managers do not value choice attributes equally such as the attractiveness of a market location, the need to access new resources, or the importance of experiential learning to reduce risk. For instance, to some, knowledge acquired from experience may be a valuable source of learning, resulting in a firm-specific advantage, whilst to others, it may represent a source of path dependency. In a similar vein, a new partner may be a source of increased opportunism and transaction costs or an opportunity to learn about the market and diversify the firm's network resources and capabilities. There is therefore a differential effect on strategic choices due to managers having different biases and points of reference when assessing strategic trade-offs associated with growth or expansion. As such, our position in this chapter is that we require a more nuanced understanding of what managerial rationality is bounded by. The different facets of bounded rationality become the focus of our next section and, we propose, a foundation for future international business management theorising.

3.3   Bounded rationality: a multi-faceted concept

An important first step forward in understanding how ideas from behavioural economics and social psychology can complement extant international management theorising, is to better understand the idea of individuals being *boundedly* rational. Bounded rationality is, itself, multi-faceted. In fact, bounded rationality has various dimensions that build on one another (Foss and Weber, 2016; Simon, 1982, 1990). Extant literature has focused on one dimension, namely the Simonian (1990) view of processing capacity that a decision-maker's ability to process and interpret existing information is limited by their short-term memory and attention. Such restricting views of the short-term horizons of managers are no longer credible. Academic thinking has moved on to acknowledge that managers are not so myopic and are able to estimate probable outcomes of strategic choices.

Behavioural and experimental economics, and more recently, social psychology, place more emphasis on the complementary dimensions of bounded rationality such as cognitive economising (Fiske and Taylor, 1991) and cognitive biases (Tversky and Kahneman, 1974; see also Weick, 1995; Weick et al., 2005). These help our understanding of what information managers prioritise to make strategic choices and why. Namely, cognitive economising refers to the use of heuristics to select a subset of the most relevant available information to make quick decisions in complex situations (Gigerenzer, 2003). Hence, instead of seeking to process all information available, managers may seek to organise the *most relevant* information; this may be the information most retrievable at a point in time (Tversky and Kahneman, 1974) or the information *most salient* to them (Frost et al., 2002).

In turn, the concept of cognitive biases recognises mainly the errors in judgement that may arise from unintentionally distorting the information available. For instance, a decision-maker may search for, interpret, and recall information that affirms their already existing beliefs (i.e. confirmation bias, see Wason, 1960; see also Weick et al., 2005 on "self-fulfilling prophecies"). To illustrate how embedded and inconspicuous cognitive biases are, we invite the reader to consider for a moment a central tenet of management theories, that, for any resource capable of serving as a source of competitive advantage, it must be "rare". Attributing disproportionate value to "rarity" is one of our longest held biases (Ditto and Jemmott, 1989; Lee et al., 2020). This cognitive bias to value rare qualities, traits and resources is central to many areas of modern ethical contention such as the procurement of rhino horns, shark fins, diamonds, lithium, oil and truthful politicians. If there is a scarce resource, is this a main source of advantage or could we be misattributing performance outcomes to those rare resources? Psychologically, individuals find it difficult to decouple "value" from "rarity" (Ditto and Jemmott, 1989). For instance, a firm that has been around for 100 years is rare. The distinction between rarity and value is important because rare resources need to be perceived as valuable; when value perceptions change, rarity alone may not constitute a source of market advantage.

Cognitive biases have been found most obvious when circumstances present humans with an unexpected threat (Kanouse and Reid Hanson, 1972). Duhaime and Schwenk (1985) explained how biases play a role in the decision to divest a business unit, noting that once divestment of a failing unit is considered, it becomes the key strategic alternative for decision-makers (see also Elia et al., 2019). When dealing with complex, uncertain decisions, rather than specifying, and rationally analysing, all the known alternatives and their associated probabilities – as traditional theory posits – managers reduce uncertainty by limiting themselves to one option and avoid the trade-offs inherent in choosing amongst complex strategic options. Importantly, cognitive biases are extensive and present throughout human behaviour, including behaviours associated with the pursuit of goals (Labroo and Kim, 2009). In order to support the attainment of goals and the reduction of threats to those goals, judgement heuristics, in addition to deliberate, rational cognition, may be deployed as a more "efficient" modality.

Judgement heuristics

Individuals rely on shortcuts or heuristics in order to make sense of the information available to them, rather than process it in a systematic and gradual manner (Kahneman and Tversky, 1979; Tversky and Kahneman, 1992). Despite the evident benefits of logic and reason, the process of deliberate rationalisation is slow and resource intensive; with the outcome of applying logic being assumed to be an "improvement" to human judgement (Gilovich et al., 2002). Heuristics are expected to enable decision-makers to make sense of highly complex phenomena (based on managerial experiences and/or expected future outcomes) (Gigerenzer, 2003; Gilovich et al., 2002; Shoham and Fiegenbaum, 2002). This is important because complexity and ambiguity typically characterise much of our experience. Therefore, a barrier to the effectiveness of deliberative rationalisation is the level of perceived uncertainty with which the judgement must be made. Particularly in such instances, we propose, heuristics are likely to be applied by managerial decision-makers (see Hamilton et al., 2009; Maitland and Sammartino, 2015).

Heuristics, thought to have evolved to support human judgement (Tversky and Kahneman, 1974), are fundamentally cognitive "shortcuts" to problem solving. In order to arrive at a "faster" and more "efficient" evaluation, heuristics draw upon our past experiences, memories and schemata (representations and theories about the world) of those experiences to arrive at a set of quick solutions. Because our experiences, memories and schemata are determined by the subjective experiences of both ourselves and others – this introduces further biases into heuristic judgements (Evans, 2008).

We found a few notable examples in the international business management literature where heuristics may be used to understand decisions made. In their study on managers assessing a potential acquisition in a high-risk African country, Maitland and Sammartino (2015) found that managers were limited in their understanding of the local environment and thus, drew on different types of heuristics to analyse potential strategic choices. These included an attempt to understand, in their case, how other institutional actors and business partners would behave, in this way, to also understand the hazard associated with an uncertain local political environment. Past experiences played a role in enriching the ability of decision-makers to create a set of different scenarios about their external context (Hamilton et al., 2009; Maitland and Sammartino, 2015). Interestingly also, during this process, decision-makers were found to perceive their contextual environments somewhat differently. The authors view these differing views of decision-makers positively and discussed the importance of having different perspectives when operating in uncertain and dynamic environments, in order to build a more complete picture of that environment and incorporate flexibility in decision-making by considering that, indeed, multiple choice scenarios are possible. Hamilton et al. (2009) proposed a similar idea with regards to companies entering distant socio-cultural environments such as China to develop compliance and ethics programmes; their study revealed differences in the manner in which these practices were perceived to be, indeed, ethical – this, in turn, required a high level of customisation of these practices to fit local needs. Beamond et al. (2016) later also reveal the importance of applying heuristics to understand the translation of corporate talent management strategies to subsidiaries in emerging economies.

Overall, the essence of these studies is that complex decisions increasingly require quick judgements to be made around the causes of a strategic problem and its potential solutions. These decisions are perhaps biased because decision-makers have varying experiences, reference points and expectations that they draw on in the absence of rich information about the potential outcome. Incorporating cognitive biases in our theorising does not mean that we reject the benefits of analytical thinking and making logical and reasonable assumptions. Rather, we recognise that, in practice, managers are exposed to combinations of routinised decisions – which may have more certain outcomes associated with them – and higher risk decisions, where outcome uncertainty is high, and decision-makers do not possess sufficient information about their environment to make unbiased choices.

Reference points and frames

Since managers may use different points of reference to develop strategic options, that introduces further biases in decision-making. Environmental and industry factors can be amongst the main points of reference that trigger preference reversals, such as when environments change and make knowledge acquisition and subsequent learning difficult for decision-makers. A firm's belonging to a strategic industry group can, for instance, act as a reference point in strategic choices (Li and Yao, 2010). Industry dynamics require fast decision-making; hence, overreliance on heuristics and past frames of reference may, in the end, lead to greater cognitive biases (Monaghan and Tippmann, 2018).

Take, for instance, firms which divest their international operations, only to re-enter the host market some years later. Frames of reference may change for firms returning to previously exited markets due to improvements in their host institutional environments and changes in competitive dynamics, which

require a re-assessment of previously held assumptions and biases and a potential unlearning of past behaviours learned from the initial investment (Surdu et
al., 2019; Surdu and Narula, in press). Since certain factors or experiences carry
a disproportionately high weight in the decision-making process (Shoham and
Fiegenbaum, 2002; Shrader et al., 2000), firms which have exited the market
due to market underperformance and inability to compete, may pay particular
attention to their competitors and thus, how they position themselves in the
market the second time around. Similarly, in the decision to divest international operations and exit a market in the first place, firms (and their managers) may place a disproportionately high value on the reputational outcomes
associated with admitting defeat in a market, and often, overstay their welcome
(Surdu et al., 2019). Surdu et al. (2018b) empirically show how negative
decisions associated with market divestment are used as reference points and
shape how and when firms reinvest into the previously exited market. Negative
experiences sped up the process of re-entering the market as the alternative
meant losing momentum into that market which would have made addressing
the causes for failure more difficult. Surdu et al. (2019) also found that the exit
experience can be associated with how much investment a firm makes into
a foreign market, irrespective of the firm's own specific resources and its prior
experience with a mode of operation.

Also important is therefore the notion that biases are dynamic and change over
time as managers interact with their environments (Kano and Verbeke, 2015;
Shapiro et al., 2007). For instance, an international manager may commit to
a course of action *ex ante* due to expectations of a payoff based on experiences
and reference points (Lumineau and Verbeke, 2016); meaning that the past
may provide a useful frame for evaluating the perceived value of future strategic choices (in fact, this provides the basis for most investment rationales). As
these choices unfold, new information and opportunities may arise that could
accrue a larger payoff, and thus be valued higher, leading to a reversal or recon-
sideration of the initial choice (Tversky et al., 1990). It does not necessarily
mean that, over time, managers acquire more experience and reduce uncertainties associated with international growth (as suggested by the Uppsala
model). In fact, over time, managers may even become uncertain about their
own preferences (March, 1978), as cognitive biases change, and MNE decisions
and contexts become more complex. In their study, Verbeke and Greidanus
(2009) provide examples of companies which, through self-evaluation biases,
overcommit to international partners, although not being able to develop the
necessary resources and capabilities to effectively serve those partners when
the time comes. Elia et al. (2019) proposed that only those experiences which
are perceived as more salient or easier to retrieve (often because they are more
recent in the minds of decision makers) have an impact on the decision to

continue using the same mode versus changing the mode of operation (Surdu et al., 2018b; 2019).

Concerning the role of time, managers may use different reference points, in different circumstances; e.g. previous experience may be useful upon initial entry where the firm is focused on potential future gains, whereas increased uncertainty associated with underperforming in the market may shape subsequent choices, leading to higher perceptions of risk. In a notable empirical study on international location selection, Buckley et al. (2007) found that the sets of international locations that managers initially consider entering may follow rational rules, whereas the choice of locations actually entered from that initial choice set, do not follow those same rules. An MNE, equipped with the same resources, at different points in time, will make different choices about international growth.

Lastly, how factors in the internal and external environments of the firm are framed, i.e. as opportunities or threats, may also have an influence on decisions made. Yet, framing – the cognitive bias leading individuals to choose between strategic options/outcomes associated with losses or gains (Tversky and Kahneman, 1981) – is almost entirely missing from our current theorising. This is particularly important because framing is a critical component of human decisions. For instance, let's look closer at the decision to re-enter a previously exited international market. The transaction costs associated with returning to a market where the firm has previously failed to perform, and where it clearly does not have a "firm-specific advantage" would make that decision improbable (i.e. re-entry is framed as a loss). Further, were the MNE to decide to re-enter, it would not be expected to commit significant financial and other resources to that previously failed market. However, when reframed as an "alternative" to missing out on a growing market, losing face, over-depending on the home market – the decision to re-enter a previously exited market appears seemingly logical, and indeed, preferable (i.e. re-entry reframed as a potential gain) to decision-makers. Though rationally we know these facets and complexities of human behaviour are ever present in "real life" (Arrow, 1982; Madrian and Shea, 2001; Odean, 1998), they are often not part of IB research designs.

3.4   Directions for future international business management research

We propose a series of research areas and questions which may be addressed by scholars interested in how behavioural theories can further our understanding of MNE choices. These research avenues, we argue, complement rather than seek to replace traditional MNE theories.

Area I: Behavioural perspectives, biases and MNE strategic choices

We explained that decisions made under conditions of increased uncertainty may require firms to draw on different types of heuristics to analyse potential choices associated with those decisions and make sense of their environments. Such a view may improve the manner in which we analyse decisions concerning international expansion. Hence, we ask the following:

- What is the role of cognitive biases in governance mode choices? Do similar biases occur while switching between governance modes?
- Are internationalisation decisions discrete choices or dynamic processes?[1] Are subsequent market investments influenced primarily by the initial entry?
- How do reference points and biases influence the risk-taking attitudes associated with international expansion? Do biases lead to more or less market commitment, and for which types of firms?
- What sources of knowledge and learning does management prioritise? Do negative/recent events tend to be more impactful for strategic decisions?
- What is the moderating role of industry factors (and their change over time) such as industry strategic groups in triggering certain reference points and frames?

Area II: Managerial biases and organisational behaviour

The link between individual behaviour and organisational behaviour must be better understood to be able to scale up our micro-foundational ideas. The Carnegie School (Simon, March and Cyert) provides a starting point to linking individual choice with MNE choice and behaviour. Scholars have observed that tacit knowledge selected and absorbed by individual decision-makers may turn into organisational "routines" (Cyert and March, 1963; Nelson and Winter, 1982). Routines are the firm equivalent of individual capabilities and cognitions (March and Simon, 1958/1993; Cyert and March, 1963), whereby the cognitive patterns that represent models of ideal behaviour are expected to be transformed into formal or informal organisational "rules" (Easterby-Smith and Lyles, 2011; Feldman, 2000; Lyles, 1994). Here, we propose that the cognitive biases of decision-makers may influence the manner in which strategic choices and experiences become incorporated into organisational routines. Thus, we invite future research to focus on the following questions:

- How do forms of behaviour arise and change in MNEs? Does individual knowledge and experience weigh more than organisational knowledge and experience?
- What is the relationship between CEO tenure and myopic MNE behaviour? Does tenure increase or decrease the likelihood of firms changing their international strategies in light of changes in their environments?
- Do certain types of organisational cultures foster recognising new forms of behaviour? How and when are old, ineffective routines replaced by new, more relevant and flexible routines? Is this always the outcome of a new or diverse management team?
- To what extent are managerial goals and expectations aligned with MNE goals? If there is misalignment, what are the short-term and long-term implications on international growth and performance?

Area III: Behavioural perspectives and firm governance

Managerial decisions are also bounded by context. We propose that a key avenue for future research would consist of understanding whether and how decision-makers in different types of firms with different ownership structures and corporate governance mechanisms might pursue different goals, have different attitudes towards risk and time-horizons to make decisions (Narula, 2012; Strange, 2018). We argue that, depending on relevant organisational contexts such as governance mechanisms, what is framed as rational and what may be used as a reference point may significantly differ. Hence, we ask:

- To what extent do emerging market MNEs rely on experience when internationalising?[2]
- To what extent do state-owned MNEs make decisions based on individual managerial biases? Do they prioritise other stakeholders (e.g. political activists) as reference points?
- To what extent do international entrepreneurs use industry reference points and benchmarks to reduce some of the risks associated with growth?
- What is the influence of family ownership in forming biases in family firm internationalisation? Do family owned MNEs use strategic reference points oriented towards the past or the future?

- Are MNEs with more flexible capital structures (i.e. private firms) less biased towards the past and more willing to experiment quickly with strategic choices compared to public MNEs?

Area IV: New methodologies

Methodologically, we fall short in making these micro-foundational concepts actionable in international business management research. In viewing the manager as human, we invite many of the complexities of human judgement and behaviour. From a rational perspective, the messy business of human unpredictability may have – historically – been somewhat inconvenient to its study. Studies on the measurements of cognitive biases and MNE strategic choices are rare. This is partly due to the limitations of current methods to measure biases in decision-making, as these cannot be operationalised by using only firm- or industry-level data. Examples of potential methods include choice experiments (Buckley et al., 2007); field studies (Maitland and Sammartino, 2015); comparative case research (Welch et al., 2011); mixed methods (Crilly, 2011); and grounded theory (Birkinshaw et al., 2011).

Whilst there are clear merits to using quantitative methodological approaches, we are increasingly confusing these methods with "hard science" (Birkinshaw et al., 2011). This has led to the growth in popularity of traditional theories that continue to be tested using quantitative methods, and a decrease in theoretical or multi-disciplinary work that stems from rich, descriptive data. We therefore propose that the dynamic and multi-institutional nature of international business management lends itself to a wider range of methodologies. More exploratory methods of research may be more suited to understand complex phenomena scattered over time and distance. Take, for instance, the study by Buckley et al. (2007) who conducted an experiment with decision-makers from top management teams in order to understand how managers make international location choices, by presenting them with a complex combination of choice attributes. They found that the attributes considered go beyond expected return on investment associated with a host location and more experienced managers were found to make different choices. Further, the attributes considered to select the initial set of location options differed from those considered in the final decision – thus also illustrating the importance of time in dynamic decision-making. Through interviews and observations, Maitland and Sammartino (2015) also attribute a large part of the heterogeneity found in the factors considered to make international business decisions to different types of experiences that managers have had in the past, and the biases stemming from those experiences. Such notable works exist and should serve as a starting point for scholars to understand how different combinations of primary and secondary data sources can be used to gain real insight into managerial decision-making. This type of advancement in our methodological approaches would help us understand not only the outcomes of managerial decision-making, but also how and why certain strategic choices are considered, and others disregarded.

3.5   Concluding remarks

Where mainstream international management theories fail, behavioural ideas may prevail! The basis for the behavioural perspective is grounded in the social psychological sciences, which likely take our typical international management reader beyond the comfort of their natural habitat. We feel that the presence of biases in decision-making is evident, none more so than in the increasingly dynamic and uncertain field of international management research. Notwithstanding the significant contributions and insights of extant management research, we have been slow to adopt and integrate behavioural concepts.

In order to lay the initial groundwork for a "behavioural perspective of international management", we hope to have provided several ways in which a behavioural perspective could complement current research. Most importantly, a behavioural theory of international management would allow researchers to explore what bounds decision-making, and why firms and their managers, when provided with the same choice attributes make different decisions. Moreover, we invite researchers and early career scholars to examine how the biases and reference points used by managers to make decisions change over time for each decision made. This, we propose, subsequently paves the way for a better understanding of multinational firm competitive advantage and survival.

In a modern business environment with ever-looming "grand challenges", a reluctance to explore social psychological solutions is a missed opportunity, when interventions in altering perception or nudging individuals to make more appropriate choices typically are more resource-efficient, and often times significantly more effective than traditional, materialist, efficiency-oriented solutions. Indeed, there will be barriers to the widespread adoption of behavioural approaches; shifting perceptions of researchers away from viewing the MNE as a mechanistic system of inputs, processes and outputs to include a human system of biases, emotion and consequences, will require a collective effort and shift in thinking. We hope that this chapter has gone some way towards convincing our readers that there is significant opportunity to be uncovered in a behavioural approach. Such a behavioural approach, we propose, will enhance and complement current international business and management research.

Acknowledgement

We would like to thank Ödül Bozkurt, Mike Geppert and Roger Strange as well as the participants at the March 2020 Paper Development Workshop in Jena for their helpful comments and suggestions on an earlier draft of this chapter.

Notes

1. The importance of using theoretical models and frameworks which enable an understanding of how firms make decisions in dynamic environments is discussed in more detail in Chapter 4 of this book.
2. Chapter 5 provides a detailed discussion concerning the effect of the home country on the internationalisation of the firm and future avenues for theorising about it.

References

Aharoni, Y., Tihanyi, L. and Connelly, B.L. (2011). Managerial decision-making in international business: A forty-five-year retrospective. *Journal of World Business*, 46(2): 135–142.

Ardalan, K. (2018). Behavioral attitudes toward current economic events: A lesson from neuroeconomics. *Business Economics*, 53(4): 202–208.

Arrow, K.J. (1982). Risk perception in psychology and economics. *Economic Inquiry*, 20(1): 1–9.

Beamond, M.T., Farndale, E. and Hartel, C.E.J. (2016). MNE translation of corporate talent management strategies to subsidiaries in emerging economies. *Journal of World Business*, 51(4): 499–510.

Benito, G.R.G., Petersen, B. and Welch, L.S. (2009). Towards more realistic conceptualisations of foreign operation modes. *Journal of International Business Studies*, 40(9): 1455–1470.

Birkinshaw, J., Brannen, M.Y. and Tung, R.L. (2011). From a distance and generalizable to up close and grounded: Reclaiming a place for qualitative methods in international business research. *Journal of International Business Studies*, 42(5): 573–581.

Brouthers, K.D. and Hennart, J.-F. (2007). Boundaries of the firm: Insights from international entry mode research. *Journal of Management*, 33(3): 395–425.

Buckley, P. (2002). Is the international business research agenda running out of steam? *Journal of International Business Studies*, 33: 365–373.

Buckley, P. and Casson, M. (1976). *The Future of the Multinational Enterprise*. London: Macmillan.

Buckley, P.J., Devinney, T.M. and Louviere, J.J. (2007). Do managers behave the way theory suggests? A choice-theoretic examination of foreign direct investment location decision-making. *Journal of International Business Studies*, 38(7): 1069–1094.

Buckley, P., Doh, J.P. and Benischke, M.H. (2017). Towards a renaissance in international business research? Big questions, grand challenges, and the future of IB scholarship. *Journal of International Business Studies*, 48(9): 1045–1064.

Casillas, J.C., Barbero, L.L. and Sapienza, H.J. (2015). Knowledge acquisition, learning, and the initial pace of internationalisation. *International Business Review*, 24(1): 102–114.

Casillas, J.C. and Moreno-Menendez, A.M. (2014). Speed of the internationalisation process: The role of diversity and depth in experiential learning. *Journal of International Business Studies*, 45(1): 85–101.

Crilly, D. (2011). Predicting stakeholder orientation in the multinational enterprise: A mid-range theory. *Journal of International Business Studies*, 42(5): 694–717.

Cyert, R.M. and March, J.G. (1963). *A Behavioral Theory of the Firm*. Englewood Cliffs, NJ: Prentice Hall.

Delios, A. and Beamish, P.W. (1999). Ownership strategy of Japanese firms: Transactional, institutional, and experience influences. *Strategic Management Journal*, 20: 915–933.

Ditto, P.H. and Jemmott, J.B. (1989). From rarity to evaluative extremity: Effects of prevalence information on evaluations of positive and negative characteristics. *Journal of Personality and Social Psychology*, 57: 16–26.

Doh, J.P. (2015). From the editor: Why we need phenomenon-based research in international business. *Journal of World Business*, 50(4): 609–611.

Dörrenbächer, C. and Geppert, M. (2017). Multinational corporations and organization theory: An introduction to post-millennium perspectives. In C. Dörrenbächer and M. Geppert (Eds), *Multinational Corporations and Organization Theory: Post Millennium Perspectives* (Vol. 49). Bingley: Emerald Publishing, 3–42.

Duhaime, I.M. and Schwenk, C.R. (1985). Conjectures on cognitive simplification in acquisition and divestment decision making. *The Academy of Management Review*, 10(2): 287–295.

Easterby-Smith, M. and Lyles, M.A. (2011). *Handbook of Organisational Learning and Knowledge Management* (2nd edition). Chichester: Wiley.

Elia, S., Larsen, M. and Piscitello, L. (2019). Entry mode deviation: A behavioural approach to internalization theory. *Journal of International Business Studies*, 50(8): 1359–1371.

Evans, J.S.B. (2008). Dual-processing accounts of reasoning, judgement, and social cognition. The Annual Review of Psychology, 59: 255–278.

Feldman, M.S. (2000). Organisational routines as a source of continuous change. Organisation Science, 11(6): 611–629.

Fiske, S.T. and Taylor, S.E. (1991). *Social Cognition* (2nd edition). New York: McGraw-Hill.

Foss, N.J. and Weber, L. (2016). Moving opportunism to the back seat: Bounded rationality, costly conflict, and hierarchical forms. *Academy of Management Review*, 41(1): 61–79.

Frost, T.S., Birkinshaw, J.M. and Ensign, P.C. (2002). Centers of excellence in multinational corporations. *Strategic Management Journal*, 23(11): 997–1018.

Gigerenzer, G. (2003). Bounding rationality to the world. *Journal of Economic Psychology*, 24(2): 143–165.

Gilovich, T., Griffin, D. and Kahneman, D. (Eds) (2002). *Heuristics and Biases: The Psychology of Intuitive Judgment.* Cambridge: Cambridge University Press.

Hamilton, J.B., Knouse, S.B. and Hill, V. (2009). Google in China: A manager-friendly heuristic model for resolving cross-cultural ethical conflicts. *Journal of Business Ethics*, 86: 143–157.

Hennart, J.-F. (1982). *A Theory of Multinational Enterprise.* Ann Arbor: University of Michigan Press.

Johanson, J. and Vahlne, J.E. (1977). The internationalization process of the firm: A model of knowledge development and increasing foreign market commitments. *Journal of International Business Studies*, 8(1): 23–32.

Kahneman, D. and Tversky, A. (1979). Prospect theory: An analysis of decision under risk. *Econometrica*, 47(2): 263–291.

Kano, L. and Verbeke, A. (2015). The three faces of bounded reliability: Alfred Chandler and the micro-foundations of management theory. *California Management Review*, 58(1): 97–122.

Kanouse, David E. and Reid Hanson, Jr., L. (1972). Negativity in evaluations. In E.E. Jones (Ed.), *Attribution: Perceiving the Causes of Behavior.* Morristown, NJ: General Learning Press.

Labroo, A.A. and Kim, S. (2009). The 'instrumentality' heuristic: Why metacognitive difficulty is desirable during goal pursuit. *Psychological Science*, 20(1): 127–134.

Lee, J., Jung, H.J. and Park, H. (2020). Rare is beautiful? Rare technological resources and value implications. *Academic of Management Proceedings*, 12962.

Li, J. and Yao, F.K. (2010). The role of reference groups in international investment decisions by firms from emerging economies. *Journal of International Management*, 16(2): 143–153.

Lumineau, F. and Verbeke, A. (2016). Let's give opportunism the proper back seat. *The Academy of Management Review*, 41(4): 739–741.

Lyles, M.A. (1994). The impact of organisational learning on joint venture formations. *International Business Review*, 3(4): 459–467.

Madrian, B.C. and Shea, D.F. (2001). The power of suggestion: Inertia in 401(k) participation and savings behavior. *Quarterly Journal of Economics*, 116(4): 1149–1187.

Maitland, E. and Sammartino, A. (2015). Managerial cognition and internationalization. *Journal of International Business Studies*, 46(7): 733–760.

March, J.H. (1978). Bounded rationality, ambiguity, and the engineering of choice. *Bell Journal of Economics*, 9: 587–608.

March, J.H. and Simon, H.A. (1958/1993). *Organisations.* Oxford: Blackwell.

Monaghan, S. and Tippmann, E. (2018). Becoming a multinational enterprise: Using industry recipes to achieve rapid multinationalisation. *Journal of International Business Studies*, 49(4): 473–495.

Mudambi, R., Narula, R. and Santangelo, G. (2018). Location, collocation and innovation by multinational enterprises: A research agenda. *Industry and Innovation*, 25(3): 229–241.

Muradoglu, G. and Harvey, N. (2012). Behavioural finance: The role of psychological factors in financial decisions. *Review of Behavioural Finance*, 4(2): 68–80.

Narula, R. (2012). Do we need different frameworks to explain infant MNEs from developing countries? *Global Strategy Journal*, 2(3): 188–204.

Narula, R. (2017). Emerging market MNEs as meta-integrators: The importance of internal networks. *International Journal of Technology Management*, 74(1–4): 214–220.

Narula, R. (2018). An extended dual economy model: Implications for emerging economies and their multinational firms. *International Journal of Emerging Markets*, 13(3): 586–602.

Narula, R., Asmussen, C., Chi, T. and Kundu, S. (2019). Applying and advancing internalization theory: The multinational enterprise in the 21st century. *Journal of International Business Studies*, 50: 1231–1252.

Narula, R. and Verbeke, A. (2015). Making internalization theory good for practice: The essence of Alan Rugman's contributions to international business. *Journal of World Business*, 50(4): 612–622.

Nelson, R.A. and Winter, S.G. (1982). *An Evolutionary Theory of Economic Change*. Cambridge, MA: Harvard University Press.

Nguyen, Q.T.K. and Almodóvar, P. (2018). Export intensity of foreign subsidiaries of multinational enterprises: The role of trade finance availability. *International Business Review*, 27(1): 231–245.

Odean, T. (1998). Are investors reluctant to realize their losses? *Journal of Finance*, 53(5): 1775–1798.

Popper, C. (1957). *The Poverty of Historicism*. London: Routledge.

Rugman, A.M. (1980). A new theory of the multinational enterprise: Internationalization versus internalization. *Columbia Journal of World Business*, 15(1): 23–29.

Schubert, T., Baier, E. and Rammer, C. (2018). Firm capabilities, technological dynamism and the internationalisation of innovation: A behavioural approach. *Journal of International Business Studies*, 49(1): 70–95.

Shapiro, D.L., Von Glinow, M.A. and Xiao, Z. (2007). Toward polycontextually sensitive research methods. *Management and Organization Review*, 3(1): 129–152.

Shoham, A. and Fiegenbaum, A. (2002). Competitive determinants of organisational risk-taking attitude: The role of strategic reference points. *Management Decision*, 40(2): 127–141.

Shrader, R.C., Oviatt, B.M. and McDougall, P.P. (2000). How new ventures exploit trade-offs among international risk factors: Lessons for the accelerated internationalization of the 21st century. *The Academy of Management Journal*, 43(6): 1227–1247.

Simon, H.A. (1955). A behavioural model of rational choice. *The Quarterly Journal of Economics*, 69(1): 99–118.

Simon, H.A. (1982). *Models of Bounded Rationality, Volume 2: Behavioural Economics and Business Organization*. Cambridge, MA: MIT Press.

Simon, H.A. (1990). Invariants of human behavior. *Annual Review of Psychology*, 41: 1–19.

Strange, R. (2018). Corporate ownership and the theory of the multinational enterprise. *International Business Review*, 27(6): 1229–1237.

Surdu, I. and Mellahi, K. (2016). Theoretical foundations of equity based foreign market entry decisions: A review of the literature and recommendations for future research. *International Business Review*, 25(5): 1169–1184.

Surdu, I., Mellahi, K. and Glaister, K.W. (2018a). Emerging market multinationals' international equity-based entry mode strategies: Review of theoretical foundations and future directions. International Marketing Review, 35(2): 342–359.

Surdu, I., Mellahi, K. and Glaister, K.W. (2019). Once bitten not necessarily shy? Determinants of foreign market re-entry commitment decisions. *Journal of International Business Studies*, 50(3): 393–422.

Surdu, I., Mellahi, K., Glaister, K.W. and Nardella, G. (2018b). Why wait? Organisational learning, institutional quality and the speed of foreign market re-entry after initial entry and exit. *Journal of World Business*, 53(6): 911–929.

Surdu, I. and Narula, R. (in press). Organizational learning, unlearning and re-internationalization timing: Differences between emerging- versus developed-market MNEs. *Journal of International Management*.

Teagarden, M.B., Von Glinow, M.A. and Mellahi, K. (2018). Contextualizing international business research: Enhancing rigor and relevance. *Journal of World Business*, 53(3): 303–306.

Tversky, A. and Kahneman, D. (1974). Judgment under uncertainty: Heuristics and biases. *Science*, 185: 1124–1131.

Tversky, A. and Kahneman, D. (1981). The framing of decisions and the psychology of choice. *Science*, 211(4481): 453–458.

Tversky, A. and Kahneman, D. (1992). Advances in prospect theory: Cumulative representation of uncertainty. *Journal of Risk and Uncertainty*, 5(4): 297–323.

Tversky, A., Slovic, P. and Kahneman, D. (1990). The causes of preference reversal. *The American Economic Review*, 80(1): 204–217.

Vahlne, J.E. and Johanson, J. (2017). From internationalization to evolution: The Uppsala model at 40 years. *Journal of International Business Studies*, 48(9): 1087–1102.

Verbeke, A. and Greidanus, N. (2009). The end of the opportunism vs trust debate: Bounded reliability as a new envelope concept in research on MNE governance. *Journal of International Business Studies*, 40(9): 1471–1495.

Wason, P.C. (1960). On the failure to eliminate hypotheses in a conceptual task. *Quarterly Journal of Experimental Psychology*, 12: 129–140.

Weick, K.E. (1995). *Sensemaking in Organizations*. Thousand Oaks, CA: Sage Publications.

Weick, K.E., Sutcliffe, K.M. and Obstfeld, D. (2005). Organizing and the process of sensemaking. *Organization Science*, 16(4): 409–421.

Welch, C., Piekkari, R., Plakoyiannaki, E. and Paavilainen-Mantymaki, E. (2011). Theorising from case studies: Towards a pluralist future for international business research. *Journal of International Business Studies*, 42(5): 740–762.

4. Outward investment from emerging markets: time for a paradigm shift?

Suma Athreye

4.1 Introduction

Almost all management scholars will readily agree that the isolation of context in the discussion of new phenomena is not water-tight but merely a theoretical device to focus more sharply on the subject of discussion. What happens when as management scholars we confront new phenomena? A common approach is to try to conform to existing theory with incremental improvements rather than improve the theory by making context explicit. Theories developed in advanced, Western economy contexts may be biased in the contextual elements they privilege and emphasise in subsequent attempts to advance theory. Context may need be brought from the background of theoretical discussion to the foreground of study in order to understand the rationale for strategy. Doing so also enables us to find broader theoretical frames that are able to accommodate multiple contexts.

This argument about confronting theory with new phenomena is an old one in the philosophy of science and dates back to the work of Kuhn (1962). Kuhn claimed that a careful study of the history of science reveals that development in any scientific field happens via a series of phases. In the first phase, a community of researchers who share a common intellectual framework – called a paradigm or a "disciplinary matrix" – engage in solving puzzles thrown up by discrepancies (anomalies) between what the paradigm predicts and what is revealed by observation or experiment. Most of the time, the anomalies – failures of the current paradigm to take into account observed phenomena – are resolved either by incremental changes to the paradigm or by uncovering observational or experimental error. As anomalies accumulate, the time

63

becomes ripe for a paradigmatic shift. The classic example is that until the theory of relativity was discovered by Einstein (which gave birth to the field of quantum mechanics), physicists only had Newtonian gravity to work with, even though physicists knew that it produced anomalous results.

This chapter is a Kuhnian analysis of the huge literature that has emerged on outward investment by emerging economies and the phenomenon of emerging multinational enterprises (EMNEs). I trace the development of theory to explain international investment by the EMNE. This theory has been marked by adherence to a canonical model of internationalisation that is drawn from the behaviour of Western firms in the post-war era. Although this adherence has been periodically challenged by new empirical analyses, internationalisation theory is also constantly adapting to the new facts. Yet the theoretical discussion has often left out/dismissed elements that are not considered as central/critical. Three contributory factors that are often overlooked in discussions of EMNE strategy are the role of improvement in the terms of trade and exports in enabling outward investment, the role of buoyant financial markets and the peculiar phenomenon of a parallel migration of high net worth individuals. I propose a broader framework based on real options theory that may present a better explanation of the unfolding reality of outward investment by both developed and emerging market multinationals.

4.2   Canonical models of internationalisation

The widely accepted model of firm internationalisation explains internationalisation as an outcome of firm-specific advantages (FSAs) and country-specific advantages (CSAs) in the home and host countries, following Collinson and Rugman (2011). CSAs are the advantages of a country which derive from its institutions (following Porter's diamond model, this could refer to the quality of suppliers, national institutions, natural resource endowments and competitive environment facing firms) while FSAs refer to the advantages of particular firms which may reside in their unique capabilities and resources (such as personnel, technology, and/or equipment). Combining those two dimensions in a matrix, we can predict the internationalisation behaviours exhibited by the firm. If the CSAs of the home country are dominant and FSAs rather weak, economic theories argue that comparative advantages of a country (or the location within an industrial cluster) will lead to exports – regardless of the specific characteristics of the company. If FSAs are strong and CSAs are weak, the focus of the international strategy is on exploiting the company's resources, without much influence from the location. In case FSAs and CSAs are both strong, a firm has an incentive to operate across borders, and to coordinate its resources across borders and needs to combine the FSA of the company with the CSA of the host country (and, maybe, the CSA of the home country) in order to be successful (Rugman et al., 2011: 766–768). Thus, the combination of FSAs with CSAs in different locations is the true challenge of international management.

The CSA–FSA framework itself was a refinement of an earlier theoretical approach by Dunning (1988, 2001) – the so-called ownership-location-internali-sation (OLI) theory – which explained the internationalisation activity of multinational enterprises (MNEs) as their attempt to extend their ownership advantages (e.g. proprietary access to a superior production technology or a valuable brand) to overseas markets by exploiting locational advantages (locating abroad to access low cost inputs or better serve local markets), and internalising the efficiency gains from economies of scale and scope by integrating the firm's activities across borders. The CSA–FSA framework succeeded in synthesising the insights of the OLI with the more mainstream strategy literature on competitive advantage, pioneered by scholars like Michael Porter, which had emphasised the role of institutions and market structures as elements of the economic environment, which influence competitive strategies. The CSA dimension was intended thus to capture many of the elements of the economic environment which could influence competitive outcomes and thus provide a theory for explaining the location of investment activity.

The rationale that foreign direct investment (FDI) enables firms to exploit their existing firm-specific assets has been challenged on both theoretical and empirical grounds. On theoretical grounds, Caves (1996) pointed out that these arguments only apply to horizontal FDI. Although the rationale for vertical FDI is similar to that of vertical integration – securing stable supply, avoiding coordination problems and reducing transaction costs – this does not need ownership advantages in the form of proprietary assets. In another important paper, Fosfuri and Motta (1999) questioned the widespread argument that firms embarking on FDI must possess some specific advantages to offset the penalties of operating across national and cultural boundaries. Using a simple model they showed that firms might invest abroad to capture local advantages through geographical proximity of plant location, rather than to exploit existing ones. Due to the spatially bounded nature of spillovers (e.g. because of movement of labour), laggard firms might use foreign investments to acquire location-specific knowledge, whereas leading firms might prefer costly exports to avoid the dissipation of their advantages.

Empirical research has found that the relationship between ownership advantages and outward FDI is often weak (see, for instance, Belderbos and Sleuwaegen, 1996 in the context of Japanese firms). The Linkage, Leverage, and Learning model developed by Mathews (2006) aims to capture the idea that "latecomer firms" (in his case he was looking at South Korea, Taiwan, Singapore and Hong Kong) will use their overseas investments and global linkages to leverage their existing cost advantage and learn about new sources of competitive advantage. If so, internationalisation may contribute to the building of ownership advantages rather than merely being an outcome of existing advantages. Thus, confronted with a context that was not Western, both the leading theoretical approaches based on firm-specific advantages were found wanting.

These matters of inconsistency came to a head when there was a large outflow of investments from India and China and other emerging market multinationals from the late 1990s. Like Mathews (2006), Child and Rodrigues (2005) found that Chinese firms had internationalised partly to exploit competitive advantages, but also to address the competitive disadvantages incurred by operating in exclusively domestic markets. Others like Kumar (2008) studying Indian firms argued that internationalisation was a natural consequence of liberalisation in these two larger emerging countries where government policies of foreign exchange control had denied the use of outward investment as a strategy. What was notable about those early arguments was that ownership advantages in the standard terminology were found wanting in their explanatory power.[1]

One response to this overwhelming evidence from EMNE contexts was to argue that the way FSA had been conceptualised in the literature was unnecessarily narrow. Ramamurti and Singh (2009), but also Kumar and Chadha (2009) argued for a broadening of the definition of FSA and elaborated the different nature of FSAs enjoyed by EMNEs that derive from an "adverse environment" for business and the EMNE ability to adapt imported technology to develop products suited to the special needs of local customers. Examples include making products cheaper and more affordable, making products that were rugged and easy to maintain in harsher road conditions, the provision of after-sales service and lastly operational and technological efficiency in the presence of poor power supply and infrastructural impediments. Yet, in this very Kuhnian resolution of inconsistencies between theory and empirical evidence, context had forced itself on the discussion – largely in the form of institutional environments that affected firm behaviours and enabled the development of unique dynamic capabilities among the EMNEs.

4.3   Institutions as context and the role of CSA in EMNE internationalisation

Although emerging markets constitute a culturally and economically hetero-geneous group of nations, their similarity rests on the distinctive and common features of poorly functioning institutional environments that hinder the growth of businesses. In the parlance of the CSA/FSA framework, they all suffer from some sort of deficit in their CSA, although this may not be uniform across sectors. Weak home country institutions which we may think of as a country-specific disadvantage (CSD) have a significant and often similar impact on emerging market firms' internationalisation strategies (Luo and Wang, 2012; Peng et al., 2008). Thus, the story of internationalisation from emerging markets has often been seen as a response to the push and pull of institutional factors (or CSD) faced by firms with non-standard FSA.

Luo and Wang (2012) identify and justify the existence of a systematic asso-ciation between country-specific ownership advantages stemming from home market and domestic firms' overseas expansion. Specifically, they show that timing, location and scale of outward investment of Chinese firms are depend-ent on the competitive advantage they gain from the home market. Similarly, Wang et al. (2012) suggest that government-related ownership advantages shape firms' level, location, and type of overseas investment. Cuervo-Cazurra (2011) finds that many EMNEs first develop domestically the knowledge to manage complexity and differences in competitive conditions and institutional environments that subsequently facilitates foreign expansion and explains these firms' non-sequential internationalisation. Thus, the disadvantages expe-rienced at home can become advantages when venturing abroad, as successful EMNE firms have learned to survive in "unfavourable" conditions. Inverting the traditional notions where the CSAs are largely seen as supporting FSA, the exciting finding in the case of EMNEs is that more successful firms develop hard to imitate FSAs, due to the deficits in CSA.

In contrast to the above studies, which have mainly looked at the pull of inter-nationalisation strategies due to distinctive FSAs of EMNE firms, a large liter-ature has also argued that institutional imperfections may push EMNE firms towards internationalisation to acquire supporting CSA in the host environ-ment. As already noted, Mathews (2006, 2017) in the context of his study on the four dragons (South Korea, Taiwan, Singapore and Hong Kong) suggested that international expansion is strategic because of the advantages that late-comer firms can access in foreign markets. According to him, firms interna-tionalise by acquiring strategic resources through linking in foreign markets, learning to expand ownership advantages and leveraging their ownership advantages in combination with new resources. Concomitantly, such firms also embrace a learning mentality and adopt novel means of learning to ensure foreign market survival. In a similar vein, Luo and Tung (2007) and Yamakawa et al. (2008) have argued that emerging market firms use internationalisation as a "springboard" to overcome their latecomer disadvantages in the global arena and are not evolutionary but radical in their international expansion. These strategic resources include advanced technology, brand name, managerial expertise, and access to the customer base in foreign markets. Boisot and Meyer (2008) and Cuervo-Cazurra and Genc (2008) add that emerging market firms may leverage "institutional arbitrage", which indicates that EMNEs search for more efficient institutions outside their home markets.

Thus, the pull and push arguments for internationalisation stemming from adverse institutional contexts suggest internationalisation may be used both to exploit and augment the distinctive FSA of EMNEs, which may also try to overcome institutional disadvantages or CSA deficits at home by exploiting CSA in the host country. This investigation of the impact of CSD on firm internationalisation strategy should be seen as another important contribution to the literature on EMNEs on the canonical models of FSA/CSA based theories.

4.4   Omitted factors in theoretical explanations of EMNE internationalisation

While it is undeniable that country-specific institutions, such as the rule of law, financial market development and protection of property, are important contextual factors that explain EMNE internationalisation, these are not the only aspects of context that matter. The economic circumstances of the late 1990s also influenced EMNE internationalisation because changes in the policy and global environment made obtaining finance for investment much easier than in the past. Growing exports at better terms of trade, the globalisation of finance markets and the accumulation of individual wealth were important antecedents to EMNE outward investment strategies. Using an analogy from statistical methods, I argue that omitting these contextual factors may have overstated the contribution of the CSA and FSA factors to internationalisation.

4.4.1   Exports, terms of trade and outward FDI from EMNEs

At the macroeconomic level, a factor that contributes to a nation's ability to make outward investments is its export performance. Mirza and Miroux

(2007) note that almost all the emerging market economies that sent investments abroad in the 1980s (such as Argentina, Brazil and India) had also seen
an improvement in export performance and terms of trade vis-à-vis the world
economy. This was also true of many emerging markets in the late 1990s,
but especially for the BRIC countries (Brazil, Russia, India and China).[2] The
accumulation of export surpluses in the current account must lead to exports
of capital and so it was to be expected that all these economies would end up
with investments abroad.

At the microeconomic level, there is much debate among scholars about the
exact relationship between exports and outward FDI. Standard models like
that of Johanson and Vahlne (1977) see the internationalisation process of
the firm as a continuum, starting from the low commitment stage of exports
and licensing and moving to the greater commitment of resources implicit
in setting up foreign subsidiaries as knowledge about markets, production
and regulation in host countries improves. In this reasoning, FDI and home
nation exports are substitutes. In vertically integrated enterprises such as steel
mills or metal producers, the home nation operations of a multinational firm
can be vertically linked with host nation operations, such that an increase
in the activity in the latter generates increased demand for intermediate
products, including capital goods, from the former. Some would argue that
this might characterise Chinese investments in Africa (Athreye and Kapur,
2009). Furthermore, marketing and distribution capabilities created by FDI
might enable the home nation operations to export final goods and services to
customers that would not be reached in the absence of FDI. To the extent that
either of these happens, home country FDI and exports will be complements.

The relation between outward FDI and terms of trade is equally important
but understudied in the context of EMNE internationalisation. Chen (2012)
estimates that between 2000 and 2010, the BRIC countries together more than
doubled their share of world trade and China accounted for over two-thirds of
that growth. In 2010, the BRICs accounted for over 17 per cent of the world
total exports and almost 14 per cent of the world total imports. Chen (2012)
also shows that the majority of the BRICs' trade was with high income economies (HIEs) – HIEs' share in the BRICs' total exports declined from 72 per cent
in 2000 to 64 per cent in 2010 while the share in total imports declined from
62 per cent in 2000 to 54 per cent in 2010, respectively. This was compensated
by the expansion of trade between the BRICs and low and middle-income
economies (LMIEs) during the period. In 2010, over 30 per cent of the BRICs'
total exports went to LMIE markets; while one-third of its total imports were
sourced from LMIEs. These increases in export volumes also went hand in
hand with improving terms of trade. Using World Bank data, Figure 4.1 shows

that Brazil, India and China saw an improvement of terms of trade from 1990 to 2000 while Russia and South Africa saw an improvement thereafter (from 2000 to 2008).

Chen (2012) also notes that the four BRIC governments are net foreign (currency) creditors. They accounted for almost 40 per cent of the world's total foreign currency reserves by 2010 (*The World Factbook* (CIA, 2011) as cited in Chen, 2012: 225). Although China was the dominant contributor, Russia, India, and Brazil also accumulated substantial volumes of reserves. With China's surplus increasing sharply, the BRICs' combined current account surplus exceeded $280 billion in 2010 (IMF, 2011). Macroeconomic theory generally predicts that such surpluses on account of trade would fuel capital outflows both in the short and long term.

Source: World Bank data: https://databank.worldbank.org/reports.aspx?source=2 &series=TT.PRI.MRCH.XD.WD.

Figure 4.1   Net barter terms of trade, BRICS economies (2000=100)

The combination of expanding exports and rising terms of trade gave several firms in emerging markets large cash balances just as the hyper-globalised world of the 1990s was emerging. What we understand less is how firms used those increased earnings. Cespedes et al. (2020) studying the US retail sector, found that following windfalls, small business owners favour internal and external growth, and for some entrepreneurs, the existing business seems to be a gateway to other ventures. Work that is more interdisciplinary, perhaps by business history scholars, can help to fully understand the potential investment responses to such a windfall of unexpected profits. It seems reasonable to assume, however, that at least some of those profits from exporting may have been channelled into outward investments in new markets that represented future growth opportunities. Fortuitously, and as we discuss below, this branching out also coincided with a period when global financial markets were more open about the possibility of lending to emerging market firms.

4.4.2   International financial markets and credit availability

It is well known that the financial systems in China and other emerging economies are underdeveloped (Buckley et al., 2007) and so failed to deliver the two important functions of any financial system, namely, the availability of a large volume of credit finance and delivery of risk-bearing investible funds. The availability of finance depends upon the presence of lenders and borrowers but the ability to spread risks depends on how deep the financial market is (thickness of buyers and sellers) and systems of monitoring that can evaluate and price risk.

The four BRIC countries are different in their experience of the financial disadvantage that a weak institutional framework creates. China and Russia have a shorter history of market-based financial transactions compared to India and Brazil. Thus, in China and Russia, the state owns most of the banks and disburses credit according to government policy and a domestic stock market is still emerging. India and Brazil – both mixed economies – may have somewhat more developed financial institutions, boasting a larger number of private sector banks and a shallow but functioning stock market. Studies on Brazil suggest the government retains a dominant control over the banking system (Ness, 2000). Financial markets in India are better developed but here too public sector lending is large and financial lending is also sensitive to the riskiness of investments, which in turn is reflected in a higher cost of capital for investments perceived to be risky (Das and Banik, 2015). This means credit is not available to a whole class of borrowers perceived as risky (small firms, young firms) and also to projects perceived as risky (technological investments and foreign investments).

That financial constraints mark EMNE internationalisation is well recognised. Buckley et al. (2007) place considerable emphasis on financial market imperfections as a significant deficit in the CSA faced by several emerging market firms (including China which is the country of their focus) but argue that such imperfections mean access to finance can confer special ownership advantages. In China and to a lesser degree in Russia, such privileged access to state resources confers special ownership advantages to state-owned enterprises which enable successful internationalisation. Other scholars like Khanna and Yafeh (2005) have argued that in many emerging markets such financial market disadvantages are overcome by organisational forms such as business groups who operate internal markets of finance for group companies.

The period from 2000 to 2008, when many EMNE outward investments were first conceived and executed, was also an era of globalised, buoyant financial markets. In an era of globalised markets and finance, adverse financial institutions at home were not a constraint to outward investment as EMNEs were able to raise money for foreign investment overseas when they could not find it domestically. Nayyar (2008) notes that international capital markets were an independent and important source of financing international investment for many EMNEs and were typically not included in official national figures for outward FDI. Kumar and Chadha (2009) and Saeed and Athreye (2014) find that liberalisation of economic policy had the effect of mitigating internal financial constraints on domestic and foreign investment for Chinese and Indian firms.

After the financial crisis of 2008, world financial markets became more cautious about lending and demand in overseas markets suddenly became weak, affecting exports. Figure 4.2 shows that the outward investment paths of BRICS firms, which had looked similar, began to diverge sharply after the financial crisis. In particular only Chinese firms have been able to sustain the growth of outward investments. If only FSAs were involved in outward investments, such a shift in trend for Brazil, India, Russia and South Africa should not have taken place. This divergence of outward FDI pattern between China and the other BRICS economies, in turn raises some interesting questions: Could it be that the whole pattern of outward FDI from emerging markets was driven by buoyant global financial markets? Does the sustained availability of finance constitute a boundary condition, where we can see the development of FSA? We do not know the answers to these questions but I pose them here because omitting this factor could overstate the role of FSA/CSA in the traditional paradigm.

4.4.3   Capital flight and its impact on outward investments

A third economic circumstance not considered in the literature is the effect of wealth accumulated in many emerging markets, including through corruption by political elites. The desire to protect this wealth for progeny (and from tax and political risk) has been a major factor fuelling the rise in offshore tax havens and secret overseas accounts. A lively literature in political science has examined the effects of tax on millionaire migration and concluded that such migration is less sensitive to tax rates than commonly thought (see Young and Varner, 2011; Young et al., 2016), but the field of EMNE internationalisation is oblivious to these trends.

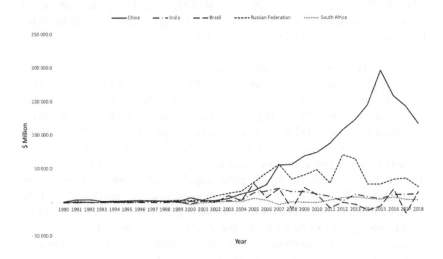

Source: UNCTAD, FDI/MNE database: https://www.unctad.org/fdistatistics.

Figure 4.2   Outward FDI from BRICS economies (1990–2019)

Since the mid-1980s, wealth migration has been a prominent feature of Russia and other transition economies. Brada et al. (2013) estimate that such capital flight[3] (as it is sometimes referred to) is almost always a result of the investor thinking that the risk-return in the host economy is more attractive than in the home economy and fuelled by financial liberalisation. This capital flight is very closely related to the development of domestic financial markets. When financial markets are poorly developed they do not have a wide variety of savings instruments to soak up domestic savings, and investible funds may seek foreign outlets/savings instruments. Brada et al. (2013) outline that the most frequent ways in which private money is moved abroad is through a sort of transfer pricing and mis-invoicing and "fictitious" outward investment. This finding raises the prospect that, depending upon the source of data, some of the EMNE investment may also be overstated/understated. Outward investment data from the home country will understate and inward investment data from the host country will overstate the volume of foreign investment.

Although in the past estimating such capital flight has been tricky, in the last four years, the Global Wealth Migration Review (GWMR) has provided a more direct measure by tracking millionaire migration (defined as the movement of high net worth persons who own assets in excess of $1 million). GWMR (2019)[4] estimates that 30 per cent of this wealth migration or capital flight happens through investor visas, where foreign nationals bring in stipulated amounts of investment in exchange for citizenship.

The truly astonishing fact about millionaire migration and the associated capital flight of recent years is clear from Figure 4.3. The figure shows that the BRIC countries and Turkey are losing more high net worth individuals, defined as persons with assets greater than $1 million, than other countries and the developed world is the chief beneficiary gaining them. The relationship between this migration and the uphill flow of investment from emerging markets to developed countries needs more attention, especially in countries where outward investment may be politically directed. Hitherto, the argument has been that EMNEs go in search of strategic assets to developed country markets. However, the data on millionaire migration may reveal the role of corruption legacies in determining the direction of outward FDI flows. Put differently, ignoring the context of wealth migration to avoid taxes, find new avenues of investment or simply to consume better quality collective goods like public health and education, might also lead one to overstate the role of CSAs in explaining the direction of outward investment.

Another reason could be that human capital and financial capital may play complementary roles in a range of service industries. Whatever the relationship between EMNE investment and wealth migration, progress in this area of study needs greater engagement with political science literature on elites and perhaps also literature in sociology on patterns of diaspora development and skilled and entrepreneurial migration. Such interdisciplinarity has been largely absent in the study of EMNE investments. Instead by looking at the phenomenon in silos, we may have overestimated the influence of FSA/CSA and ignored the links of outward foreign capital with the rewards to human capital in emerging markets.

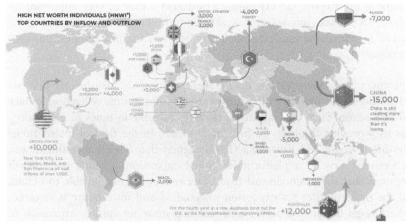

Source: https://www.visualcapitalist.com/millionaire-migrants-countries-rich
-people-flocking/.

Figure 4.3   Millionaire migration

4.5   Time for a paradigm shift? Real options theory as a better lens for understanding EMNE behaviours

The foregoing section has shown that contemporary EMNEs and political elites in emerging markets have enjoyed a range of exogenously created opportunities brought about by exceptionally buoyant global financial markets and export market successes that have created favourable country of origin effects. Yet the effect of these on firm investment behaviours cannot really be accommodated fully in the canonical models currently in use. Being relative newcomers to global competition, many EMNE outward investments were initially exploratory in nature, trying to discover those markets and locations where they could leverage or augment their limited advantages – a different starting point from Western MNEs that had already established firm advantage they could leverage from the outset. Additionally, EMNE outward investments faced uncertainty on various counts: institutional disruptions when they entered new countries, fluctuations in currency value and unexpected changes in demand. Their outward investment activity, undertaken in response to sudden windfalls (such as an export boom or significant increase in private earnings) or access to global finance, is better analysed using a framework that incorporates potential uncertainty and rewards to investment activity. The exploratory nature of investments may also mean flexibility across a range of responses to uncertainty – such as switching the location of resources, divestment of investment and expanding investment – may be very important for the EMNE to take into account. Real options thinking which is popular in the analysis of financial asset portfolios may be a very useful framework for such analysis.

Bowman and Hurry (1993) define "real options" as investments that are discretionary in that they offer firms the right, but not the obligation, to take future action. Such options are particularly valuable in times of uncertainty as they provide flexibility to firm investments. In the field of international business, Kogut and Kulatilaka (1994) suggest that foreign investments can effectively serve as a platform for future expansion, creating real growth options that the multinational firm otherwise would not be able to obtain. If the opportunities for expansion materialise, and uncertainty is resolved, the foreign investment serves as a stepping-stone for further expansion of operations in the target country. Such a perspective is very consistent with the Johanson/Vahlne argument of gradually increasing commitments in a staged process of internationalisation.

Defining a real option, however, requires a consideration of the types of uncertainty and growth options associated with particular investments. Without uncertainty, there would be no option value that is different from the present value of an investment. The more detailed the uncertainty and growth profiles can be, the better is the description of the real options (for action) that the EMNE faces. Thus, a key requirement for using the real options approach is to identify the sources of uncertainty, which in turn give rise to strategies that enable a firm to keep (investment) options open: either by increasing investment in some activity lines or locations, switching investment across activity line/locations, or withdrawing from activity lines/locations.

While discussing a real options framework, a distinction is often made between exogenous and endogenous sources of uncertainty. Chi et al. (2019: 541) provide the clearest definition of this distinction using the language of stochastic variables with mean (μ) and standard deviation (σ).

> To make the distinction between exogenous and endogenous uncertainty clearer, we need to determine whether the action under consideration (e.g. market entry) would influence the parameters (i.e., μ and σ) of the distribution of the stochastic state variable (e.g. cost, demand, profit or project value).

Exogenous uncertainty is present when there are parameters that affect a firm's revenue stream, which the investing firms' action cannot influence. Buckley et al. (2020) consider as exogenous risks all those that influence MNEs and other actors in a uniform way. Prior studies on advanced country EMNEs have confirmed that multinational firms do adjust operations of affiliates in response to changes in relative cost and market conditions. Rangan (1998) finds that changes in exchange rate movements lead to shifts in manufacturing and intra-firm imports of US foreign subsidiaries. Fisch and Zschoche (2012) observe uncertain labour costs as an antecedent of German firms' foreign divestment. Song et al. (2014) find that labour cost differentials are a reason for intra-firm production shifts within Korean multinational networks. The impact of disasters (including war) can also be considered an exogenous uncertainty that impacts upon MNEs' strategic commitments (Dai et al., 2017; Oetzel and Oh, 2014). Exogenous uncertainty is often location-specific and closely related to CSA in the host country.

The important property shared by all sources of exogenous uncertainty is that the MNE can passively, through experience, find more information and act on that basis to lower the impact of that uncertainty on the state variable of inter-est, profits, market share, etc. The ability to wait is crucial to the resolution of exogenous uncertainty and having deep pockets may help with the waiting. In the context of EMNEs, the close relations between the state and EMNEs (as in the case of state-owned enterprises) may mean that this ability to wait is greatly enhanced. Certainly, Chinese and Russian EMNEs seem to be privileged in this regard.

Endogenous uncertainty on the other hand relates to uncertainty that is unequal between firms and which firms can influence through their own actions. Endogenous uncertainty is strongly related to the strength of a firm's competitive position and its FSA. For example, an MNE making a small initial commitment through a joint venture in order to enter a new market is faced with endogenous risk. Although the market seems attractive, it may take more active learning in the form of selling in the market to fully understand the costs and benefits of the investment as well as the attributes of the product that are attractive (relative to competitor offerings) in the foreign market. A small initial commitment (with a local partner) secures a future growth option. Chi et al. (2019) also argue that when there is the potential to invest in stages, i.e. starting small and growing the investment, endogenous uncertainty can give rise to powerful learning effects. Such effects are noted in Mathews' Linkage, Leverage, and Learning model based on the internationalisation of the four dragons or Luo's Springboarding model based on the experience of more recent EMNEs from the BRICS countries.

EMNE firms being new to the international market, probably face higher degrees of endogenous uncertainty because of not knowing where exactly their competitive advantages lie and their weaker FSA. (In contrast, one could argue that MNEs in advanced economies were more sensitive to exogenous uncertainties as they had a clearer idea of their own markets and competencies.) EMNEs were therefore more likely to hedge their (investment) bets by making investments in both developed and developing countries. In turn, this meant they faced different levels of country risk in their portfolio of international investments.

In response to endogenous and exogenous uncertainty, EMNE firms could deploy a number of different strategies, e.g. expanding investments, delaying investments, switching investments or divesting investments. In the case of each action, other factors would come into play. Thus, expanding investments were more likely to be employed when there was a positive shock in the form of new growth opportunity. However, foreign exchange uncertainty or labour costs uncertainty (due to strong unions for example) may give rise to switching and divestment behaviours. Anecdotal evidence exists of the difficulties of dealing with local labour unions by Chinese firms (Zhu, 2015). One problem in the EMNE literature is also that the various actions of the EMNE beyond initial (entry) or expanding investment are not that well studied – more careful data on the survival and divestment of EMNE investments is needed to expand the menu of actions.

Do political and country risk constitute exogenous or endogenous uncertainty in the location decisions of MNEs? Early studies often assumed political risk to be exogenous to MNEs, as MNEs were thought to respond passively to the environmental characteristics of the host country (Buckley et al., 2007; Globerman and Shapiro, 2003; Loree and Guisinger, 1995). More recent work in Buckley et al. (2020) argues that country and political risk is an endogenous uncertainty as firms can lobby governments and mitigate adverse impacts. A similar argument can be made for institutional difference and uncertainty.

The real options framework with its emphasis on uncertainty and flexibility is capable of nesting within it the two major approaches discussed in sections 4.2 and 4.3 (these are the CSA-FSA and springboarding behaviour explanations of the phenomenon of internationalisation respectively). It enables the incorporation of several other contextual factors largely ignored in the discussion of EMNE internationalisation. However, this approach also requires a clearer delineation of context (type of uncertainty and advantage) and a range of actions (entry, expanding, switching and divestment of investments).

4.6   Why does it matter?

One might reasonably ask, since all theory is in some way a simplification of reality, can one really incorporate all contextual factors and finally what does paradigm shift achieve? This question recalls the philosophical arguments posed by Borges (1946) and Eco (1994) on the impossibility of drawing a map that accounts for every aspect of reality. Equally dangerous is the tendency to regard the map or conceptual model as the territory/reality. This was explained by Baudrillard (1981/1994: 1) in the following way:

> Today abstraction is no longer that of the map, the double, the mirror, or the concept. Simulation is no longer that of a territory, a referential being, or a sub-stance. It is the generation by models of a real without origin or reality: a hyperreal. The territory no longer precedes the map, nor does it survive it. It is nevertheless the map that precedes the territory – precession of simulacra – that engenders the territory, and if one must return to the fable, today it is the territory whose shreds slowly rot across the extent of the map.

It is of course possible that adherents of the first school will not be persuaded by the fears of the second. Disciplines like physics and economics have accom-modated both sorts of thinkers by distinguishing empirical and theoretical contributions as a division of labour within the discipline. This has been an efficient sorting and the pace of discovery in both sub-disciplines has increased over time but has come at a cost because the dialogue between the two schools (theory and empirics) is minimal.

In the international business space too one can see the beginnings of such a bifurcation with the two leading journals, namely, *Journal of International Business Studies* (JIBS) and *Journal of World Business* (JWB). While JIBS prides itself on theoretical contributions and has several to its credit, JWB has estab-lished a strong reputation for study of phenomena – grounded in theory but still looking to articulate what is new in the empirical reality. As in the case of other disciplines, such bifurcation can come at the cost of a dialogue between context and theory and paradigm shift may potentially lead to a third way that unifies theory and empirics.

The real options framework is proposed as a less restrictive theoretical framework that is capable of incorporating the realities of EMNE expansion far better than the FSA/CSA framework. However, in order to develop the framework in a realistic way we need to commit ourselves to a research program that builds the theoretical and empirical foundations of a new para-digm. Theoretically, the new paradigm should reflect better understanding of both the options available for investment and the uncertainties faced by the MNE and EMNE actors involved. This is consistent with bringing the context back in and making it the foreground of any discussion of international strategy. Empirically, there should be a commitment to study a wider range of actions – beyond the initial foray into a new market. Expansion, switching of investment and divestment should all be observed with as much care as the initial entry. Further understanding the uncertainties, risks and rewards of international investment needs much closer attention to contextual details and to understand the debates in neighbouring disciplines like political science and business history. Interdisciplinary study of context should ultimately shape the direction of theoretical evolution that helps us generalise from new realities.

Acknowledgement

This chapter is part of a programme of work on the study of Chinese and Indian multinational investment, divestment and survival and draws on ideas in papers that I have written jointly with Abubakr Saeed and Mohammad Saad, both of COMSATS University, Pakistan. I am very grateful to the editors for their valuable comments that have helped improve the chapter. The usual disclaimer applies.

Notes

1. See also the debate in the *Asia Pacific Journal of Management* in 2006 (Dunning, 2006; Mathews, 2006; Narula, 2006), where Mathews emphasised that he saw his LLL as a strategic framework which far from displacing microeconomic reasoning of OLI, was a way of complementing the timeless insights of OLI with the strategic necessities of latecomer firms that were seeking to become players in the globalised economy.
2. Some authors include South Africa in this group and the acronym used then is BRICS.
3. Capital flight can be defined as unregistered private capital flows which may be for legal (economically profitable activities) or for illegal activity (think money laundering).
4. The report is produced by the AfrAsia Bank and available online from https://www .afrasiabank.com/en/about/newsroom/global-wealth-migration-review-2019.

References

Athreye, S. and Kapur, S. (2009). Introduction: The internationalization of Chinese and Indian firms – trends, motivations and strategy. *Industrial and Corporate Change*, 18(2): 209–221.

Baudrillard, J. (1981/1994). *Simulacra and Simulation*, trans. S. F. Glaser. Ann Arbor: University of Michigan Press.

Belderbos, R. and Sleuwaegen, L. (1996). Japanese firms and the decision to invest abroad: Business groups and regional core networks. *The Review of Economics and Statistics*, 78(2): 214–220.

Boisot, M. and Meyer, M.W. (2008). Which way through the open door? Reflections on the internationalization of Chinese firms. *Management and Organization Review*, 4(3): 349–365.

Borges, J. (1946). On exactitude in science. In *Collected Fictions*, trans. Andrew Hurley. New York: Penguin Books.

Bowman, E.H. and Hurry, D. (1993). Strategy through the option lens: An integrated view of resource investments and the incremental-choice process. *Academy of Management Review*, 18(4): 760–782.

Brada, J.C. Kutan, A.M. and Vukšić, G. (2013). Capital flight in the presence of domestic borrowing: Evidence from Eastern European economies. *World Development*, 51: 32–46.

Buckley, P.J., Chen, L., Clegg, L.J. and Voss, H. (2020). The role of endogenous and exogenous risk in FDI entry choices. *Journal of World Business*, 55(1): 101040.

Buckley, P., Clegg, L.J., Cross, A., Lie, X., Voss, H. and Zheng, P. (2007). The determinants of Chinese outward foreign direct investment. *Journal of International Business Studies*, 38(2): 499–518.

Caves, R.E (1996). *Multinational Enterprise and Economic Analysis*. Cambridge: Cambridge University Press.

Cespedes, J., Huang, X. and Parra, C. (2020). The 'jackpot' question: How do cash windfalls affect entrepreneurial activities? https://ssrn.com/abstract=3301451 or http://dx.doi.org/10.2139/ssrn.3301451.

Chen, L. (2012). The BRICS in the global value chains: An empirical note. *Cuadernos de Economía*, 31(SPE57): 221–239.

Chi, T., Li, J., Trigeorgis, L.G. and Tsekrekos, A.E. (2019). Real options theory in international business. *Journal of International Business Studies*, 50: 525–553.

Child, J. and Rodrigues, S. (2005). The internationalization of Chinese firms: A case for theoretical extension? *Management and Organization Review*, 1(3): 381–410.

CIA (2011). *The World Factbook*. Washington, DC: CIA. https://www.cia.gov/library/publications/the-world-factbook/index.html.

Collinson, S.C. and Rugman, A.M. (2011). Relevance and rigor in international business teaching: Using the CSA-FSA matrix. *Journal of Teaching in International Business*, 22(1): 29–37.

Cuervo-Cazurra, A. (2011). Selecting the country in which to start internationalization: The non-sequential internationalization model. *Journal of World Business*, 46(4): 426–437.

Cuervo-Cazurra, A. and Genc, M. (2008). Transforming disadvantages into advantages: Developing-country MNEs in the least developed countries. *Journal of International Business Studies*, 39(6): 957–979.

Dai, L., Eden, L. and Beamish, P.W. (2017). Caught in the crossfire: Dimensions of vulnerability and foreign multinationals' exit from war-afflicted countries. *Strategic Management Journal*, 38(7): 1478–1498.

Das, K.C. and Banik, N. (2015). Outbound foreign direct investment from China and India: The role of country-specific factors. *China Report*, 51(3): 204–229.

Dunning, J.H. (1988). The eclectic paradigm of international production: A restatement and some possible extensions. *Journal of International Business Studies*, 19(1): 1–31.

Dunning, J.H. (2001). The eclectic (OLI) paradigm of international production: Past, present and future. *International Journal of the Economics of Business*, 8(2): 173–190.

Dunning, J.H. (2006). Towards a new paradigm of development: Implications for the determinants of international business. *Transnational Corporations*, 15(1): 173–227.

Eco, U. (1994). On the impossibility of drawing a map of the empire on a scale of 1 to 1. In *How to Travel with a Salmon and other Essays*, trans. William Weaver. New York: Harcourt Brace and London: Secker, 95–106.

Fisch, J.H. and Zschoche, M. (2012). The effect of operational flexibility on decisions to withdraw from foreign production locations. *International Business Review*, 21(5): 806–816.

Fosfuri, A. and Motta, M. (1999). Multinationals without advantages. *Scandinavian Journal of Economics*, 101(4): 617–630.

Globerman, S. and Shapiro, D. (2003). Governance infrastructure and US foreign direct investment. *Journal of International Business Studies*, 34: 19–39.

IMF (2011). *World Economic Outlook 2011*. Washington, DC: IMF.

Johanson, J. and Vahlne, J.E. (1977). The internationalization process of the firm: A model of knowledge development and increasing foreign market commitments. *Journal of International Business Studies*, 8(1): 23–32.

Khanna, T. and Yafeh, Y. (2005). Business groups and risk sharing around the world. *Journal of Business*, 78(1): 301–340.

Kogut, B. and Kulatilaka, N. (1994). Options thinking and platform investments: Investing in opportunity. *California Management Review*, 36(2): 52–71.

Kuhn, T. (1962). *The Structure of Scientific Revolutions*. Chicago: University of Chicago Press.

Kumar, N. (2008). Emerging MNCs: Trends, patterns, and determinants of outward FDI by Indian enterprises. In R. Rajan, R. Kumar and N. Virgill (Eds), *New Dimensions of Economic Globalization: Surge of Outward Foreign Direct Investment from Asia*. Singapore: World Scientific, 141–167.

Kumar, N. and Chadha, A. (2009). India's outward foreign direct investments in steel industry in a Chinese comparative perspective. *Industrial and Corporate Change*, 18(2): 249–267.

Loree, D.W. and Guisinger, S.E. (1995). Policy and non-policy determinants of US equity foreign direct investment. *Journal of International Business Studies*, 26(2): 281–299.

Luo, Y. and Tung, R. (2007). International expansion of emerging market enterprises: A springboard perspective. *Journal of International Business Studies*, 38(4): 481–498.

Luo, Y. and Wang, S.L. (2012). Foreign direct investment strategies by developing country multinationals: A diagnostic model for home country effects. *Global Strategy Journal*, 2(3): 244–261.

Mathews, J.A. (2006). Dragon multinationals: New players in 21st century globalization. *Asia Pacific Journal of Management*, 23(1): 5–27.

Mathews, J.A. (2017). Dragon multinationals powered by linkage, leverage and learning: A review and development. *Asia Pacific Journal of Management*, 34: 769–775.

Mirza, H. and Miroux, A. (2007). Third world multinationals revisited. https://vi
.unctad.org/fdiCD/sessions/Session3/MirzaMiroux.pdf.

Narula, R. (2006). Globalization, new ecologies, new zoologies, and the purported death
of the eclectic paradigm. *Asia Pacific Journal of Management*, 23(2), 143–151.

Nayyar, D. (2008). The internationalization of firms from India: Investment, mergers
and acquisitions. *Oxford Development Studies*, 36(1): 111–131.

Ness, W.L. (2000). Reducing government bank presence in the Brazilian financial
system: Why and how. *The Quarterly Review of Economics and Finance*, 40(1): 71–84.

Oetzel, J.M. and Oh, C.H. (2014). Learning to carry the cat by the tail: Firm experience,
disasters, and multinational subsidiary entry and expansion. *Organization Science*,
25(3): 732–756.

Peng, M.W., Wang, D.Y. and Jiang, Y. (2008). An institution-based view of international business strategy: A focus on emerging economies. *Journal of International
Business Studies*, 39(5): 920–936.

Ramamurti, R. and Singh, J.V. (2009). Indian multinationals: Generic internationalization strategies. In R. Ramamurti and J.V. Singh (Eds), *Emerging Multinationals in
Emerging Markets*. Cambridge: Cambridge University Press, 110–166.

Rangan, S. (1998). Do multinationals operate flexibly? Theory and evidence. *Journal of
International Business Studies*, 29(2): 217–237.

Rugman, A.M., Verbeke, A. and Nguyen, Q.T. (2011). Fifty years of international business theory and beyond. *Management International Review*, 51(6): 755–786.

Saeed, A. and Athreye, S. (2014). Internal capital markets and outward foreign investment from India and China. In Y. Temouri and C. Jones (Eds), *International Business
and Institutions after the Financial Crisis*. Basingstoke: Palgrave Macmillan, 93–108.

Song, S., Makhija, M. and Lee, S.-H. (2014). Within-country growth options versus
across-country switching options in foreign direct investment. *Global Strategy
Journal*, 4(2): 127–142.

Wang, C., Hong, J., Kafouros, M. and Wright, M. (2012). Exploring the role of
government involvement in outward FDI from emerging economies. *Journal of
International Business Studies*, 43(7): 655–676.

Yamakawa, Y., Peng, M.W. and Deeds, D.L. (2008). What drives new ventures to internationalize from emerging to developed economies? *Entrepreneurship Theory and
Practice*, 32(1): 59–82.

Young, C. and Varner, C. (2011). Millionaire migration and state taxation of top
incomes: Evidence from a natural experiment. *National Tax Journal*, 64(2, Part 1):
255–284.

Young, C., Varner, C., Lurie, I.Z. and Prisinzano, R. (2016). Millionaire migration
and taxation of the elite: Evidence from administrative data. *American Sociological
Review*, 81(3): 421–446.

Zhu, J.S. (2015). Chinese multinational corporations' responses to host country trade
unions: An eclectic approach. *Journal of Industrial Relations*, 57(2): 232–249.

PART II

Changing roles of nation-states and MNEs

5. The role of the home country in international business and management research: state of the art and future research directions

Florian Becker-Ritterspach and Khaled Fourati

5.1 Introduction

Most classical theories on firm internationalisation initially showed little concern for the role of the home country, let alone home country support, in understanding the prerequisites and patterns for firm internationalisation. However, the growing foreign direct investment (FDI) by emerging market multinationals (EMNEs) led to considering the role of the home country in firm internationalisation. More specifically, it was difficult to account for these firms' internationalisation motivation and pattern without reference to their home country conditions.

The global shift in FDI patterns gave rise to two changes in theory development. First, it led proponents of classical theories of internationalisation to pay closer attention to the role of the home countries and their institutions (e.g. Dunning et al., 2008; Dunning and Lundan, 2008; Rugman, 2009). Second, it led to the emergence of a new class of theories specifically tailored towards understanding the internationalisation of emerging market firms (e.g. Cuervo-Cazurra and Genc, 2008; Hennart, 2012; Luo and Tung, 2007, 2018; Mathews, 2002, 2006; Ramamurti, 2009, 2012). While amended classical theories and new theories held different positions on EMNEs' internationalisation drivers and competitive advantages (cf. Hennart, 2012), they shared an increasing attention to the constraining or enabling role of home country conditions. These home country conditions were often seen as intimately linked with the behaviour of home country governments.

In the constraint perspective, failing governments, poor institutions as well as competitive disadvantage explain how difficult market and non-market conditions at home push firms out for internationalisation. In the enabling perspective, the home country provides economic policies, infrastructure and institutions that are conducive to firm internationalisation. In this view, governments play a pivotal supporting role as they create competitive learning conditions for firms, for instance, through market liberalisation and FDI policies fostering inward internationalisation (Cuervo-Cazurra et al., 2018; Luo and Tung, 2007, 2018; Luo and Wang, 2012). In short, in all these contributions, home countries either directly or indirectly support or constrain domestic firm internationalisation.

In this chapter, we take stock of recent insights on the role of the home country in firm internationalisation. However, while the home country perspective has come a long way, there are still blind spots that deserve attention in future research. We would like to focus on three areas and suggest a related research agenda.

The first area centres on developing a better understanding about the antecedents, patterns and consequences of home country measures that support firm internationalisation. The second area relates to opening the black box of home-institutional imprinting and host country deployment of non-market firm capabilities. Relatedly, the third area focuses on the extension of home institutions to host contexts in support of firm internationalisation.

In the next sections, we review three bodies of literature. Section 5.2 briefly discusses major theories of internationalisation and asks about the role that the home country plays in these theories. Section 5.3 looks more closely at international business and management (IB/M) perspectives that have focused on the country-of-origin or home country effects. Section 5.4 examines recent theories that have emerged in and around the internationalisation of emerging market firms and asks about the role of the home country in these theories. Section 5.5 presents future research directions based on the gaps identified in the previous sections.

5.2   Mainstream IB theories and the role of the home country

Hymer's theory of the multinational firm, Johanson and Vahlne's Uppsala model and Dunning's eclectic paradigm, also known as the OLI model, and Rugman's FSA-CSA matrix are among the most iconic theories of internationalisation. We shall, therefore, focus on these approaches in this section.

Hymer's theory of the multinational firm

Hymer's (1960) theory asks why the firms invest abroad. Hymer (1960) argues that multinational enterprises (MNEs) need to have monopolistic advantages that allow them to overcome their liability of foreignness abroad. These may include privileged access to capital or other resources, economies of scale or government concessions (Forsgren, 2009). In this view, firms are able to venture abroad because they possess monopolistic advantages that they can exploit internationally (Forsgren, 2009: 28). While Hymer's work is not particularly interested in how and why countries actively promote firm internationalisation, Hymer's focus on market imperfections in different industries and what he calls "firms' special advantages" suggest the importance of the home country where firms' resources are developed in the first place. Yet, Hymer did not elaborate much on the types of advantages that firms develop at home and how they are leveraged abroad. His focus was primarily on market imperfections at home that defined monopolistic advantages that firms could exploit internationally.

Johanson and Vahlne's Uppsala model

Johanson and Vahlne (1977) aim at understanding the internationalisation process of the firm by drawing primarily on the learning perspective. Johanson and Vahlne (1977) see firm internationalisation as a gradual process wherein firms move from more to less familiar foreign contexts and from low to increasingly high commitment activities in the host context. While the former involves moving initially into neighbouring countries, before more distant markets are entered, the latter involves an establishment chain, starting with exports and ending with production facilities abroad (Becker-Ritterspach et al., 2019). The explanatory mechanisms for this incremental pattern rest on the concept of "psychic distance". "Psychic distance" denotes the linguistic, cultural, economic and political-legal differences between countries. "Psychic distance" causes uncertainty or a "liability of foreignness" that acts as a barrier for rapid internationalisation. While the Uppsala model does consider the home country through the concept of home/host country distance, the home context plays only a subordinate role, that is, merely as a reference point for the psychic distance to other foreign contexts. In the revised Uppsala model, the home context receives a little more consideration by being seen as a context that might host important network relationships that enable or constrain firm internationalisation (Johanson and Vahlne, 2009).

Dunning's OLI model

The third iconic theory of firm internationalisation is Dunning's (1988) "eclectic paradigm". Dunning is interested in the question of what conditions are required for a firm to cross borders and engage in FDI. Dunning argues that three conditions need to be met for firms to engage in FDI. These are ownership advantage, locational advantage and internalisation advantage (OLI). While Dunning (1988) is among the first to emphasise and name the specific conditions that allow firms to internationalize, there is initially only modest concern for the enabling or constraining role of the home country. Dunning's work faced a wide range of critique. Especially, within the context of emerging market firm internationalisation, questions were raised whether MNEs would always require organisational advantages to venture abroad. In a similar vein, questions were raised about the contextual constitution of organisational advantages pointing to the importance of home institutional contexts in building organisational advantages or acting as a functional equivalence in their absence (Becker-Ritterspach et al., 2019). While Dunning and colleagues came to acknowledge more recently the role of home country institutions in enabling and constraining firm internationalisation (Dunning et al., 2008; Dunning and Lundan, 2008), this recognition did not receive a differentiated treatment or theoretical integration into Dunning's extended OLI model. As we shall see next, this is different in Rugman's work where the nexus between country and firm specific advantages is of central concern.

Rugman's FSA-CSA framework

Rugman's FSA-CSA framework (1981) is the fourth major theory of internationalisation that we shall briefly explore in terms of the role of the home country. The goal of the framework is to understand the drivers and the competitive advantages of internationalising firms. The distinction between firm-specific (FSA) and country-specific (CSA) advantages are the main building blocks of the theory. Although the FSA-CSA framework shows some similarity to Dunning's OLI approach, it contrasts with it in focusing on the link between different types of firm- and country-specific advantages. This is particularly the case in recent work. In these contributions, Rugman and colleagues (e.g. Collinson and Rugman, 2011) not only underline that FSAs and CSAs are often intimately related, but also suggest that CSAs are often connected to national institutional conditions. It is important to note for the purpose of this chapter that CSAs can be either home and host country based and take on equal importance in the framework. Moreover, the relationship between CSAs and FSAs is not a deterministic one. While some FSAs are bound to the home or host country location, others are not. Accordingly, Rugman and colleagues distinguish location bound from non-location bound FSAs.

5.3   Contributions on the country-of-origin effect

In contrast to the grand internationalisation theories, the field of IB/M has seen a range of contributions that were explicitly interested in the influence of the home countries on different aspects of international business and management (e.g. Ferner, 1997; Noorderhaven and Harzing, 2003; Sethi and Elango, 1999; Zhu et al., 2014). These contributions can be broadly labelled as country-of-origin perspectives. The theoretical foundations underpinning country-of-origin perspectives have shown a substantial variance ranging from institutional and cultural to economic and socio-political perspectives. Sethi and Elango (1999), for instance, in their landmark conceptual paper on the country-of-origin effect on firm internationalisation identify three different sets of factors. These include a country's economic and physical resources along with particular industrial capabilities; the cultural values and institutional norms of a country; and a country's economic and industrial policies.

The explanation of the country-of-origin effect has seen a variety of theoretical foundations. Most contributions, however, have drawn on either culturalist or institutionalist explanations (cf. Zhu et al., 2014) with some notable exceptions in combining the two (see particularly Harzing and Sorge, 2003; Noorderhaven and Harzing, 2003). Among institutionalist perspectives, both new institutionalism and comparative institutionalism (also labelled here as comparative capitalism) have found entry into the theorisation of the country-of-origin effect (Noorderhaven and Harzing, 2003). While new institutionalists see cognitive, normative and regulatory institutions (cf. Scott, 1995) of the home country at play that influence managerial behaviour in MNEs, comparative institutionalists focus on the MNEs' embeddedness in formal institutions (e.g. the educational system, the financial system, the political and industrial relation systems) of the home country (Noorderhaven and Harzing, 2003). In this view, national institutional settings coin the organisational designs and practices of firms. As firms internationalise, their managers' hold on to home country organisational practices and reproduce them intentionally or unintentionally within the MNEs and its global network of subsidiaries. The persistence of home country practices has been attributed to different factors including ethnocentrism, organisational inertia (e.g. Noorderhaven and Harzing, 2003; Pauly and Reich, 1997) or seeing transfers as the very basis of a firm's competitive advantage (Sethi and Elango, 1999). The latter rests on the idea that firm practices – along with their embeddedness in home country institutions – define the competitive advantage of the firms and require, therefore, their transfer and reproduction overseas (Whitley, 2001, 2012; Zhu et al., 2014).

With regard to the question how the country-of-origin effect influences MNEs, institutionalist scholars have looked at a wide range of organisational dimensions and behaviours. These range from the home country's influence on internationalisation patterns, organisational designs, and forms of coordination and control (e.g. Harzing and Sorge, 2003; Morgan, 2001; Whitley, 1999, 2001), to the propensity of transferring home country organisational practices and policies to subsidiaries (e.g. Almond, 2011; Almond et al., 2005; Almond and Ferner, 2006; Edwards et al., 2010; Ferner, 1997; Ferner and Quintanilla, 1998; Zhu et al., 2014). A particular focus has been on the transfer of human resource management (HRM) practices.

Culturalist research in IB/M has equally looked at the country-of-origin effect. Much of this work rest on Hofstede's seminal work on national cultural differences (Hofstede, 1980, 2001). The principal explanatory mechanism is that the home country management's cultural values – particularly with regard to power distance and uncertainty avoidance – correspond with organisational preferences that shape the MNE's organisational design and behaviour (Noorderhaven and Harzing, 2003). Culturalists have also related a wide range of international management themes to the cultural set up of the home country. These include, among others, the internationalisation strategy, entry mode preferences, preferred modes of coordination and control as well as typical headquarter–subsidiary relations (e.g. Lubatkin et al., 1998; Mayrhofer, 2004; Noorderhaven and Harzing, 2003; Stevens and Dykes, 2013). Culturalists have also looked at how the country-of-origin influences the diffusion of HRM practices in MNEs (e.g. Ngo et al., 1998).

It should be finally noted that contributions on the country-of-origin effect have discussed a range of variables that moderate the effect. While it is beyond the scope of this chapter to discuss these variables in detail, suffice it to mention that there are three principal sources of moderators. These are home country conditions (e.g. homogeneity of institutions and culture), host country conditions (e.g. strength, cohesiveness or diversity of institutions) and firm-level conditions (e.g. ownership, internationalisation path and pattern of MNE, subsidiary integration and autonomy) (Becker-Ritterspach et al., 2017; Dörrenbächer, 2003; Geppert et al., 2003; Morgan, 2009; Noorderhaven and Harzing, 2003; Tüselmann et al., 2010; Whitley, 1998).

In summary, in contrast to the iconic theories of firm internationalisation, IB/M's country-of-origin effect literature has advanced our understanding on how home country conditions influence the motivations and paths, strategies and structures, organisational design and operational modes of internationalising firms. Still, what is lacking in this body of work (both in culturalist and institutionalist perspectives) is how home countries encourage and support firm internationalisation directly and intentionally.

5.4   Recent IB/M theory advancements and the role of the home country

The rapid internationalisation of emerging market multinational enterprises brought forward a scholarly debate on the interactions between home country institutions and the nature of advantages these multinationals harness (Cuervo-Cazurra and Genc, 2008; Deng, 2012; Guillén and García-Canal, 2009; Ramamurti, 2009). Along with amended classical theories, new theories were advanced to probe the strategic behaviour of EMNEs (Becker-Ritterspach et al., 2019) (see also Chapter 8).

EMNEs and the home country

The past decade has seen a proliferation of research on the strategic behaviour of multinationals from emerging markets. In contrast to internationalisation patterns of firms from developed economies, EMNEs were seen to venture abroad more rapidly and invest in both developed and emerging markets at the same time (Mathews, 2006). Importantly, questions were raised about what allowed these firms to internationalise, as they seemed to lack the ownership advantages that developed country MNEs typically possessed (e.g. big brand names or proprietary technology). IB/M scholars sought to better understand the market and particularly the non-market advantages that enabled these firms to operate abroad (Cuervo-Cazurra and Genc, 2008; Cuervo-Cazurra et al., 2018; Gammeltoft et al., 2010; Gaur and Kumar, 2010; Guillén and García-Canal, 2009; Luo and Tung, 2007, 2018; Mathews, 2002, 2006; Ramamurti, 2009, 2012). Along with the increasing focus on understanding EMNEs' competitive advantages, IB/M scholars came to realise that these were institutionally imprinted (Cantwell et al., 2010) which, in turn, engendered further interrogations on the influence of the home country (e.g. Cuervo-Cazurra et al., 2018).

IB/M literature has come to see EMNEs' market and non-market advantages as rooted in a country's home context (Cuervo-Cazurra and Genc, 2011). Examples of market advantages include operational flexibility, production efficiencies, the capacity to be agile and adapt products and services to meet the needs of price sensitive consumers in emerging markets, and the ability to build and leverage networks and relationships (Guillén and García-Canal, 2009; Ramamurti, 2009, 2012). Non-market advantages are rooted in resources enabling firms to operate in weak institutional contexts and uncertain legal regimes and regulations, to deal with heavy bureaucracy and political risks, and to cope with weak infrastructure and other supporting resources (Cuervo-Cazurra and Genc, 2008; Guillén and García-Canal, 2009). While market advantages have been widely studied, non-market advantages have been less widely explored (Cuervo-Cazurra and Genc, 2008, 2011; Kothari et al., 2013). Overall, however, research suggests that EMNEs that have developed capabilities to manage home country institutions will be better equipped than others at handling similar environments abroad (Contractor, 2013; Cuervo-Cazurra, 2006; Cuervo-Cazurra and Genc, 2008; Guillén and García-Canal, 2009; Kothari et al., 2013). This is particularly the case when EMNEs compete with other Western or developed countries in other emerging markets (Cuervo-Cazurra, 2011; Cuervo-Cazurra and Genc, 2008; Cuervo-Cazurra and Ramamurti, 2014; Guillén and García-Canal, 2009; Ramamurti, 2009, 2012). Ramamurti (2009, 2013) argues, for instance, that Indian MNEs develop FSAs or "adversity advantages" that stem from their ability to cope with institutional voids and infrastructure constraints in their home country (e.g. unreliable power, congested ports and roads, corrupt bureaucracies, political and regulatory uncertainties, and weak educational institutions). This implies that when Indian MNEs venture into similar environments abroad, they hold a competitive advantage over developed and/or Western MNEs.

In summary, while new theories on emerging market multinationals as well as amended classical theories may differ on the nature of EMNEs' advantages, they share a common interest in understanding the enabling and constraining home country conditions that influence the multinational's behaviour (Becker-Ritterspach et al., 2019).

Enabling and constraining perspective

Home market constraining conditions may limit the capacity of the MNEs to access needed resources externally. Building on this perspective, some scholars argue that EMNEs will internationalise to escape poor competitive conditions in the home country (e.g. weak innovation systems) and capture resources abroad (Cuervo-Cazurra and Ramamurti, 2014; Cuervo-Cazurra et al., 2018; Luo and Rui, 2009; Luo and Tung, 2007; Peng, 2012a, 2012b). Luo and Tung (2007) show, for instance, that South African MNEs internationalise to escape the home government's foreign exchange controls and the limited domestic market. In terms of capturing resources abroad, Luo and Tung (2007) illustrate that internationalisation is often used as a springboard (e.g. Tata's acquisition of Jaguar Land Rover) to acquire strategic assets such as prestigious brands or state-of-the-art technology that may not be available in the home market. EMNEs may also find an advantage in escaping underdeveloped institutions, uncertainty in the enforcement of rules and regulations, corruption, and poor infrastructure (Luo et al., 2010).

Yet, home market characteristics can also enable the internationalisation of domestic firms. Home country governments can facilitate privileged access to resources, cheap capital, or labour (Hennart, 2012; Ramamurti, 2009; Rugman, 2009). Rugman (2009) and Hennart (2012) note that while Russian and Brazilian MNEs have benefited from home country access to natural resources, Chinese and Indian MNEs could take advantage of cheap labour markets at home. What is more, home country governments can put policies in place to support the development of infrastructure and national innovation systems helping firms to upgrade their capabilities (Becker-Ritterspach et al., 2019; Ramamurti, 2013). Governments can – as was the case in China – encourage collaboration between international and local firms and facilitate competitive learning and capacity development (e.g. Cuervo-Cazurra et al., 2018). They can also be more proactive and provide support through overseas direct investment policies (Hope et al., 2011; Hoskisson et al., 2013; Li et al., 2013; Luo and Tung, 2007; Peng, 2012a, 2012b; Ramamurti, 2009; Wang et al., 2012; Zubkovskaya and Michailova, 2014). Various types of incentives can be put in place including access to cheap capital, reduced taxation, simplified administrative procedures, and information and guidance (Luo et al., 2010; Peng, 2012a, 2012b). These policies often benefit specific industries or state-owned enterprises (SOEs) as can be seen exemplarily in the case of China (Luo and Tung, 2007; Ramamurti, 2013).

Home country measures (HCMs)

The closer investigation of EMNEs, looking at the motivations and patterns of their internationalisations, has also brought about a closer concern with the specific measures that countries employ to support the internationalisation of their firms. In this regard, the work of Luo et al. (2010) is particularly worth noting. Luo et al. (2010) elaborate on the specific portfolio of support measures that is employed by the Chinese government to facilitate firm internationalisation. These include:

> (a) fiscal incentives (e.g., tax incentives, tax deductions, low-interest loans), (b) insurance against political risk, (c) assistance for the private sector in international expansion through government agencies (e.g., a Chamber of Commerce or National Business Council), (d) double taxation avoidance agreements, (e) bilateral and regional treaties to protect investment abroad, (f) bilateral or multilateral frameworks to liberalise investment conditions in host countries, (g) assistance in dealing with host country governments or legislative institutions, and (h) conformity with international agreements required for free trade access, such as WTO protocols and the U.S. Foreign Corrupt Practices Act. (Luo and Rui, 2009: 57)

In a similar vein, Sauvant et al. (2014) discuss a wide range of HCMs that countries employ to promote outward FDI. In this context, HCMs are defined as:

> [T]he granting of specific advantages by the home country government (or one of its public institutions) in connection with the establishment, acquisition and expansion of an investment by a home country firm in a foreign economy […]. They are meant to facilitate, support or promote outward FDI – in other words, to help firms establish foreign affiliates. (Sauvant et al., 2014: 10)

Sauvant et al. (2014) suggest that HCMs often come with eligibility and conditionality criteria. Such criteria specify the types of firms (e.g. nationality, size or industry) eligible for support as well as the types of internationalisation activities that are being supported. Sauvant et al. (2014) indicate that eligibility and conditionality criteria are generally reflective of a supporting government's objectives (e.g. home country national security, economic or geopolitical interest or developmental goals for the host country).

SOEs and the home country

One of the most direct ways for home countries to support firm internationalisation is through state owned enterprises (SOEs). SOEs are important FDI players. The UNCTAD 2019 World Investment Report identified 1,500 SOEs, including 16 among the top 100 MNEs, 5 from China and 11 with shareholding from developed countries (including Germany, France, Italy, Japan and

Norway). State ownership from European countries accounted for 33 per cent, while China and other developing Asian countries accounted for 45 per cent. Governments held majority ownership in 73 per cent of the cases. SOEs can be owned directly by governments or indirectly through other state-owned entities such as sovereign wealth or government pension funds or central banks. In some strategic industries such as in the energy sector, SOEs are dominant controlling 90 per cent of oil and gas reserves and 75 per cent of oil and gas production (Bass and Chakrabarty, 2014).

Again, home market characteristics can influence SOEs' internationalisation patterns since political considerations rather than economic performance might be driving their investments abroad (Peng, 2012a, 2012b). This is particularly the case for fully owned and majority owned SOEs that may seek to internationalise to advance the economic development, the national security, and geopolitical position of their home country (Bass and Chakrabarty, 2014; Cuervo-Cazurra et al., 2014). Cuervo-Cazurra et al. (2014) note that Russian Gazprom sought to strategically expand its presence in COMECON countries and the central Asian republics as a way to reduce the influence of Western power. Similarly, the expansion of infrastructure and mining Chinese SOEs to Africa enabled the Chinese government to access not only resources but also to increase its influence in the continent. The literature highlights that SOEs tend to be more tolerant towards risk, and will not shy away from incurring short-term losses for longer-term gains (Cuervo-Cazurra et al., 2014; García-Canal and Guillén, 2008).

Home governments may have dedicated measures that are tailored to support the internationalisation of SOEs. These include preferential government purchases, cheap financial resources such as loans or subsidised loans to the host country that can be used to retain the services of the SOEs (Bass and Chakrabarty, 2014; García-Canal and Guillén, 2008). Governments may also use their diplomacy and political power to negotiate with the host country investment treaties that favour their SOEs (Cuervo-Cazurra et al., 2014). However, SOEs may also face a liability of origin in foreign markets if they are perceived to be advancing the political interests of their country-of-origin. A case in point are the investment bans that Huawei faces with certain products and its 5G network development projects in a range of Western countries. In a similar vein, SOEs may be restricted from investing in specific sectors or from buying firms to prevent technology transfers. In these situations, the host country will claim national security interests to stop these investments. It is important to note that overall, the effects of home country government measures on the internationalisation of SOEs have not been widely explored in IB (Estrin et al., 2016).

In summary, IB/M research agrees on the importance of the home country in imprinting firm capabilities as well as in enabling and constraining firm internationalisation. It has also started to conceptualise HCMs that directly facilitate firm internationalisation. However, we believe there are three areas that have remained under researched. First, there is little systematic knowledge on how, why and with what consequences countries differ in their firm internationalisation support measures. Second, little is known on how countries imprint firms institutionally and thereby allow them to internationalise with more or less success into particular contexts. Lastly, little is known on how and why countries differ in the extensions of home country support to host contexts and to what extent this forms a basis for a competitive advantage in firm internationalisation (see Chapter 6). We will explore these issues in more detail below.

5.5   Future directions

Understanding antecedents, patterns and consequences of HCMs

IB scholars have started to map the measures that home governments use to incentivise firm internationalisation. However, the overall IB/M literature has studied primarily the type of measures developed to attract FDI rather than mechanisms tailored to support outward FDI. Importantly, although HCMs can have a direct effect on domestic firms' internationalisation, they are still underexplored in IB/M research (Sauvant et al., 2014).

First, there is little knowledge on how countries differ with regard to their portfolios of HCMs. Second, there is a little knowledge about why countries HCMs' differ and third, there is a very limited understanding about the consequences of HCMs. While there is some rudimentary work that compares countries in terms of their HCM portfolios (Sauvant et al., 2014), there is little knowledge as to why this is the case. Sauvant et al. (2014) suggest that the level of development, the nature of business–government relations and economic priorities of home countries may be important factors. Drawing on Comparative Capitalism (CC) literature, Becker-Ritterspach et al. (2019) theorise that the type of market economy or the dominant form of economic coordination in a market economy are important explaining variables. Still, there is little systematic empirical research on how and particularly why HCMs differ across countries.

Importantly, there is a particular dearth in research with regard to the consequences of HCMs at the micro- and macro-level. At the micro-level, key questions relate to how effective HCMs are in the support of firm internationalisation. For instance, are some countries better prepared than others to help their SMEs to internationalise into high risk environments? We lack comprehensive knowledge about the effectiveness and performance of different HCMs at the firm level. At the macro-level, questions arise about positive and negative effect for home and host countries as well as the international geopolitical and economic order (Witt, 2019). This entails the question about the economic, (geo)political, socio-developmental objectives of HCMs (e.g. opening up new markets, accessing natural resources abroad, acquiring capabilities, technologies, brands, hegemonic goals of nation-states, and sustainable development goals in developing countries) and whether these objectives are met by the measures in place. With sustainable FDI becoming a growing field of interest in IB/M, questions as to how effective HCMs are in supporting sustainable FDI define another important field of research (cf. Sauvant and Gabor, 2019). This would entail a systematic review of eligibility and conditionality criteria of HCMs and to what extent these succeed in incentivising sustainable FDI.

Lastly, we have a limited understanding of the micro- and macro-level antecedents, patterns and consequences of HCMs that governments develop in support of their SOEs. Further research is needed to better understand the underlying causes, objectives, modes as well as the consequences of these SOEs supporting HCMs (see also Chapter 6). With regard to the latter, the effect on international economic relations and on geopolitical power shifts appears to be of particular salience (see also Chapter 8).

Imprinting and leveraging non-market advantages from home

The IB/M literature has expanded on the nature of MNE market advantages and how they are deployed abroad. At the same time, it has paid limited attention to how non-market advantages arise at home and how they are leveraged abroad (Cuervo-Cazurra and Genc, 2011; Kothari et al., 2013). Addressing this gap is particularly relevant to comprehend the behaviour of EMNEs. Relatedly, while there is consensus that EMNEs do leverage their home-rooted institutional capabilities to effectively operate in other emerging markets (Cuervo-Cazurra and Genc, 2008, 2011; Ramamurti, 2009), we still know little about how these deployed resources translate into competitive outcomes. There is also only scant research as to whether EMNEs differ in their capacity to use their home-rooted capabilities to compete in other challenging institutional contexts. Clearly, EMNEs are not a homogeneous group (Ramamurti,

2009); some might be better than others at leveraging their home-rooted capabilities.

In order to better understand the nature of non-market advantages, how they arise at home and how they are deployed abroad, we suggest that future studies should draw on the CC perspective to adopt a thick rather than a thin analysis of institutions (Aguilera and Grøgaard, 2019; Jackson and Deeg, 2008, 2019). The IB/M literature has predominantly conceptualised institutions into variables limiting the institutional agency of the multinational enterprise (Becker-Ritterspach et al., 2017; Jackson and Deeg, 2008; Saka-Helmhout et al., 2016). Research has started to draw on an institutional agency perspective to study MNEs (Kostova et al., 2008; Ramachandran and Pant, 2010). The adoption of a broad view of agency would facilitate the integration of responses beyond institutional fit and adaption to include actions of institutional entre-preneurship and influence (Doh et al., 2017). Understanding the variety of responses in relation to institutions will provide a deeper understanding of the strategic behaviour of the multinational in different settings. For example, the extant literature has suggested that institutional agency in emerging market contexts may require subtle and unaggressive strategies since governments have generally more control over key resources and may be unsympathetic with firms that convey dissent with public policy too loudly (Marquis and Raynard, 2015). Perceived as a threat, firms may be forced to abandon oper-ations; their assets may be seized, while their management may face jail time.

A thick perspective of institutions suggests the study of institutional dynamics and formal institutional configurations at the industry level. As firms seek to deploy their business operations whether at home or abroad, they interact with customers, suppliers, formal institutions (financial, educational etc.) and government agencies and will have to deal with regulative, normative or cog-nitive institutions that guide their interactions (Kostova et al., 2008; Phillips et al., 2009; Regnér and Edman, 2014). These manifest themselves in contractual agreements, laws, regulations, norms or standards and beliefs or logic of actions. As such, industry institutional structures (formal and informal) may have a direct effect on the capacity of MNEs to develop non-market advantages at home and to deploy these abroad. Very few studies have chosen to investi-gate the interactions between home and host country institutional contexts and their effects on MNEs' capability development and deployment (Cantwell et al., 2010; Gammeltoft et al., 2012). We lack in particular a comprehensive understanding of how the relationship between the parent and the subsidiary could influence the ways home-rooted institutional capabilities are deployed in the host market.

In summary, future work should investigate both how non-market advantages are developed by the parents at home as well as how the subsidiaries redeploy these advantages in the host market. For example, some parent companies might be challenged to export their institutional capabilities and some subsidiaries might be challenged to redeploy or reconfigure these in the host market context (Geppert et al., 2003). As such, the subsidiary might not be able to build on the experience of its parent to secure an advantage in a host market context. This suggests a greater investigation of the enabling and constraining factors of transferring home country non-market advantages.

Home country extensions and institutional entrepreneurship in host countries

We see as a last promising field of research in IB/M in the question how home countries and their HCMs in particular serve to extend home country institutions to host contexts. This also harks back to the previous issue of institutional imprinting. Its starting point is CC's insight that firm capabilities and competencies are embedded in specific economic relations and institutional settings (e.g. Hall and Soskice, 2001). The CC literature – irrespective of whether it is the national business system, the varieties of capitalism or the societal effect approach – suggests that firm capabilities and strategies can only be understood by analysing the influence of home country institutional configurations, which differ depending on the forms of capitalism (Hall and Soskice, 2001; Maurice et al., 1980; Whitley, 1999). The CC approaches suggest that firms from different market economies coordinate interactions within institutional domains such as capital, labour and other firms in fundamentally different ways. Being embedded in different institutional configurations and interdependencies implies that firms also vary in terms of competencies and capabilities. CC literature helps us to better understand how home country institutional arrangements constitute capability development. Hence, these institutionally imprinted capabilities will vary depending on how home country institutional domains are structured (Jackson and Deeg, 2008). For instance, depending on the type of home market economy or forms of capitalism, firms may rely to different degrees on collaborative relationships with business partners, government partners or other institutions (e.g. research or educational institutions). Hence, when specific forms of institutional embeddedness define the competitive advantage of firms, the question arises to what extent firms and supporting home country actors – such as governments or business associations – engage in host country institutional entrepreneurship to extend the needed home country institutions into the host context (Becker-Ritterspach et al., 2017). This, in turn, raises the question to what extent host countries are open and willing to allow home country institutionalisation efforts. Among other things, the strength, cohesiveness or diversity of host context institutions, home/host country institutional and cultural proximity as well as the economic and geopolitical relations or struggles between home and host countries have to be considered in answering this question (see also Witt, 2019).

In summary, there is only limited theorisation about how and why home country institutional extensions to host contexts differ. Relatedly, we know very little about the importance and effectiveness of home country institutional extensions for internationalising firms. Specifically, what role do home country extensions play in reducing the risks and liability of foreignness for internationalising firms? What role do home country extensions play in reproducing firm capabilities abroad? We know also very little about the effect of home country extensions on the institutional environments of host countries. For instance, to what extent do institutional transfers (e.g. transfer of vocational training institutions) improve the institutional infrastructure of a host country and how does it affect the competitiveness of domestic firms and of the host economy? Lastly, we know very little how host countries differ in accepting or welcoming home country institutional extensions. The last question harks back to a wider array of research questions that would investigate home country internationalisation support and related institutional extensions as geopolitical tools that are employed by certain countries in pursuance of hegemonic ambitions (see Chapter 8).

References

Aguilera, R.V. and Grøgaard, B. (2019). The dubious role of institutions in international business: A road forward. *Journal of International Business Studies*, 50(1): 20–35.

Almond, P. (2011). Re-visiting 'country of origin' effects on HRM in multinational corporations. *Human Resource Management Journal*, 21(3): 258–271.

Almond, P., Edwards, T., Colling, T., Ferner, A., Gunnigle, P., Müller-Camen, M. and Wächter, H. (2005). Unraveling home and host country effects: An investigation of the HR policies of an American multinational in four European countries. *Industrial Relations: A Journal of Economy and Society*, 44(2): 276–306.

Almond, P. and Ferner, A. (2006). *American Multinationals in Europe: Human Resource Policies and Practices*. Oxford: Oxford University Press.

Bass, A.E. and Chakrabarty, S. (2014). Resource security: Competition for global resources, strategic intent, and governments as owners. *Journal of International Business Studies*, 45(8): 961–979.

Becker-Ritterspach, F., Allen, M., Lange, K. and Allen, M. (2019). Home-country measures to support outward foreign direct investment: Variation and consequences. *Transnational Corporations Journal*, 26(1): 61–85.

Becker-Ritterspach, F., Lange, K. and Becker-Ritterspach, J. (2017). Divergent patterns in institutional entrepreneurship of MNCs in emerging economies. *critical perspectives on international business*, 13(3): 186–203.

Cantwell, J., Dunning, J.H. and Lundan, S.M. (2010). An evolutionary approach to understanding international business activity: The co-evolution of MNEs and the institutional environment. *Journal of International Business Studies*, 41(4): 567–586.

Collinson, S.C. and Rugman, A.M. (2011). Relevance and rigor in international business teaching: Using the CSA-FSA matrix. *Journal of Teaching in International Business*, 22(1): 29–37.

Contractor, F.J. (2013). Punching above their weight. *International Journal of Emerging Markets*, 8(4): 304–328.

Cuervo-Cazurra, A. (2006). Who cares about corruption? *Journal of International Business Studies*, 37(6): 803–822.

Cuervo-Cazurra, A. (2011). Global strategy and global business environment: The direct and indirect influences of the home country on a firm's global strategy. *Global Strategy Journal*, 1(3-4): 382–386.

Cuervo-Cazurra, A. and Genc, M.E. (2008). Transforming disadvantages into advantages: Developing country MNEs in the least developed countries. *Journal of International Business Studies*, 39(6): 957–979.

Cuervo-Cazurra, A. and Genc, M.E. (2011). Obligating, pressuring, and supporting dimensions of the environment and the non-market advantages of developing-country multinational companies. *Journal of Management Studies*, 48(2): 441–455.

Cuervo-Cazurra, A., Inkpen, A., Musacchio, A. and Ramaswamy, K. (2014). Governments as owners: State-owned multinational companies. *Journal of International Business Studies*, 45(8): 919–942.

Cuervo-Cazurra, A., Luo, Y., Ramamurti, R. and Ang, S.H. (2018). The impact of the home country on internationalization. *Journal of World Business*, 53(5): 593–604.

Cuervo-Cazurra, A. and Ramamurti, R. (Eds.) (2014). *Understanding Multinationals from Emerging Markets*. Cambridge: Cambridge University Press.

Deng, P. (2012). The internationalization of Chinese firms: A critical review and future research. *International Journal of Management Reviews*, 14(4): 408–427.

Doh, J., Rodrigues, S., Saka-Helmhout, A. and Makhija, M. (2017). International business responses to institutional voids. *Journal of International Business Studies*, 48(3): 293–307.

Dörrenbächer, C. (2003). Grenzüberschreitender Modelltransfer in multinationalen Unternehmen. In C. Dörrenbächer (Ed.), *Modelltransfer in multinationalen Unternehmen*. Berlin: Edition Sigma, 151–171.

Dunning, J.H. (1988). The theory of international production. *The International Trade Journal*, 3(1): 21–66.

Dunning, J.H., Kim, C. and Park, D. (2008). Old wine in new bottles: A comparison of emerging-market TNCs today and developed-country TNCs thirty years ago. In K.P. Sauvant (Ed.), *The Rise of Transnational Corporations from Emerging Markets: Threat or Opportunity?* Cheltenham, UK and Northampton, MA, USA: Edward Elgar Publishing, 158–180.

Dunning, J.H. and Lundan, S.M. (2008). Institutions and the OLI paradigm of the multinational enterprise. *Asia Pacific Journal of Management*, 25(4): 573–593.

Edwards, T., Edwards, P., Ferner, A., Marginson, P. and Tregaskis, O. (2010). Multinational companies and the diffusion of employment practices from outside the country of origin. *Management International Review*, 50(5): 613–634.

Estrin, S., Meyer, K.E., Nielsen, B.B. and Nielsen, S. (2016). Home country institutions and the internationalization of state owned enterprises: A cross-country analysis. *Journal of World Business*, 51(2): 294–307.

Ferner, A. (1997). Country of origin effects and HRM in multinational companies. *Human Resource Management Journal*, 7(1): 19–37.

Ferner, A. and Quintanilla, J. (1998). Multinationals, national business systems and HRM: The enduring influence of national identity or a process of 'Anglo-Saxonization'. *International Journal of Human Resource Management*, 9(4): 710–731.

Forsgren, M. (2009). *Theories of the Multinational Firm: A Multidimensional Creature in the Global Economy*. Cheltenham, UK and Northampton, MA, USA: Edward Elgar Publishing.

Gammeltoft, P., Filatotchev, I. and Hobdari, B. (2012). Emerging multinational companies and strategic fit: A contingency framework and future research agenda. *European Management Journal*, 30(3): 175–188.

Gammeltoft, P., Pradhan, J.P. and Goldstein, A. (2010). Emerging multinationals: Home and host country determinants and outcomes. *International Journal of Emerging Markets*, 5(3/4): 254–265.

García-Canal, E. and Guillén, M.F. (2008). Risk and the strategy of foreign location choice in regulated industries. *Strategic Management Journal*, 29(10): 1097–1115.

Gaur, A. and Kumar, V. (2010). Internationalization of emerging market firms: A case for theoretical extension. *Advances in International Management*, 23(9): 603–627.

Geppert, M., Williams, K. and Matten, D. (2003). The social construction of contextual rationalities in MNCs: An Anglo-German comparison of subsidiary choice. *Journal of Management Studies*, 40(3): 617–641.

Guillén, M.F. and García-Canal, E. (2009). The American model of the multinational firm and the "new" multinationals from emerging economies. *Academy of Management Perspectives*, 23(2): 23–35.

Hall, P.A. and Soskice, D. (2001). An introduction to varieties of capitalism. In P.A. Hall and D. Soskice (Eds), *Varieties of Capitalism: The Institutional Foundations of Comparative Advantage*. Oxford: Oxford University Press, 1–68.

Harzing, A.W. and Sorge, A. (2003). The relative impact of country of origin and universal contingencies on internationalization strategies and corporate control in multinational enterprises: Worldwide and European perspectives. *Organization Studies*, 24(2): 187–214.

Hennart, J.M.A. (2012). Emerging market multinationals and the theory of the multinational enterprise. *Global Strategy Journal*, 2(3): 168–187.

Hofstede, G. (1980). Culture and organizations. *International Studies of Management & Organization*, 10(4): 15–41.

Hofstede, G. (2001). *Culture's Consequences: Comparing Values, Behaviors, Institutions and Organizations across Nations*. Thousand Oaks, CA: Sage Publications.

Hope, O.K., Thomas, W. and Vyas, D. (2011). The cost of pride: Why do firms from developing countries bid higher? *Journal of International Business Studies*, 42(1): 128–151.

Hoskisson, R.E., Wright, M., Filatotchev, I. and Peng, M.W. (2013). Emerging multinationals from mid-range economies: The influence of institutions and factor markets. *Journal of Management Studies*, 50(7): 1295–1321.

Hymer, S. (1960). *On Multinational Corporations and Foreign Direct Investment: The Theory of Transnational Corporations*. London: Routledge for the United Nations.

Jackson, G. and Deeg, R. (2008). Comparing capitalisms: Understanding institutional diversity and its implications for international business. *Journal of International Business Studies*, 39(4): 540–561.

Jackson, G. and Deeg, R. (2019). Comparing capitalisms and taking institutional context seriously. *Journal of International Business Studies*, 50(1): 4–19.

Johanson, J. and Vahlne, J.-E. (1977). The internationalization process of the firm: A model of knowledge development and increasing foreign market commitments. *Journal of International Business Studies*, 8(1): 23–32.

Johanson, J. and Vahlne, J.-E. (2009). The Uppsala internationalization process model revisited: From liability of foreignness to liability of outsidership. *Journal of International Business Studies*, 40(9): 1411–1431.

Kostova, T., Roth, K. and Dacin, M.T. (2008). Institutional theory in the study of multinational corporations: A critique and new directions. *Academy of Management Review*, 33(4): 994–1006.

Kothari, T., Kotabe, M. and Murphy, P. (2013). Rules of the game for emerging market multinational companies from China and India. *Journal of International Management*, 19(3): 276–299.

Li, J., Newenham-Kahindi, A., Shapiro, D.M. and Chen, V.Z. (2013). The two-tier bargaining model revisited: Theory and evidence from China's natural resource investments in Africa. *Global Strategy Journal*, 3(4): 300–321.

Lubatkin, M., Calori, R., Very, P. and Veiga, J.F. (1998). Managing mergers across borders: A two-nation exploration of a nationally bound administrative heritage. *Organization Science*, 9(6): 670–684.

Luo, Y. and Rui, H. (2009). An ambidexterity perspective: Toward multinational enterprises from emerging markets. *Academy of Management Perspectives*, 23(2): 49–70.

Luo, Y. and Tung, R. (2007). International expansion of emerging market enterprises: A springboard perspective. *Journal of International Business Studies*, 38(4): 481–498.

Luo, Y. and Tung, R.L. (2018). A general theory of springboard MNEs. *Journal of International Business Studies*, 49(2): 129–152.

Luo, Y. and Wang, S.L. (2012). Foreign direct investment strategies by developing country multinationals: A diagnostic model for home country effects. *Global Strategy Journal*, 2(3): 244–261.

Luo, Y., Xue, Q. and Han, B. (2010). How emerging market governments promote outward FDI: Experience from China. *Journal of World Business*, 45(1): 68–79.

Marquis, C. and Raynard, M. (2015). Institutional strategies in emerging markets. *Academy of Management Annals*, 9(1): 291–335.

Mathews, J.A. (2002). *Dragon Multinationals: A New Model of Global Growth*. New York: Oxford University Press.

Mathews, J.A. (2006). Dragon multinationals: New players in 21st century globalization. *Asia Pacific Journal of Management*, 23(1): 5–27.

Maurice, M., Sorge, A. and Warner, M. (1980). Societal differences in organizing manufacturing units: A comparison of France, West Germany, and Great Britain. *Organization Studies*, 1(1): 59–86.

Mayrhofer, U. (2004). The influence of national origin and uncertainty on the choice between cooperation and merger-acquisition: An analysis of French and German firms. *International Business Review*, 13(1): 83–99.

Morgan, G. (2001). The multinational firm: Organizing across institutional and national divides. In G. Morgan, P.H. Kristensen and R. Whitley (Eds), *The Multinational Firm: Organizing Across Institutional and National Divides*. New York: Oxford University Press, 1–26.

Morgan, G. (2009). Globalization, multinationals and institutional diversity. *Economy and Society*, 38(4): 580–605.

Ngo, H.Y., Turban, D., Lau, C.M. and Lui, S.Y. (1998). Human resource practices and firm performance of multinational corporations: Influences of country origin. *International Journal of Human Resource Management*, 9(4): 632–652.

Noorderhaven, N.G. and Harzing, A.W. (2003). The "country-of-origin effect" in multinational corporations: Sources, mechanisms and moderating conditions. *Management and International Review*, 43: 47–66.

Pauly, L.W. and Reich, S. (1997). National structures and multinational corporate behavior: Enduring differences in the age of globalization. *International Organization*, 51(1): 1–30.

Peng, M.W. (2012a). Accelerated internationalization by MNCs from emerging economies: Determinants and implications. *Organizational Dynamics*, 41(4): 318–326.

Peng, M.W. (2012b). The global strategy of emerging multinationals from China. *Global Strategy Journal*, 2(2): 97–107.

Phillips, N., Tracey, P. and Karra, N. (2009). Rethinking institutional distance: Strengthening the tie between new institutional theory and international management. *Strategic Organization*, 7(3): 339–348.

Ramachandran, J. and Pant, A. (2010). The liabilities of origin: An emerging economy perspective on the costs of doing business abroad. In T.M. DeVinney, T. Bach Pedersen and L. Tihanyi (Eds), *The Past, Present and Future of International Business & Management*. Bingley: Emerald Group Publishing, 231–266.

Ramamurti, R. (2009). What have we learned about emerging market multinationals? In R. Ramamurti and J.V. Singh (Eds), *Emerging Multinationals in Emerging Markets*. Cambridge: Cambridge University Press, 399–426.

Ramamurti, R. (2012). What is really different about emerging market multinationals? *Global Strategy Journal*, 2(1): 41–47.

Ramamurti, R. (2013). Cross-border M&A and competitive advantage of Indian EMENs. In P.J. Williamson, R. Ramamurti, A. Fleury and M.T.L. Fleury (Eds), *The Competitive Advantage of Emerging Market Multinationals*. Cambridge: Cambridge University Press, 239–260.

Regnér, P. and Edman, J. (2014). MNE institutional advantage: How subunits shape, transpose and evade host country institutions. *Journal of International Business Studies*, 45(3): 275–302.

Rugman, A.M. (1981). *Inside the Multinationals: The Economics of Internal Markets*. New York: Columbia University Press.

Rugman, A.M. (2009). Theoretical aspects of MNEs from emerging countries. In R. Ramamurti and J.V. Singh (Eds), *Emerging Multinationals in Emerging Markets*. Cambridge: Cambridge University Press, 42–63.

Saka-Helmhout, A., Deeg, R. and Greenwood, R. (2016). The MNE as a challenge to institutional theory: Key concepts, recent developments and empirical evidence. *Journal of Management Studies*, 53(1): 1–11.

Sauvant, K., Economu, P., Gal, K., Lim, S. and Wilinski, W. (2014). Trends in FDI, home country measures and competitive neutrality. In A. Bjorklund (Ed.), *Yearbook on International Investment Law and Policy 2012-2013*. New York: Oxford University Press, 3–107.

Sauvant, K.P. and Gabor, E. (2019). Advancing sustainable development by facilitating sustainable FDI, promoting CSR, designating recognized sustainable investors, and giving home countries a role. Available at: https://ssrn.com/abstract=3496967 or http://dx.doi.org/10.2139/ssrn.3496967.

Scott, W.R. (1995). *Institutions and Organizations*. Thousand Oaks, CA: Sage Publications.

Sethi, S.P. and Elango, B. (1999). The influence of "country of origin" on multinational corporation global strategy: A conceptual framework. *Journal of International Management*, 5(4): 285–298.

Stevens, C.E. and Dykes, B.J. (2013). The home country cultural determinants of firms' foreign market entry timing strategies. *Long Range Planning*, 46(4–5): 387–410.

Tüselmann, H.J., Heise, A., McDonald, F. and Allen, M. (2010). Employment relations in German multinational companies in the UK and the future of the German model: Empirical evidence on country-of-origin effects and industry internationalization. *International Journal of Public Policy*, 5(4): 390–408.

Wang, C.Q., Hong, J.J., Kafouros, M. and Wright, M. (2012). Exploring the role of government involvement in outward FDI from emerging economies. *Journal of International Business Studies*, 43(7): 655–676.

Whitley, R. (1998). Internationalization and varieties of capitalism: The limited effects of cross-national coordination of economic activities on the nature of business systems. *Review of International Political Economy*, 5(3): 445–481.

Whitley, R. (1999). *Divergent Capitalisms: The Social Structuring and Change of Business Systems*. Oxford: Oxford University Press.

Whitley, R. (2001). How and why are international firms different? The consequences of cross-border managerial coordination for firm characteristics and behaviour. In G. Morgan, P.H. Kristensen and R. Whitley (Eds), *The Multinational Firm: Organizing Across Institutional and National Divides*. New York: Oxford University Press, 27–68.

Whitley, R. (2012). Internationalization and the institutional structuring of economic organization: Changing authority relations in the twenty-first century. In G. Morgan and R. Whitley (Eds), *Capitalisms and Capitalism in the Twenty-First Century*. Oxford: Oxford University Press, 211–236.

Witt, M.A. (2019). De-globalization: Theories, predictions, and opportunities for international business research. *Journal of International Business Studies*, 50(7): 1053–1077.

Zhu, J.S., Zhu, C.J. and De Cieri, H. (2014). Chinese MNCs' preparation for host-country labor relations: An exploration of country-of-origin effect. *Human Resource Management*, 53(6): 947–965.

Zubkovskaya, A. and Michailova, S. (2014). The development of Russian multinational enterprises from the 1990s to the present. *Organizations and Markets in Emerging Economies*, 5(2): 59–78.

6. The diplomatic imperative: MNEs as international actors

Brent Burmester

6.1 Introduction

In February 2017, Rex Tillerson, CEO of Exxon-Mobil, became Secretary of State of the United States of America. Despite having no prior government service, he was endorsed by President George W. Bush, together with Bush's former Vice-President, Defence Secretary, Secretary of State, and National Security Advisor (Seib, 2016). This array of experienced senior politicians recognised Tillerson, the international businessman, as a denizen of their world.

Contemporary international business (IB) does not dwell upon that recognition. The discipline has forgotten something it knew when multinational enterprises (MNEs) began to contend with an expanded universe of competing sovereign interests (Penrose, 1989). The MNE distinguished itself then as an unprecedented species of geopolitical actor, simultaneously participating across markets and international society. The intuition that diplomatic conduct set the MNE apart from other firms carried far-reaching implications, and, in response, IB might have become an alloy of business science and international specialisations in law, sociology, history and politics.

This chapter argues diplomacy is not an *option* for MNEs: internationalisation admits them to a society of actors whose interactions are definitively diplomatic. IB's determinedly apolitical treatment of the MNE must be challenged when governments concede this point, as witnessed in Tillerson's appointment; Denmark's establishment of a technology ambassador to interface with infotech MNEs (Jacobsen, 2017); and the "summit meeting" between France's President and 140 MNE CEOs at the Palace of Versailles (Rose, 2018). Over the last half century, in an "explosion" of diplomatic and quasi-diplomatic activity,

MNEs have constituted one of the major new sources of power (Hamilton and Langhorne, 2011).

Conforming to an outdated conception of the international order, IB typically reduces the MNE to a *firm* exposed to multiple sovereignties (Sundaram and Black, 1992), necessarily subordinate to nation-states. Three decades of theoretic developments in the analysis of structure, process and agency in international governance require that this view is revised. IB must contend with the ontological implications of the incompleteness and contestability of global governance and confront the MNE as a *governor* beyond the market (Burmester et al., 2019).

In the first half of 2020 alone, during the worldwide pandemic, major inter-nationalised companies, such as Huawei (McCabe, 2020), Facebook (Scott, 2020), and Apple (FE Online, 2020) repeatedly featured in headlines about the fracture and repair of relations between states. Notable among them was 3M's struggle to limit antagonism between governments in reaction to US capriciousness over the supply of personal protective equipment. The Trump administration insisted that 3M give priority to its home country in supplying respirators, denying Canada and South American states in the process. For 3M, sales were guaranteed regardless of destination, but the company stood its ground, reminding the President of his country's duty to not worsen the situation for its regional allies in a global crisis (Breuninger, 2020). Corporations conceal the greater part of their political activity, so these visible interactions only hint at the depth and definitiveness of MNE diplomacy. Indeed, the silence speaks volumes as to the true scope of their diplomatic engagement. International legal instruments seem wholly unaware of the profound depend-ency of the global political economy on MNEs and the corporate form on which they depend, except when conferring unique privileges to them (Whyte, 2020).

Others have urged academia to re-evaluate the political distinctiveness of MNEs (cf. Clegg et al., 2018). This might be in expectation that MNEs sup-plement the role of governments, remodelling democracy in the process (e.g. Scherer and Palazzo, 2011), or in the conviction that MNEs exist to commit social harm and misappropriate wealth on a global scale (e.g. Tombs and Whyte, 2015). Without taking sides, this chapter employs international theory to revive the international political-economic conceptualisation of the MNE. In so doing it considers the MNE's credentials as a member of the genus, *international actor*. Nation-states are the most recognised species of that genus and boast the longest and deepest experience of diplomacy, but MNEs can be conceived as a related species, distinctive in their capacities and priorities.

Both further their interests in the disputatious international sphere, subject to common constraints. Without over-stretching the analogy, this chapter transposes emergent diplomacy theory onto the MNE to learn how the research agenda of IB might be advanced.

6.2   Paradigm shift

IB was in paradigmatic flux in the early 1970s. Stephen Hymer (1972) abandoned liberal economic ontology to critique MNEs as weapons of global class warfare; Raymond Vernon (1971) voiced cautious optimism that MNEs had the upper-hand in relationships with host governments; at the United Nations (UN), debate raged over the containment of MNEs' monopolistic and neo-colonial power (cf. Yackee, 2008); and, from Paris, Servan-Schreiber (1967) warned that MNEs were rewriting the grammar of liberal political economy.

MNE–host dyads were featured subjects of academic analysis (cf. Moran, 1974; Penrose, 1968; Smith, 1974; Vaitsos, 1970; Vernon, 1971), and the nascent field drew contributions from sociologists, legal scholars, geographers, business historians, and students of politics. To managerial economists and professors of corporate policy, IB was becoming strange and unwieldy, but help was at hand. Hymer's doctoral thesis (1960/1976) characterised foreign direct investment (FDI) as a means of transaction-cost minimisation, proffering a "hard" social scientific foundation for IB. The full ontological, theoretical and methodological potential of transaction-cost economics (TCE) was delivered in the works of Williamson (1975) and Buckley and Casson (1976). By "sterilising" the MNE, rendering it a tractable economic phenomenon and marginalising its political character, TCE relieved IB of the noise and normativity of neighbouring disciplines.

TCE's appeal to MNE theorists is evinced by the flurry of books published in the early 1980s (e.g. Dunning, 1981; Hennart, 1982; Rugman, 1981). IB became dependent on a body of economics lacking acquaintance, or sympathy, with the models, methods or concerns of disciplines grappling with non-market power. By 1990, the detachment of IB from the intellectual worlds of sociology, public administration, international law and international relations was almost complete, if never quite completed. Neighbouring fields retained their interest in the MNE in international society, but as IB began a new conversation they talked amongst themselves.

6.3   The firm as diplomat

Early fascination with the political character and capacity of the MNE faded, but did not vanish. There is resurgent interest in firm-level diplomacy, with intersecting perspectives differing in derivation, motivation and substance (Ruël et al., 2013). To reconcile these differences, it helps to first assign business diplomacy to the domain of IB. Diplomacy properly describes interactions between international actors and IB is uniquely positioned to problematise the firm's international operating context.

Corporate diplomacy, per L'Etang (2006) and Ordeix-Rigo and Duarte (2009), is inspired by the practice of public and cultural diplomacy, and treats the firm as a diplomat when it seeks to influence public opinion. L'Etang reviews work in international relations and discerns obvious parallels in the work of diplomats and public relations (PR) practitioners, both employing "rhetoric, oratory, advocacy, negotiation, peacemaking, counselling, intelligence gathering" (L'Etang, 2006: 374). However, she does not find in these similarities evidence that diplomats and PR professionals serve the same ends. Indeed, L'Etang speculates that the title "corporate diplomat" merely lends a veneer of respectability to the PR practitioner. Others prescribe a range of management practices under the banner of "corporate diplomacy", but do not equate the concept with PR (Henisz, 2014; Steger, 2003). For Steger (2003: 7), corporate diplomacy is ultimately about ensuring that "business is done smoothly", granting firms a "licence to operate" and enhancing legitimacy. Without legitimacy, corporations lack "social power" and lose their licence to operate in multi-stakeholder contexts where profit maximisation is insufficient justification (Ordeix-Rigo and Duarte, 2009: 557). While these authors acknowledge that international operations entail an increased diplomatic workload, they do not see diplomacy as the exclusive preserve of the MNE.

Hillman and Hitt (1999) define "constituency building", a category of corporate political strategy (CPS) that overlaps with Ordeix-Rigo and Duarte's idea of corporate diplomacy. CPS deals with firm-level acquisition, augmentation and retention of competitive advantage by scripting the rules of competition (Hillman et al., 2004). In this light, diplomacy is constructive engagement with rule-makers, overcoming non-market resistance to the firm's realisation of market objectives. Although it does not engage with international theory, research in the CPS tradition acknowledges that operating across borders demands more from the firm as a political actor (Hillman et al., 2004; Holtbrügge and Berg, 2004; Keillor et al., 1997; Wan and Hillman, 2006).

Finally, the *business diplomacy* school is inspired by governmental practice of economic and commercial diplomacy. Ruël (2013) and Saner et al. (2000) adopt the diplomacy scholar's focus on the diplomat and her office, and conceptualise business diplomacy as a practice or profession resolving conflicts of interest between corporations and governments. Business diplomacy attends closely to the human and organisational competencies needed to work through conflicts often arising from a lack of corporate understanding of the governmental universe. Here, diplomacy is the grammar of discourse between governments that firms must learn in order to prevail against them. Politics is the higher domain, the master, not the servant, and one that MNEs must navigate with care and respect.

Business diplomats are distinguished by their mindset: strategic, long-term oriented, and, most distinctively, intent on geopolitical risk management (Kesteleyn et al., 2014). They analyse risk at the international level, build influence networks, and form alliances with other political actors. Practitioners of business diplomacy are essential to "global firms" (Saner and Yiu, 2003), firms "operating abroad" (Kesteleyn et al., 2014), or "international businesses" (Ruël, 2013, 2015). Business diplomacy is emphatically an IB specialisation.

Can these alternative perspectives on firm-level diplomacy be reconciled or unified? They agree in one important respect: diplomacy establishes and maintains "positive relationships" with governing entities in order to maximise legitimacy, a critical resource obviating strategically disadvantageous regulation. Business diplomacists would add that legitimacy is also a means of attenuating geopolitical risk. Accordingly:

> Business diplomacy is the practice of establishing and maintaining positive relationships with internal and external business and non-business stakeholders, including employees, businesses, governments and civil society actors, to create and maintain legitimacy and a social licence to operate, create alliances, and shape and influence the environment. (Alammar and Pauleen, 2016: 9)

Conceived thus, firm-level diplomacy licenses the firm to shape and influence "the environment" and might be any action yielding a legitimacy payoff. Conspicuously, *international* relationships, stakeholders, or social licensors are not afforded privileged analysis in the current framing of the field. It remains unclear what behaviour uniquely constitutes diplomacy, or on what body of theory its students and practitioners should depend. Nevertheless, this definition creates a vantage point from which to assess the contribution of international theory.

6.4   The MNE as international actor

Unsurprisingly, the firm-level diplomacy literature takes little notice of international theory. The same is true of IB, where the "I" connotes private economic exchange between transactors separated by state borders, rendering it quantitatively and qualitatively distinct. Quantitatively, because distances exacerbated by borders engender misunderstanding and mistrust, and qualitatively, in that border-defending states lay competing claims to determining the parties' rights. IB takes the states and their borders for granted, and instead wonders at the MNE's ability to be, simultaneously, all of the private parties implicated in these transactions.

By contrast, the MNE construed as "international actor" inhabits a unique social domain in which states, and the state-like, contend with one another's existence. This invites adaptation of theories of inter-state relations to relations between the MNE and other international actors, including other MNEs. The analogy between MNE and state defies IB's ontology, as the state's territorial sovereignty, extensive non-economic responsibilities, and power to deploy violence give it an alien quality, despite the role violence played in the prototype for the contemporary MNE (cf. Clegg, 2017). Indeed, to pursue this analogy it is necessary to allow for the possibility that an MNE's power is not derived solely from its capacity to withhold resources, but might extend to the assertion of force when the opportunity arises.

International actors, including states, intergovernmental organisations (IGOs), non-governmental organisations (NGOs), and MNEs all weigh in the balance of power in the international system: their alliances and enmities impinge on the maintenance of a particular international order (Simonovic, 2001). As members of this highly select society, international actors are capable of enforcing standards of appropriate behaviour in international relations (Kelly, 2006). This characterises the MNE as an international law-maker and enforcer, as all large corporations are to the extent that they "establish and enforce rules within their jurisdiction beyond those of the laws of the land" (Ciepley, 2013: 141). In this sense, the MNE, comprised of corporations in multiple jurisdictions, makes and enforces "international law" and so influences the formalisation of norms in the international public domain. However, this does not qualify the MNE as an international actor. That qualification stems from its contributions to issue-prioritisation on the international diplomatic agenda, and its authorship and integral role in the implementation of international policy.

When IB took shape as an academic field, international politics was about what nation-states did with, and to, one another (cf. Singer, 1961). It was possible to conceive of corporations as international actors (e.g. Wolfers, 1962), but a tidy state-centric model of international politics had too great an appeal to theorists and policymakers (Turner, 1998). In the dominant realist school of international relations, MNEs could only be interesting as instruments of home-state foreign policy. Indeed, Behrman (1969) concluded that no truly "international" companies could exist until MNEs possessed the autonomy to disengage from this exploitation. Meanwhile, scholars in the liberal or rational-choice schools of IR, where the economic interests of non-state actors were given more weight, could not foresee the change wrought by increasingly assertive MNEs. In the 1970s, a still more inclusive and holistic school of thinking about international relations gained momentum under the rubric of the "English School" (e.g. Bull, 1977). This promoted a concept of *international society*, inspired by the European state-system where a collective, rules-based diplomatic culture maintained international order. Acknowledging that violence can erupt in international relations, the English School rejected the supposition that states wage perpetual war on one another. It laid particular emphasis on the uniqueness of international society, discouraging application of models drawn from domestic politics (Alderson and Hurrell, 2000). However, this perspective came too late to influence IB's retreat from the geopolitical firm.

An MNE's international agency, like that of a state, is derived from its recognition by a plurality of states. However, statehood depends on formal mutual recognition between states, whereas the MNE, as a plurality of corporations, first constructs its economic, legal and political identity in multiple states, before gaining *de facto* recognition among them. Their existence is not merely contingent on a joint and separate "authorisation" by states, they are, as jurisdictionally diversified constellations of corporations, accorded a status unlike any other non-state actor. The MNE exploits its enigmatic status of corporate "republic" (Ciepley, 2013) – multiplied, magnified and convoluted – in its assertion of international personality. Its network of foreign subsidiaries is a Matryoshka of nationally diverse republics: in effect, a corporate empire autarkic insofar as it chooses its own leaders, and autonomous insofar as it legislates within an exclusive jurisdiction that interleaves with those of multiple states. Virtually every state has acceded to MNEs' corporate override of the conventions of property, contract and liability that grants them their exceptional status in international capitalism (Ciepley, 2013). Ultimately, the entitative dependence of the MNE on *the* nation-state is dissolved, rendering it constituted by *international* consensus. This reality is evident in the inability of any state, home or host, no matter its reach, to extinguish any sufficiently globalised MNE (what we might think of as a "true" MNE). The threatened

MNE simply reassigns property and control rights between its geopolitically diversified components, rendering any such attempt futile.

The corporation always had the potential to "metastasize into a world power" (Ciepley, 2013: 139). It can therefore be argued that the MNE assumes shared responsibility for the provision of global public goods. Today MNEs are active in securing capital account liberalisation, recognition of private property rights, currency convertibility, macroeconomic coordination, freedom of navigation, adoption of industrial standards, and the establishment of a lender of last resort (Kindleberger, 1986). But these are a narrow subset of the public goods that international actors are expected to provide. The wider list includes the manifold dimensions of issue areas like peace, conflict resolution without resort to force (see also Chapter 9), justice, public health, biodiversity, climatic stability, preservation of cultural heritage, knowledge diffusion, and human rights protection (per Kaul et al., 2003). Too much remains unknown of MNEs' contribution in these domains.

Attributing international public responsibilities to MNEs may no longer be controversial in global governance circles, but in IB the idea remains subversive. A strict private/public distinction obscures MNE power in international society (Cutler, 1997). Even in the case of state-owned MNEs, IB scholars reduce public status to constrained strategic autonomy and atypical stoicism in the face of disappointing profits (cf. He et al., 2016). This is not IB's failing: the public-purpose origins of the business corporation were obliterated in the nineteenth century and their private status rendered legally unassailable (Horwitz, 1981). By the 1960s, any lingering interest in ascribing corporate duties to anyone but shareholders was diverted into advocacy for corporate social responsibility (CSR), where public service is promoted as a means of maximising shareholder wealth. Ironically, the divestiture of public duties from large-scale organisations, despite their obvious regulatory capacity and provision of essentials, was conclusive proof of their ability to influence public policy. The apparent disjuncture between the citizen's experience of corporations and their theorisation in law and economics led Adolf Berle (1959) to call for a political theory of the corporation. Neoliberal economics, however, was committed to the opposite course, and by the mid-1970s the firm could be construed entirely as a nexus of contracts, completing its ontological "privatisation" (Jensen and Meckling, 1976). This gave further impetus to IB's retreat from the international political corporation.

As IB began to turn away from the geopolitical corporation, a steady ontological shift began in international relations. Nye and Keohane (1971) observed that the international arena was expanding to accommodate a new class of "somewhat autonomous" actors strategically deploying "substantial" resources across state lines in the execution of private foreign policy in conflict with state preferences. The small population of self-described IB specialists might have noted parallels with Vernon's (1971) "sovereignty at bay" thesis, which positioned MNEs and states as rivals. There remained, however, a sense in Nye and Keohane that MNEs were more of a contaminant of inter-state relations than an equal and entitled participant in global politics.

By the 1990s, the strategic theatre of international relations accommodated an expanded cast of characters. As Cerny (2010) put it, the borders that mattered segregated interests, not territories, and groups aligned by interest could be very diverse in their composition. As the century closed, international theorists began to set aside state-centric models of global political economy (Slaughter, 2004). The end of the Cold War granted MNEs new liberties extracted from states in the name of globalisation (Avant et al., 2010). As economic growth, education, and efficiency supplanted the projection of military force as bases of international influence, states had no alternative but to treat MNEs as equals. This elicited increasingly "statesmanlike" behaviour from the corporations (Stopford et al., 1991). Some in IB were attuned to the re-emergent diplomatic MNE. Kobrin (1998), for example, contemplated the revival of a "medieval" world system in which MNEs pursued their interests within an emergent global heterarchy.

Despite the broad agreement among international theorists that MNEs are eligible members of international society, IB continues to treat them as strictly subordinate to states. Thus, their influence in international relations must be channelled, and muted, through domestic political machinery (Noortmann et al., 2015). MNEs' exclusion from IGOs seems confirmation of this subordination, but MNEs cooperate within their own global collectives, such as the International Chamber of Commerce and Business and Industry Advisory Council, which states are ineligible to join. Legal formality trends behind political reality, and here the lag proves advantageous to MNEs. They have no appetite for IGO membership: it would blow their cover. For seven decades, major international firms have been influential in specifying the scope and practice of IGOs without bearing the accountability entailed in voting rights.

6.5   Diplomacy in international theory

In review of these facts and arguments, we conclude that diplomacy is no longer a "uniquely stately activity" (Melissen, 2005: 12). However, diplomacy, understood in international theory, bears little resemblance to the concept used in business academia. Der Derian (1987a, 1987b), for example, defines it as *mediation between estranged or alienated powers in the international domain*. The reference to "powers", if disconcerting, works very much to the advantage of the present synthesis, as it includes international actors of any stripe. *Mediation* restores, retains or resets a multi-dimensional equilibrium between international actors. It is a process in which they defend their individuality as they bargain with one another, guaranteeing the cohesion of the system as a whole. Diplomacy preserves freedoms or evades constraints, but is modulated so as not to strain the fabric of a rules-based international society.

Estrangement describes the fundamental disunity implied by a world of competing claimants to resources, loyalties and authority (Der Derian, 1987b). International society is understood to be in perpetual tension between tendencies towards universalism, entailing empire or a one-world state, and particularism, characterised by autarky and isolation. Thus, estrangement is inevitable and liberating, achieved consensually and maintained through mutual effort. The collapse of empires in the mid-twentieth century, which launched the MNE as an international actor, was a profusion of estrangement, but nonetheless regarded as a positive step for both newly emancipated nation-states and international society itself. The nature and degree of estrangement determines what an international actor can expect of its peers, and what is expected of it. MNEs work extremely hard to legally distance themselves from states, insisting that their private national character disqualifies them from duties imposed by, for example, international human rights law (Muchlinski, 2001). Yet the same MNEs do not hesitate to assert their public international character in designing international legal regimes such as the Regional Comprehensive Economic Partnership and Comprehensive and Progressive Agreement for Transpacific Partnership.

In their theorisation of diplomacy, Jönsson and Hall (2005) elaborate on estrangement and its mediation amongst international actors, or "polities". The persistence and evolution of a social order constituted of, and simultaneously constituting, international actors, is explained by diplomacy itself. That order depends on the array of specific estrangements between individual actors, and between international society and its alternatives. Thus, diplomacy entails (1) communication, essential to the mediation process, (2) representation, which alludes to the fact that individuals engaged in diplomatic communication are not themselves international actors, and, most critically, (3) reproduction of international society. Membership and identity within international society is secured through diplomacy. In consequence, the boundaries and relational norms of that society are defined and redefined. This is clear in the context of the MNE, which first had to assert and defend its status as international actor over the preceding century, and then, as it rapidly evolved as a political and economic actor, maintain and advance its privileges in international society. The powerful home state sponsorship granted MNEs, alluded to in Chapter 5 in this volume, implies that they reciprocated through deliberate constructive contribution to international society, and their status is contingent on continuing to do so as the needs and composition of that society change.

6.6   International business as diplomacy

International theory confronts IB with a conceptualisation of diplomacy framed very differently to its firm-level namesake. There are, however, points of contact. Business diplomacy exponents agree with Jönsson and Hall on the importance of the relationship between the human agents practising diplomacy and their non-human principals possessed of international standing. As the Vienna Convention on Diplomatic Relations (United Nations, 1961) clarifies in relation to states, diplomats are assigned a mission to promote and protect the interests of their international actor. MNEs, like states, must be represented by professionals acculturated in the ritual and ceremony of diplomacy, who understand its institutions well enough to ensure their preservation or constructive modification. Lacking embassies and consulates, and formal diplomatic status, MNEs communicate with international actors through alternative channels constructed in collaboration therewith. While extant business diplomacy research touches on this theme, it is not informed by the present ontology, so cannot take account, for example, of the corporate diplomat's potentially conflicting sense of duty to international society itself, or where business-to-business relations tend more to the diplomatic than the commercial.

Another overlap is in the agreement that diplomacy entails influence over the society in which the diplomatic actor is embedded. From the business perspective, that society is construed in national or, occasionally, multinational terms. In international theory, however, the salient social environment is irreducibly international and excludes most stakeholders captured by environmental analyses prescribed in the business literature, and is thus more certain and determinative.

Firm-level theory insists that diplomacy is a means to acquire legitimacy, a firm-specific attribute sustaining strategic liberty derived from conformity with social norms (Oliver, 1996). However, it remains unclear how "society" should be understood by a firm that transects so many, both horizontally and vertically. Nor is it obvious how diplomacy, as opposed to PR, CSR, or basic legal compliance, is uniquely capable of securing legitimacy. Insisting that diplomacy is exclusive to MNEs, as international actors, offers new clarity. To be sure, there is no simple formula by which legitimacy is bestowed on an international actor, although Collingwood (2006) observes that the legitimacy of non-state actors does not depend on their institutional isomorphism with liberal states in terms of transparency, accountability and representation. An international actor operates within fields of undefined and contested rights, and participates in the formulation and enforcement of new standards. Consequently, its legitimacy depends on its recognition of social reproduction as a constraint on its power. Social reproduction necessitates innovation as international society confronts new challenges that disrupt equilibria in estrangements. This might, for example, entail advancing democratisation of the global order (Clark, 2003). Diplomacy is a process whereby new norms are consciously constructed through mediation between actors that strive at all times to guarantee their qualified independence. In form it has a legitimising aspect insofar as its practitioners comply with diplomatic formalities. In substance, diplomacy can be provocative, even defiant. Thus, as Olins (2000) observes, legitimation is more than compliance with prevailing norms, it is anticipation of those norms.

Business scholars prescribe diplomacy as means of repairing de-legitimisation, brought about by errors such as marketing unsafe products, operating in countries with poor human rights records, tax evasion, environmental degradation, or a culturally insensitive promotional strategy. These errors are often the catalyst for CSR. However, although marketing blunders alienate consumers and trigger regulatory sanctions, the required acts of contrition and rehabilitation are indistinguishable from PR, reminding us of L'Etang's deliberate conflation of the two practices. Compare this with the occurrence of de-legitimisation in a genuinely international sense. Estrangement is not *necessarily* induced by errors within an international actor's own "territory". Here, the market domain of the firm is analogous to the geographic domain of the state. International society, as a legitimising community, is far more concerned about the MNE's service to the functioning of that society than it is in how the MNE governs its nested "republics". At some threshold, misconduct in the MNE's private domain threatens to disorder international society itself, but, until then, the restorative purpose of diplomacy concerns the specific estrangements the MNE mediates with its fellow international actors. Diplomacy, however self-serving, should not detract from the provision of core global public goods: peace, security, order, continuity and institutional adaptation.

CSR scholars, Palazzo and Scherer, see legitimacy as a function of the democratisation of the corporation mandated by the incipient sovereignty of transnational civil society (Palazzo and Scherer, 2008; Scherer and Palazzo, 2011). Their thesis intersects with the present argument where they contend that companies, especially MNEs, must contribute to governance, "and help to solve political problems in cooperation with state actors and civil society actors" (Palazzo and Scherer, 2008: 19). They do not see the corporate political imperative in specifically international terms: on the contrary, they insist that globalisation has rendered the national/international distinction increasingly anachronistic. Thus, the corporation must exert itself to guarantee individual rights, or fail in its public duty. This chapter does not argue that the global regulatory framework is defective, necessitating reform both from corporations and of corporations. Rather, the MNE as international actor adopts a contingent stance with respect to human rights. It calibrates its behaviour to reflect the value of championing them, depending on their extant issue-salience, as it manoeuvres to secure its allocation of the global commons.

A violation of norms governing the conduct of international actors, most particularly an act, or failure to act, that puts the actor's commitment to those norms in question, requires the mediation of estrangement. What forms of MNE conduct generate estrangement in this sense, creating a *need* for a diplomatic mediation? An example is undermining multilateral sanctions by continuing to do business with sanctioned states or their nationals. Others include the exploitation of slave labour, the encouragement of extrajudicial killings to deter unionisation, facilitating terrorism, undermining national development, triggering global economic recession, or espionage. That is, actions inconsistent with the reproduction of international society. Notably, MNEs in breach of these norms are likely to be found in breach again before long, and this nine-lived nature is strongly suggestive of how adept they are at mediating estrangements generated by their malfeasance.

Diplomacy can also be instrumental in establishing a position of relative invulnerability. Business diplomacy scholars emphasise building "positive relationships" in order to deflect risk and retain market power. International diplomacy, however, necessitates taking sides, pulling away from certain actors, drawing closer to others. Furthermore, as alluded to above, retaining or deploying market power need not be the MNE's exclusive concern. As an international actor the MNE is distinguished by its specialisation in the exploitation of marketable technologies, and *market* power is the form most readily developed and deployed. Yet while MNEs are not states, they too have multiple policy fronts, a fact which can become obscured by understanding them exclusively in terms of the profit-maximising firm. There is no *prima facie* reason to suppose that MNEs eschew other bases of power when the opportunity arises. Violence is the antithesis of diplomacy, and MNEs would be unwise to consider it a means of resolving conflict with international peers, but MNEs can, for example, deploy information and propaganda, and, crucially, legitimacy to their advantage.

To maintain their status as international actors, MNEs must be prepared to mediate estrangements between their fellow international actors, mindful of their self-interest and that of international society. When are they moved to assert themselves? What can they achieve in this capacity, and by what means besides acts of public diplomacy like that of 3M's mollification of the Trump administration during the COVID-19 pandemic? While it is unlikely an MNE will be invited to adjudicate in an inter-state dispute, MNEs are quite capable of diplomatically interceding on behalf of their international peers or to prevent destabilisation of the international system. As the global balance of power shifts, and international commitment to liberalism erodes (Witt, 2019), how will MNEs adjust their diplomatic positions?

To close this section, reconstructing the MNE as an international actor requires greater focus on diplomatic interaction *between* MNEs. Stopford et al. (1991) were impressed by MNEs negotiating with states as equals, but they were amazed that MNEs bargain with one another with a view to improve their standing with states. Their ability to distance themselves from mutual antagonism in the market to strengthen their hand in negotiating outcomes with states revealed an unrecognised political sophistication. Consequently, exchanges of promise between states and firms and indeed between firms were intelligible as "international treaties" (Stopford et al., 1991: 23). Although it is no secret that MNEs collude to increase their political bargaining power, the preceding discussion suggests it is necessary to account for their status as international actors to fully understand the purpose and limit of their alliances.

6.7   Concluding discussion

This chapter has sought to establish the credentials of the MNE as an international actor, and on that basis adapt a theory of diplomacy to the MNE. The work is formative, and more questions are raised than answered. Whatever is made of the claimed centrality of diplomacy to IB, the point is to more precisely delimit the scope of IB diplomacy theory, giving it a political foundation to complement established bodies of research. The annexation of business diplomacy by IB is historically justified, but existing research, grounded in microeconomic ontology, employs competing and unreconciled conceptualisations of political behaviour. While these problems can be circumvented by adopting a concept of diplomacy from international relations, micro-level inquiry addressing the MNE in the non-market domain remains essential, and as IB edges towards accommodating the political distinctiveness of the MNE, it will find the necessary ontological adaptation gets easier.

All internationalised firms, however unwittingly, play a vital part in the reproduction of a liberally constituted international society. MNEs are especially important in this regard because they, more than any other international actor, enact the totality of practices that characterise the contemporary global political economy. They are dominant traders, practitioners of FDI, gatekeepers of production technology, and governors of global supply chains. Moreover, they are conscious of their power in international society. Accordingly, MNEs have been granted diplomatic rights, but these are not unassailable. Mediations that gradually facilitated the building of diplomatic capabilities and entitlements in MNEs occurred over decades, between firms and states, between states in bilateral and multilateral contexts, and, in still undiscovered ways, between MNEs themselves. All of this was underpinned by power in service to the liberal ideology championed at the core of the OECD and replicated in the culture of diplomacy. As economic and commercial diplomacy rose to prominence in the post-war era, and internationalised firms asserted themselves in political space, the MNE was elevated from the status of *technology*, an instrument helping maintain a liberal international order, to a *personality* whose entitlements should be respected. This separation of MNEs from their home states arguably represents the most significant and carefully mediated estrangement of the post-decolonisation era.

As a result of the estrangement of MNEs from their states of origin, international business diplomacy does not exclude MNE interactions with home states: both qualify as international actors. Even in interactions concerning home state domestic policy, MNE interests are indivisibly international. By the same token, international business diplomacy excludes non-MNEs dealing with proximate regulatory agencies or publics. These relationships are not less important, but neither are they conditioned by anarchy, the defining feature of the international domain. Standing firm on this point helps considerably in sifting and sorting the competing perspectives on political engagement at the level of the firm.

Despite the comparison drawn between states and MNEs as international actors, there is no reason to suppose MNEs practise diplomacy as states do. MNE representatives do not enjoy the legal immunities granted ambassadors, nor can MNEs assume membership of intergovernmental organisations. Indeed, we know far too little about the forms of diplomacy deployed by MNEs, although some small proportion is observable, or very nearly. We can identify issue domains in which MNEs inevitably take an interest in revising and enforcing norms, but the realm of diplomacy is far larger than negotiating national market access or the enforceability of patents, and in this larger space we have much to learn about how and with whom MNEs communicate, by what means of representation, and how they acknowledge their responsibilities with respect to the reproduction of international society.

Clearly, overlaying a state-level concept of diplomacy on the MNE has rami-fications for the theory of the MNE itself. The class of actor meriting the term "MNE" might be far smaller than currently envisaged. How much smaller? Are "true" MNEs the 147 entities controlling almost 40 per cent of global corporate shareholdings identified by Vitali et al. (2011), two thirds of which are financial institutions? Are they the 737 controlling 80 per cent? Or are the diplomatic credentials of internationalised firms only partly established by economic scale and scope? Small states can wield influence vastly disproportionate to the size of their economies or destructive potential of their military forces, and inter-national NGOs possess far fewer resources. Certainly, the number of MNEs qualifying as international actors, on which basis they are genuinely distinct from other species of business entity, is only a fraction of the population of firms engaged in FDI.

Theoretical development necessitates two interrelated tasks: (1) deeper immer-sion in the literatures of international relations, foreign policy and diplomacy for insights into the MNE's participation in mediated estrangement; and (2) original research to explore the diplomatic imperative in IB practice. The territory is unfamiliar, and MNEs resist full disclosure of their diplomatic involvement, so data collection will be challenging. However, developing this line of theorising may attract scholars working in neighbouring international fields. IR theorists, sociologists and legal theorists can be encouraged by signs of IB drawing inspiration from their discourses. Putting the "international" back into IB encourages interdisciplinary research and cross-fertilises thinking in multiple directions. This means a reinvigorating injection of new ideas from fields that are increasingly excited about the diplomatic MNE, and, perhaps, the revival of that excitement in IB.

References

Alammar, F.M. and Pauleen, D.J. (2016). Business diplomacy management: A conceptual overview and an integrative framework. *International Journal of Diplomacy and Economy*, 3: 3–26.

Alderson, K. and Hurrell, A. (2000). *Hedley Bull on International Society*. London: Macmillan.

Avant, D.D., Finnemore, M. and Sell, S.K. (Eds) (2010). *Who Governs the Globe?* Cambridge: Cambridge University Press.

Behrman, J. (1969). *Some Patterns in the Rise of the Multinational Enterprise*. Research Paper No. 18. Chapel Hill: Graduate School of Business, University of North Carolina.

Berle, A.A. (1959). *Power without Property: A New Development in American Political Economy*. New York: Harcourt, Brace & Co.

Breuninger, K. (2020). 3M warns Trump: Halting exports under Defense Production Act would reduce number of masks available to US. *CNBC*, 3 April. https://www.cnbc.com/2020/04/03/coronavirus-3m-tells-trump-halting-exports-would-reduce-number-of-masks.html.

Buckley, P. and Casson, M. (1976). *The Future of the Multinational Enterprise*. London: Macmillan.

Bull, H. (1977). *The Anarchical Society: A Study of Order in World Politics*. London: Red Globe Press.

Burmester, B., Michailova, S. and Stringer, C. (2019). Modern slavery and international business scholarship: The governance nexus. *critical perspectives on international business*, 15(2/3): 139–157.

Cerny, P.G. (2010). *Rethinking World Politics: A Theory of Transnational Neopluralism*. Oxford: Oxford University Press.

Ciepley, D. (2013). Beyond public and private: Toward a political theory of the corporation. *American Political Science Review*, 107: 139–158.

Clark, I. (2003). Legitimacy in a global order. *Review of International Studies*, 29: 75–95.

Clegg, S. (2017). The East India Company: The first modern multinational? *Research in the Sociology of Organizations*, 49: 43–67.

Clegg, S., Geppert, M. and Hollinshead, G. (2018). Politicization and political contests in and around contemporary multinational corporations: An introduction. *Human Relations*, 71(6): 745–765.

Collingwood, V. (2006). Non-governmental organisations, power and legitimacy in international society. *Review of International Studies*, 32(3): 439–454.

Cutler, A.C. (1997). Artifice, ideology and paradox: The public/private distinction in international law. *Review of International Political Economy*, 4: 261–285.

Der Derian, J. (1987a). Mediating estrangement: A theory for diplomacy. *Review of International Studies*, 13: 91–110.

Der Derian, J. (1987b). *On Diplomacy: A Genealogy of Western Estrangement*. Oxford: Blackwell.

Dunning, J.H. (1981). *International Production and the Multinational Enterprise*. London: Allen & Unwin.

FE Online (2020). Trump threatens Apple; derails Modi's plan to lure companies away from China to Make in India. *Financial Express*, 15 May. https://www.financialexpress.com/industry/donald-trump-threatens-apple-derails-narendra-modis-make-in-india-plan/1960054/.

Hamilton, K. and Langhorne, R. (2011). *The Practice of Diplomacy: Its Evolution, Theory, and Administration.* Abingdon: Routledge.

He, X., Eden, L. and Hitt, M.A. (2016). The renaissance of state-owned multinationals. *Thunderbird International Business Review,* 58(2): 117–129.

Henisz, W.J. (2014). *Corporate Diplomacy: Building Reputations and Relationships with External Stakeholders.* Sheffield: Greenleaf Publishing.

Hennart, J.F. (1982). *A Theory of Multinational Enterprise.* Ann Arbor: University of Michigan Press.

Hillman, A.J. and Hitt, M. (1999). Corporate political strategy formulation: A model of approach, participation, and strategy decisions. *Academy of Management Review,* 24: 825–842.

Hillman, A.J., Keim, G.D. and Schuler, D. (2004). Corporate political activity: A review and research agenda. *Journal of Management,* 30(6): 837–857.

Holtbrügge, D. and Berg, N. (2004). How multinational corporations deal with their socio-political stakeholders: An empirical study in Asia, Europe, and the US. *Asian Business & Management,* 3(3): 299–313.

Horwitz, M.J. (1981). History of the public/private distinction. *University of Pennsylvania Law Review,* 130: 1423–1428.

Hymer, S.H. (1960/1976). *The International Operations of National Firms: A Study of Direct Foreign Investment.* Cambridge: MIT Press.

Hymer, S. (1972). The multinational corporation and the law of uneven development. In J. N. Bhagwati (Ed.), *Economics and World Order from the 1970s to the 1990s.* London: Macmillan, 113–140.

Jacobsen, S. (2017). Silicon Valley giants outrank many nations says first techplomat. *Reuters,* 19 June. http://www.reuters.com/article/us-denmark-tech/silicon-valley-giants-outrank-many-nations-says-first-techplomat-idUSKBN19A17A?il=0.

Jensen, M.C. and Meckling, W.H. (1976). Theory of the firm: Managerial behavior, agency costs and ownership structure. *Journal of Financial Economics,* 3(4): 305–360.

Jönsson, C. and Hall, M. (2005). *Essence of Diplomacy.* Basingstoke: Palgrave Macmillan.

Kaul, I., Conceicao, P., Le Goulven, K. and Mendoza, R.U. (2003). *Providing Global Public Goods: Managing Globalization.* Oxford: Oxford University Press.

Keillor, B.D., Boller, G.W. and Ferrell, O.C. (1997). Firm-level political behavior in the global marketplace. *Journal of Business Research,* 40(2): 113–126.

Kelly, C. (2006). Power, linkage and accommodation: The WTO as an international actor and its influence on other actors and regimes. *Berkeley Journal of International Law,* 24: 79–128.

Kesteleyn, J., Riordan, S. and Ruël, H. (2014). Introduction: Business diplomacy. *The Hague Journal of Diplomacy,* 9(4): 303–309.

Kindleberger, C.P. (1986). International public goods without international government. *The American Economic Review,* 76(1): 1–13.

Kobrin, S.J. (1998). Back to the future: Neomedievalism and the postmodern digital world economy. *Journal of International Affairs,* 51(2): 316–386.

L'Etang, J. (2006). Public relations as diplomacy. In M. Pieczka (Ed.), *Public Relations: Critical Debates and Contemporary Practice.* London: Psychology Press, 373–388.

McCabe, D. (2020). F.C.C. designates Huawei and ZTE as national security threats. *The New York Times,* 4 July. https://www.nytimes.com/2020/06/30/technology/fcc-huawei-zte-national-security.html.

Melissen, J. (2005). The new public diplomacy: Between theory and practice. In J. Melissen (Ed.), *The New Public Democracy.* Basingstoke: Palgrave Macmillan, 3–27.

Moran, T. (1974). *Multinationals and the Politics of Dependence: Coer in Chile*. Princeton, NJ: Princeton University Press.

Muchlinski, P.T. (2001). Human rights and multinationals: Is there a problem? *International Affairs*, 77(1): 31–47.

Noortmann, M., Reinisch, A. and Ryngaert, C. (Eds) (2015). *Non-State Actors in International Law*. London: Bloomsbury.

Nye, J.S. and Keohane, R.O. (1971). Transnational relations and world politics: An introduction. *International Organization*, 25(3): 329–349.

Olins, W. (2000). Why companies and countries are taking on each other's roles. *Corporate Reputation Review*, 3: 254–265.

Oliver, C. (1996). The institutional embeddedness of economic activity. *Advances in Strategic Management*, 13: 163–186.

Ordeix-Rigo, E. and Duarte, J. (2009). From public diplomacy to corporate diplomacy: Increasing corporation's legitimacy and influence. *American Behavioral Scientist*, 53: 549–564.

Palazzo, G. and Scherer, A.G. (2008). Corporate social responsibility, democracy, and the politicization of the corporation. *Academy of Management Review*, 33(3): 773–775.

Penrose, E. (1968). *The Large International Firm in Developing Countries: The International Petroleum Industry*. London: Allen & Unwin.

Penrose, E. (1989). History, the social sciences and economic theory with special reference to multinational enterprise. In A. Teichova. M. Lévy-Leboyer and H. Nussbaum (Eds), *Historical Studies in International Corporate Enterprise*. Cambridge: Cambridge University Press, 7–13.

Rose, M. (2018). With Versailles business summit, Macron seeks to bank on global appeal. *Reuters Business News*, 23 January. https://de.reuters.com/article/us-france-business/with-versailles-business-summit-macron-seeks-to-bank-on-global-appeal-idUSKBN1FB1VE.

Ruël, H. (2013). Diplomacy means business. *Windesheimreeks Kennis en Onderzoek*, 46.

Ruël, H. (2015). *Business Diplomacy: A Definition and Operationalization*. Zwolle: Windesheim University of Applied Sciences.

Ruël, H., Betlam, F., Wolters, T. and van der Kaap, H. (2013). Business diplomacy in MNCs: A study into its determinants. Presentation at European International Business Academy, Bremen, 12–14 December.

Rugman, A. (1981). *Inside The Multinationals: The Economics of Internal Markets*. London: Croom Helm.

Saner, R. and Yiu, L. (2003). *International Economic Diplomacy: Mutations in Post-Modern Times* (Discussion Papers in Diplomacy). Wassenaar: Netherlands Institute of International Relations.

Saner, R., Yiu, L. and Sondergaard, M. (2000). Business diplomacy management: A core competency for global companies. *Academy of Management Executive*, 14: 80–92.

Scherer, A.G. and Palazzo, G. (2011). The new political role of business in a globalized world: A review of a new perspective on CSR and its implications for the firm, governance, and democracy. *Journal of Management Studies*, 48(4): 899–931.

Scott, M. (2020). Facebook slaps labels on state-controlled media amid anger over Trump's posts. *Politico*, 4 June. https://www.politico.com/news/2020/06/04/facebook-labels-state-controlled-media-trump-posts-300957.

Seib, G. (2016). Why Rex Tillerson has the GOP foreign-policy establishment's support. *The Wall Street Journal*, 20 December. https://blogs.wsj.com/washwire/2016/12/20/why-rex-tillerson-has-the-gop-foreign-policy-establishments-support/.

Servan-Schreiber, J.J. (1967). *Le défi américain*. Paris: Denoel.

Simonovic, I. (2001). Relative sovereignty of the twenty first century. *Hastings International & Comparative Law Review*, 25: 371–382.

Singer, D. J. (1961). The level-of-analysis problem in international relations. *World Politics*, 14: 77–92.

Slaughter, A.M. (2004). Sovereignty and power in a networked world order. *Stanford Journal of International Law*, 40: 283–328.

Smith, R. (1974). Private power and national sovereignty: Some comments on the multinational corporation. *Journal of Economic Issues*, 8: 417–447.

Steger, U. (2003). *Corporate Diplomacy: The Strategy for a Volatile, Fragmented Business Environment*. Hoboken: John Wiley & Sons.

Stopford, J., Strange, S. and Henley, J. (1991). *Rival States, Rival Firms: Competition for World Market Shares*. Cambridge: Cambridge University Press.

Sundaram, A. and Black, J. (1992). The environment and internal organization of multinational enterprises. *Academy of Management Review*, 17: 729–757.

Tombs, S. and Whyte, D. (2015). *The Corporate Criminal: Why Corporations Must Be Abolished*. London: Routledge.

Turner, S. (1998). Global civil society, anarchy and governance: Assessing an emerging paradigm. *Journal of Peace Research*, 35(1): 25–42.

United Nations (1961). Vienna Convention on Diplomatic Relations (18 April 1961). *United Nations Treaty Series*, 500: 95–220.

Vaitsos, C.V. (1970). Bargaining and the distribution of returns in the purchase of technology by developing countries. *Institute of Development Studies Bulletin*, 3: 16–23.

Vernon, R. (1971). *Sovereignty at Bay: The Multinational Spread of US Enterprises*. New York: Basic Books.

Vitali, S., Glattfelder, J.B. and Battiston, S. (2011). The network of global corporate control. *PloS ONE*, 6(10): e25995.

Wan, W.P. and Hillman, A.J. (2006). One of these things is not like the others: What contributes to dissimilarity among MNE subsidiaries' political strategy? *Management International Review*, 46(1): 85–107.

Whyte, D. (2020). *Ecocide: Kill the Corporation before It Kills Us*. Manchester: Manchester University Press.

Williamson, O.E. (1975). *Markets and Hierarchies*. New York: Free Press.

Witt, M.A. (2019). De-globalization: Theories, predictions, and opportunities for international business research. *Journal of International Business Studies*, 50(7): 1053–1077.

Wolfers, A. (1962). *Discord and Collaboration*. Baltimore, MD: Johns Hopkins University Press.

Yackee, J.W. (2008). Pacta sunt servanda and state promises to foreign investors before bilateral investment treaties: Myth and reality. *Fordham International Law Journal*, 32: 1550–1613.

PART III

International management, power
relations and ideology

7. Treating ideology seriously in international business and management research: a textual analysis of the global "self-management" fad

Leo McCann, Brian Wierman and Edward Granter

7.1   Introduction

"First, let's fire all the managers."

A suggestion like this wouldn't be out of place at a trade union strike meeting or street demonstration. In fact, it is the title of an article by management guru Gary Hamel in the *Harvard Business Review* (Hamel, 2011). How do we make sense of this? Why would a management expert criticise this elite cadre of managers which has for decades been regarded as the expert technocrats governing our firms, corporations and institutions (Gantman, 2005; McCann, 2016, 2020; Mills, 1956/2000)?

What Hamel is doing, in keeping with many others in the management, strategy and leadership guru "tradition" (Collins, 2001; Kanter, 1990; Peters and Waterman, 1982/2004), is identifying a deep sense of organisational malaise. He describes management as "the least efficient activity in your organization" (Hamel, 2011: 50). Senior leaders are remote, costly, insensitive and impractical. They lack the agility required to function effectively in a rapidly changing, hypercompetitive global economy. Their tendency towards micro-management, to command and control, to pointless reorganisations, and to metric-based tunnel vision leads to weak performance and resentful employees (Carney and Getz, 2010; Collins, 2001). Mid-level and senior managers themselves struggle with exhaustion, overload and cynicism (Hassard et al., 2009; Laloux, 2015). This downbeat appraisal of organisational life is not solely the view of critically minded analysts, but is widely accepted in mainstream sources (Hamel, 2009), deeply rooted in daily experience and widely reproduced in popular culture (Rhodes and Parker, 2008).

Such business writings, we argue, are forms of *ideology*. Ideology is an academic concept with an extraordinarily long, rich and controversial history (Seeck et al., 2020). A famous introductory text suggests no fewer than sixteen types of conceptual definition (Eagleton, 1991: 1–2). One particularly parsimonious author defines ideology as "the pattern of beliefs and concepts (both factual and normative) which purport to explain complex social phenomena with a view to directing and simplifying socio-political choices facing individuals and groups" (Gould, 1964: 315). For our purposes, that definition is as good as any.

We accept that the real-world impacts of ideology cannot be read off from the mere fact of its existence and circulation. Powerful traditions in international business and political economy have long highlighted the resilience of different national managerial and economic models (Dore, 2000; Hall and Soskice, 2001). The official intended "adoption" of new managerial ideas across regions and workplaces is often met with indifference and failure as ideas are ignored, circumvented and "translated" (Benders and van Veen, 2001; Frenkel, 2005; Ralston et al., 2008). Nevertheless, we suggest that serious investigations of ideology are of considerable potential value to international business management (IB/M) scholarship. Business ideology – in our case the writings of consultants and "gurus" – can play a powerful, cross-national role in establishing agendas, forming a language and setting the tone of a "spirit of capitalism" (Boltanski and Chiapello, 2005); usually one of boundless energy, change, creativity, transformation, liberation and agility. Business ideology is a powerful example of what the anthropologist Arjan Appadurai calls the "ideoscapes" of global capitalism (Appadurai, 1990).

A central element of these leadership and management guru texts is their ability to capitalise on their readers' frustration and dissatisfaction with current working methods. They highlight the limitations of the status quo, meaning that the latest, more effective, approaches are promoted by the "seller" (the guru) for the "buyer" (the manager, entrepreneur or even the employee) to adopt. These new products have included Management By Objectives, Balanced Scorecard, Six Sigma, Zero-Based Budgeting, transformational leadership, lean, Agile, and dozens of others (Mills et al., 2009; Sturdy, 2004). The latest offerings in the "airport bookstall radicalism" (Parker, 2018: 51) category propose moving in a dramatic new direction, one in which management itself becomes redundant (Hamel, 2009). This chapter explores the rise of this "self-management" approach to managing organisations, discussing the extent to which this model is starting to proliferate across a range of international regions and markets. It will focus primarily on two recent concepts – Brian Robertson's "Holacracy" and Frederic Laloux's "Teal" – similar products that offer a radical solution to organisational malaise: strip out as much management as possible and let the organisation run itself.

This "no-managers" approach is not an entirely new idea. One of its main influences is the concept of self-managed teams, which features heavily in literature on Japanese production and lean systems (Graham, 1995; Suzaki, 2012) and arguably goes further back to Trist and Bamforth (1951) and the Tavistock Institute studies on the "longwall method" of coal extraction (Bernstein et al., 2016). It also repackages the teachings of "radical" entrepreneurs such as Richard Semler at Semco (1989), or Paul Orfalea at Kinko's (Orfalea and Marsh, 2005) who aimed at the elimination of hierarchies and bureaucracy (Sennett, 2007). It has considerable overlap with 1980s literature on culture change and culture management, often celebrating a Tom Peters-style "throw out the rule book" approach, where there is no time for memos or organisational charts (Nordstrom and Ridderstrale, 2007; Peters, 1992). This lineage surfaces in the "trendy" and "zany" feel of some (but not all) of the case study companies used by Robertson and Laloux – small start-ups, the tech sector – long-term bastions of a "just be yourself", and "authentic" approach to work and management (Fleming and Sturdy, 2009, 2010). Robertson's Holacracy shares the tech sector's interest in operating systems, evolution, upgrades and complex architecture. But the no-managers oeuvre also features some organisations with much more basic operations that have also successfully adopted self-management. Examples include the Morning Star tomato packing company (Carney and Getz, 2010; Hamel, 2011; Laloux, 2014, 2015), the clothing company Patagonia, and the manufacturers FAVI and Sun Hydraulics (Carney and Getz, 2010; Laloux, 2014, 2015). The Dutch "Corporate Rebels" consultants list over one hundred other companies worldwide claiming to use similar "self-management" approaches.[1]

We suggest that these "no-manager" solutions are ideological manifestations of a cultural milieu that draws influence both from a tech zeitgeist and a faux counterculture of self-development (Ekman, 2015). Sensitive to discussions around the "needs" of "millennials", gurus and leaders feel an unease in managing people and performance. In an effort to be egalitarian or otherwise "better" they try to mitigate the most obviously coercive and hierarchical elements of capitalism but fail to recognise any inherent structural issues. Hence we see a range of major multinationals claiming to have dropped annual appraisals (GE, Cargill, Eli Lilly), with these claims handily inflated and circulated by the leadership gurus, academics and journalists writing for titles such as *Fortune* and *Fast Company*; the large and growing body of thought leaders that constitute and construct the ideological landscape of global business.[2]

In addition to its egalitarian feel, the no-managers approach also has some peculiar political connections to deeper ideological, anarcho-capitalist and right libertarian roots around the idea that management isn't needed at all; that hierarchy, bureaucracy and regulation get in the way of market calculation and enterprise; management is thus a blocker of creativity, individualism and free competition. The early roots of this tradition can be seen in such work as Burnham's *The Managerial Revolution* (Burnham, 1941). It has re-emerged in much more recent forms such as the Koch brothers' system of "Market-Based Management" (Koch, 2007). These approaches are hostile to worker organisation and extremely politically conservative.

We explore the textual practices of two prominent examples of "no-managers" writings within a critical approach sensitive to the role of ideology in general, and informed by the literature on "fads and fashions" at a more specific level. We argue that these supposedly "radical" and "liberatory" management ideas constitute a form of ideology that formats itself as new, progressive and practical, but in reality exists to further cement the dominance of senior leaders and the doctrine of managerialism alongside the continued marginalisation and exploitation of workers and professionals. We recognise that the existence of ideology does not mean its uncritical acceptance. Indeed, a very long stream of research has already argued that "best practice" is extraordinarily difficult to implement and that local level cultures and practices are enduring (Benders and van Veen, 2001; Dore, 2000). Nevertheless, we argue that IB/M as a discipline has largely circumvented questions of ideology, and we suggest there is great value in exploring the ideological formations and textual devices which influence and structure the theories and practices of any increasingly globalised managerial ideoscape.

7.2 Ideological formations and textual practices: towards a more discursive approach in international business

Delios (2017: 391) accuses academic international business research of being "staid and boring: helpful for sedation, but uninformative for knowledge generation". IB/M research and publishing – in keeping with the approaches taken in many other business school disciplines (Parker, 2018; Tourish, 2020) – has strongly adopted positivistic, "hard science" approaches in efforts to bolster the academic legitimacy of its knowledge claims. Recent years have seen increasing disquiet about the literature being dominated by large-scale quantitative data sets, applied microeconomics and complex statistical modelling. Several authors advocate much greater plurality, such as the use of ethnography and discourse analysis (Birkinshaw et al., 2011; Hassard et al., 2007). We strongly support such a broadening of the research frontier in IB/M. In this chapter we respond to the call for plurality and for fresh directions in IB/M research and writing. We do this by considering not only the general conceptual notion of ideology, but also the more specific and practical approaches of paying attention to the textual practices that inform the products created by "thought leaders", such as Holacracy and Teal. Our approach is necessarily discursive. We cannot be sure of causation and efficacy and we cannot model variables and hypotheses. However, we do argue that all manner of meaningful and rich lines of inquiry can be explored through critical exploration of the managerial texts that circulate the global knowledge economy. Analysing these texts as ideological constructs is one way in which new and evocative forms of IB/M writing can be generated, in addition to a long overdue return to in-depth, qualitative research in actual organisational settings (Delios, 2017: 397; Hassard et al., 2007).

The notion of "fads and fashions" is already very well known, and appears in both "critical" and mainstream management scholarship (Abrahamson, 1991; Birnbaum, 2001; Furnham, 2004; Piazza and Abrahamson, 2020; Røvik, 2011; Spicer, 2017; Sturdy, 2004). Management knowledge is often critiqued for being oversold, unoriginal and superficial. When "adopted" in a company, these "new" systems and concepts often have limited real impact before they die off or get superseded by the next fad. But proponents of management concepts such as Teal, Holacracy, lean, Agile, or Market-Based Management position their offerings as breakthroughs in management thought which are applicable to organisations around the world. For Laloux, Teal is a highly progressive concept that has emerged only after hundreds of years of human development. For Robertson, Holacracy is a practical and effective "operating system" that provides organisations with clarity and functionality, allowing creativity and innovation to flourish.

Critical literature on management fads and fashions is sceptical of the value of these, or any other, managerial concepts. It suggests that the adoption of fads is often superficial, acting as little more than a marketing device designed to make the company and its leadership appear progressive, evidence-based and modernised (Abrahamson, 1996; Abrahamson and Fairchild, 1999; Parker, 2018). Significant parts of the company are unaffected by, indifferent to, or cynical about the insertion of the new fad; just "going through the motions". Sometimes a company's management does not fully understand the new system it is implementing, but pushes ahead with it anyway more in hope than expectation (Brunsson, 2006). Newly introduced systems frequently don't "fit" the company's pre-existing personnel, operations and culture. It is quite common for the incoming management system to sit awkwardly among the existing ones or their legacies and remnants – what Birnbaum (2000) calls the "fad residuals".

Both Holacracy and Teal sit squarely within a broader international publishing phenomenon that has strong ideological influence. Related texts such as *Humanocracy* (Hamel and Zanini, 2020) enjoy large sales. Equally prominent are TED talks on similar themes and events such as the "Conscious Capitalism" conference.[3] Themes of management revolution are also present in consultant, coaching and training providers with active social media presences, such as the "Corporate Rebels" team (strapline: "Make Work More Fun").[4]

We argue that behind the "funky" and "conscious" façade lie powerful ideological currents. The "spirit" of the no-managers approach is seductive in its appeals to workplace democracy, individualism, creativity, and engagement, but it places the deep burden of organisational "sensemaking" onto the employees themselves. This aims to reduce management expense in organisations by turning workers into their own quasi-managers. Accountability, responsibility and decision-making move into the abstract. Everyone is encouraged to "be part of the team," and "have fun but work hard," sometimes at the expense of fair wages and treatment. Lines between work and life blur, as the no-managers fad develops a pervasive new form of industrial relations unitarism; workers are encouraged to view themselves and their interests as inseparable from those of their employer. This sums to a "pulling" of workers into managerialism itself (Klikauer, 2015). The following two sections describe and evaluate two of these "no-managers" philosophies in depth, focusing closely on their textual practices, in an effort to reveal their broader ideological aims and trends.

7.3   Holacracy

Holacracy is a new and popular take on self-management. Created in the United States, it has since developed an international following. Its name is derived from the notion of the "holon" – a whole that is part of a larger whole (Robertson, 2015: 38). Holacracy is the coordinated operation of autonomous and self-managed holons.

Founded in 2007 by Brian Robertson, a tech entrepreneur, the consulting company HolacracyOne promulgates Holacracy throughout the world through training, publishing and webinars. The *Holacracy Constitution* provides the rules and design for Holacracy, available free online at Holacracy. org. Robertson also wrote a 2015 book and released it contemporaneously with the adoption of Holacracy by what is now one of its best-known proponents – Zappos, a Las Vegas e-commerce firm wholly owned by Amazon. Tony Hsieh, Zappos' CEO, was a celebrity entrepreneur well known for experimenting with "progressive" and "radical" organisational styles (Hsieh, 2010). The move to Holacracy is the most well-known and documented (Groth, 2017). Robertson's book *Holacracy: The Revolutionary Management System That Abolishes Hierarchy* (2015) describes the system in detail. Holacracy's goal is to "[move] beyond bolting on changes and instead focus on upgrading the most foundational aspects of the way the organization functions" (2015: 10). Holacracy's phraseology speaks to an audience of tech and related e-companies like Zappos where its most ardent supporters reside, and the language of "operating systems" and "upgrading" are common textual devices in Holacratic rhetoric.

Political and clinical metaphors also feature heavily. In typical hierarchical organisations, "corporate antibodies come out and reject" creativity when an organisation seeks innovation. Holacracy, however fundamentally reworks

> the way power and authority are formally defined and exercised, the way the organization is structured, and the way we establish who can expect what, and from whom – or who can make which decisions, and within what limits (Robertson, 2015: 11)

Mechanically, Holacracy creates work "Circles" that are ostensibly egalitarian. There is a "Lead Link," who inherits "the Purpose and any Accountabilities on the Circle itself, and controls any Domains defined on the Circle, just as if the Circle were only a Role and the Lead Link filled that Role".[5] Circles are comprised of varying "Roles", which suggests a division of labour. All of these terms are defined in the *Constitution*, for example, "Accountabilities" and, ongoing "activities of the Organization that the Role will enact".[6]

Holacracy also leverages artificial intelligence to some degree. Glassfrog is "official software to support and advance your Holacracy practice". It is aimed at helping organisations develop "[C]lear structure, agile governance, efficient meetings".[7] In theory, a Holacracy organisation member would enter a variety of data on their roles, accountabilities and other descriptors specific to the type of work they do. If everyone enters good data, the software will assist in identifying "tensions"; areas where roles, accountabilities and other pieces of the organisation may overlap or otherwise conflict. Resolving tensions then becomes the main function of meetings. HolacracyOne, the Holacracy design and promotion company, states that 82 per cent of the 174 "official" Holacracy adopters are outside the United States, mostly in Europe.[8] But never has the shift to Holacracy been as well-known as in the case of Zappos. Business press in the United States and beyond documented the somewhat controversial transition,[9] with some highlighting high numbers of employees who had left Zappos since Holacracy was introduced (Groth, 2017).

Holacracy's core logic speaks to the notion of traditional capitalist organisation as something which can be "upgraded" through changes to its structural design and core cultural set-up. Thus the pathologies of the corporate capitalist work-place can be mitigated by altering its operation, rather than its essential form in terms of ownership or capital/labour relations. Corporate governance through adherence to generally agreed upon rules is seen by proponents of Holacracy and other management innovations as the main vehicle for this upgrading of work and organisation. Holacracy could be seen as something of a "Magna Carta" for the contemporary international business organisation, including the multinational. It blunts the monarch's reign ever so slightly, but it does not meaningfully restructure the real vectors of power and decision-making.

Advocates of Holacracy claim it has an international appeal, with the doctrine of flat hierarchies spread even to nations well-known for authoritarian govern-ance and very high managerial "power distance" in Hofstedian terms. Several companies in China have supposedly "adopted" Holacracy. In late 2018, two Chinese businesspeople organised "The Second China Organizational Evolution Forum", and "attracted [500] participants and a stellar, international line-up of speakers, including Frederic Laloux, John Bunch of Zappos, many Chinese thought leaders, and Enlivening Edge's own George Pór".[10] In keeping with the spirit of Holacracy, "Instead of sitting in rows and listening to one sage-on-the-stage after the other, 500 chairs were organized in small circles and participants were given some generative ques-tions with guidance for deep listening". The participants eagerly consumed and circulated Frederic Laloux's book *Reinventing Organizations*, a text that explains and promotes Teal; another "no-managers" approach that is intimately connected with Holacracy.

7.4   Evolutionary-Teal

"Self-management." "Wholeness." "Purpose." These are the three concepts that lie at the heart of "Teal" – the management programme developed and popularised by Belgian organisational consultant Frederic Laloux. In *Reinventing Organizations*, Laloux (2014) continues with the by-now familiar complaints about the chronic limitations of traditional hierarchical organisations. "[T]he current way we run organizations has been stretched to its limits. We are increasingly disillusioned by organizational life" (Laloux, 2014: 3). Organisations are blighted by "resignation, resentment and apathy", and by "posturing" and "drudgery" (Laloux, 2014: 13). We need to find "productive, fulfilling and meaningful" workplaces that are "soulful" places "where our talents can blossom and our callings can be honored" (Laloux, 2014: 13).

Laloux embeds his critique of the workplace into a long preamble about progressive stages of human consciousness. He asserts that humanity has evolved through seven broad developmental stages, each represented by a colour (Laloux, 2014: 37–42). We have moved from Reactive-Infrared (primal, prehistoric bands), to Magic-Magenta (tribal, shamanic, childlike) during the periods 1000,000–50,000 BCE to 13,000 BCE. From there we progressed to the "first proto-empires" of the Impulsive-Red paradigm, where "the ego is now fully hatched" and where, interestingly, "the first forms of organizational life" emerged – Red Organisations. Divisions of labour have arrived, and with them the first forms of role and hierarchy; Red Organisation is redolent of violence and domination. Impulsive-Red is a concept that Laloux's readers can easily recognise as something no well-run or ethical organisation would want to emulate.

Next up is the Conformist-Amber paradigm. Here we have the beginnings of a rational, ordered, mass society, where people exercise some sort of self-control and self-discipline, where organisations plan ahead and structure themselves according to formal rules, roles and bureaucratic procedures. "According to developmental psychologists, a large share of today's adult population in developed societies operate from this paradigm" (Laloux, 2014: 18). Amber organisations are well-suited to stability, favour standardisation and routine, but are ill-equipped to handle change and competition.

Amber then evolves into "Achievement-Orange", a paradigm associated with rationality, progress and the Enlightenment. Traditional forms of authority are questioned, and scientific investigation ushers in an era of "unprecedented levels of prosperity" (Laloux, 2014: 24). Standards of health, education and efficiency all climb rapidly. However, the dark side of Orange is its "corporate greed, political short-termism, overleverage, overconsumption, and the reckless exploitation of the planet's resources and ecosystems" (Laloux, 2014: 24–25). The focus on science, rationality and efficiency also diminishes and delegitimises any concerns for "spirituality and transcendence" (Laloux, 2014: 25). Achievement-Orange has no room for "deep soulful questions" (Laloux, 2014: 25). Large multinational corporations are the best examples of Orange organisations, and the organising principles are those of the inhuman machine: "inputs and outputs", "moving the needle", "scaling solutions", "downsizing" (Laloux, 2014: 28).

The next stage of the evolution is "Pluralistic-Green". This paradigm is "sensitive to people's feelings" (Laloux, 2014: 30). Organisational decisions are based on collective discussion and "relationships are valued over outcomes" (Laloux, 2014: 31). Consensus is the aim and leaders should be servants. Staff should be empowered. Authority should be devolved. While an advance in humanistic terms, Green also has its weaknesses. Its "relationship to rules is ambiguous and conflicted" and it would like to "do away with" power and hierarchy altogether (Laloux, 2014: 31). According to Laloux, Green is worthy but ultimately dysfunctional. There are things to learn from Green, but as an organisational system for international business, it cannot work.

Eventually we arrive at the paradigm that can work. This is Teal, a kind of turquoise – the colour of the future. Teal is a self-management system that promises to redefine business and commerce, harnessing the most progressive elements of Green while fusing them into a workable and efficient operating structure. The textual devices of colours and stages in Laloux's writing create a dynamic whereby Teal is placed at the end of a teleological series of progressions. But, as we know from the heterodox writer on organisations Timon Beyes, colours are deceptive. The Latin root of the word "colour" is *celare*, meaning to conceal or hide (Beyes, 2017: 1468).

The turns to colour, evolution, consciousness and developmental psychology perform similar, if more expressive and ambitious, roles to the circles, upgrading and lead links in Robertson's Holacracy; organisational improvements are sitting below the surface, waiting to come out if only companies could give up on their addiction to control, hierarchy and coercion. Self-management will occur naturally, like evolution, if only senior leaders would give up the desire to control and manage and embrace spontaneous evolutionary processes. Doing so will result in flourishing, success, better results, less resentment, and a reality where owners and staff can finally answer their calling. It removes all the pointless meetings, metrics, paperwork and targets (Carney and Getz, 2010; Hamel, 2011; Laloux, 2014; Robertson, 2015).

Laloux mentions his research on twelve companies which have adopted Teal principles. But this isn't research in an academically recognised sense. There is no methods section and no systematic presentation and analysis of findings. He tends to "research" a company simply by talking to the CEO and taking their word for it. His accounts, therefore, effectively serve only to repeat the senior leaders' promotion and celebration of that company. He reports almost nothing bad about them or their leadership.

The enthusiasm for Teal sometimes borders on cult-like, making reference to higher levels of human consciousness and stages of human growth. Much of it is based around Laloux's interpretation of "Integral Theory" – a "theory of everything" developed by the "transpersonal psychologist" Ken Wilber. While employing a kind of academic form and tone, these ideas are on the very outer fringes of academia, more likely to emanate from self-run "values centers" and consultancies than university departments. Laloux's case study companies include HolacracyOne. Robertson's work also features regularly in *Reinventing Organizations*, although Zappos itself appears in only two brief passages.[11]

The absence of any notion of organisation power is a disturbing feature of Laloux's paradigm. Despite these serious weaknesses, the influence of such writing is considerable. Like previous management fads, the ideology of Holacracy and Teal has spread globally. This happens through a process where companies deliberately take on and implement these notions, and also through a process of local emulation. Two examples provide some illustration. One is described in a blog posted on Medium by a member of Enspiral – a consulting company that promotes self-management. In this post, Basterfield[12] writes Laloux's Teal into her experience of Indian paper and packaging company Yash Pakka, whose vision statement is "Packaging with a Soul".[13] Another recent manifestation of the no-managers fad is *Results from the Heart*, a book from Kiyoshi Suzaki (2010) that combines Japanese-style lean management with a more ambiguous notion of self-run "mini-companies". Again we see references to self-realisation, to some kind of enlightened experience redolent of the "free" and "empowered" digital nomad (Aroles et al., 2020), or the "do it yourself" capitalist (Aroles et al., 2019; Murphy, 2016). As we go on to argue below, these (and other) ideological productions of global business deserve close, critical scrutiny. Further in-depth unpacking and deconstruction of such texts could be a powerful way to contribute to a broadening of the scope and remit of academic IB/M, bringing it into closer contact with other scholarly traditions in wider use across the disciplines of sociology, anthropology, political economy and cultural studies.

7.5   Towards an ideologically informed IB/M? A possible research agenda

> The primary aim of an ideology is not to understand or interpret society, but to change it by acting politically on it. (Béteille, 2009: 196)

Our analysis of the new consultant/guru literature on "self-management" interprets these texts as ideological constructs designed with explicit political purposes (Seeck et al., 2020). Holacracy is "a new way of structuring and running your organization that replaces the conventional management hierarchy [where] power is distributed throughout the organization – giving individuals and teams freedom while staying aligned to the organization's purpose."[14] Teal organisations are places where "no one holds power over anyone else, and yet, paradoxically, the organization as a whole ends up being considerably more powerful" (Laloux 2014: 62). These are seductive ideas.

We used the "airport bookstall" metaphor to indicate these texts' popular but shallow nature, and to highlight their proliferation and viral-like spread in predominant managerial thinking. As a facet of Western neo-imperialism (Boussebaa et al., 2012; Boussebaa and Morgan, 2014; Klikauer, 2015), guru ideas take hold in prominent Western business schools and popular consulting practices – Laloux is a Belgian born, INSEAD of Paris-educated MBA who writes and acts primarily in the United States – to germinate and flower elsewhere. Western guru ideas are well positioned for viral-like spread, penetrating China and other developing economies where ambitious managers look to adopt the dominant discourse.

These discourses spread in and out of global academia in the form of business school research, teaching and writing. Recent work published in the "world-leading" journal *Human Relations* includes a study of "be yourself" approaches to management in China (David et al., 2021). Authenticity and self-expression are positioned as tools for effective management, whatever the local context, and without recognition of their historical construction and particular roots in specific Western cultural, political and ideological contexts (Cooke and Alcadipani, 2015; Marens, 2010; Westwood and Jack, 2007, 2008).

Laloux trades on the currency of authenticity with "being yourself" a crucial element of effective, ethical and just forms of (self-) management. In our research with Zappos, a consistent trope was how Zappos and Holacracy "allow one to be who they really are", as if capitalist structures without Holacracy and Teal as barriers or salves would otherwise disallow this.

While Laloux and others represent these manifestations as new, their lineage and connection to older ideas is evident. Roberto Semler's Semco in 1980s Brazil, which although quite "socialist" and even critical of "regular" capitalism, was celebrated by the *Harvard Business Review* (Semler, 1989) as an advancement, demonstrating its international, vanguard appeal. Semler's innovation was removing unnecessary management layers and encouraging workers to self-manage. But cooperatives, guilds and worker owned and managed firms have been permanent fixtures of pre- and (post-) industrial economies (Parker, 2018: 24, 116–119). The newness of self-management ideas is itself an important topic, suggesting and highlighting the penchant for international capitalism to adopt and co-opt challenges to it (Boltanski and Chiapello, 2005) in order to ward off deeper structural questioning or opposition.

These "radical" models have been broadcast worldwide, although to a considerable extent, they radiate from the "sender" nations – North America, Europe – to the "receiver" nations – the Global South (Alcadipani and Caldas, 2012; Cooke and Alcadipani, 2015; Sturdy and Gabriel, 2002). Creating and broadcasting management models is in itself a profitable enterprise. Multinational companies don't only produce their physical products or services, they also create and broker new management ideologies within the context of a knowledge economy. Their writings set the tone, lexicon and agenda, from *The War for Talent* to *Reinventing Organizations*.

We argue, therefore, that the academic discipline of international business should not confine itself solely to studying the practices of international management, such as the "organization-environment fit" (Boussebaa and Morgan, 2014). In a world where the hypermediated "ideoscapes" (Appadurai, 1990) of global capitalism are becoming ever more prominent, it is vital also to critically explore the ideologies that underpin and promote international business (Alcadipani and Caldas, 2012; Westwood and Jack, 2008). We suggest that IB/M as a field of study should encapsulate not only the actual practices of management, but also its ideologies, how international business structures what is known, what there is to emulate, and how to be.

We suggest four areas in which the discipline of IB/M could become more sensitised to the ideoscapes associated with the global economy.

Firstly, IB/M could benefit from a closer connection to the rich range of literature on the promotion, circulation and translation of management knowledge. While these connections have already been made in organisation studies and sociology of work literatures, as well as in more mainstream management circles (Abrahamson and Fairchild, 1999; Piazza and Abrahamson, 2020; Whitehead and Halsall, 2016), the connections to texts in IB/M tend to be more tenuous, especially as the discipline has increasingly favoured positivistic statistical analysis where hypotheses and variables can be neatly isolated and where causation and effect can be "proved". It seems somewhat perverse that such powerful and highly globalised business guru literatures are effectively shunned by the academic educators and researchers of international management.

Secondly, we argue that IB/M scholarship could be enlivened by closer exploration of the nature of the discourses that constitute business ideology such as Holacracy, Teal, Market-Based Management, or any other prescriptive managerial approach. There is huge potential for critical analysis of the linguistic and textual devices that feature in this literature: the metaphors, imagery, examples and logics. Business ideology is one of the most powerful examples we have of one of the "ideoscapes" of globalisation. While the vacuity, imprecision and emptiness of much of the guru literature is frequently obvious and can be off-putting to the "scientific" sensibilities of IB/M scholars, there is considerable value in identifying and critically exploring precisely these weaknesses and limitations. There are also important analytical connections that can be made to the socio-political lineage of these ideas. What are the broader political and ideational backgrounds that these management texts draw from and contribute to? In our case, as scholars exploring the specific case of "self-management", we found ourselves roaming over all kinds of ideological borderlands, from the 1960s counterculture to right-wing libertarianism. Where do the other, more taken-for-granted, constructs, such as "firms" and "managers" sit amid this complex interaction of ideas and concepts?

Thirdly, another potentially rich avenue of investigation is to explore the realms of business ideology *as the global business that it is*. There is much to learn from in-depth exploration of the geographical and political locations from where this literature originates, not only in terms of its conceptual roots as noted above, but also in more prosaic and practical senses. How does the generation and proliferation of business ideology happen, in terms of the behaviour of the "thought leaders" who devise and perform this ideology, the designers and editors who package it up, the publishers who disseminate and sell it, and the practitioners and academics who teach it? What are the strategic, financial, management and marketing and communication models employed in this particular part of the global knowledge industry?

Fourthly, there is a pressing need to better understand the real-world impacts of business ideology. IB/M scholars are potentially very well positioned to contribute to our understandings of the reception, rejection and translation of managerial fads and fashions, especially in a global business environment still very much characterised by regional power differentials and enduring varieties of capitalism, but where the global economic and political environment nevertheless remains structured into uneven relations between the "senders" and "receivers" of business knowledge (Cooke and Alcadipani, 2015). At a macro-level, other contributions to this present volume advocate the broadening of IB's focus to encompass diplomacy and the roles of governments and states, and a much greater sensitivity to postcolonial perspectives (see Chapters 6 and 8). At a more micro-level, an excellent example of a piece of research on the everyday and practical enactment of business ideology is Whitehead and Halsall's (2016) paper on how the notion of "global nomadism" is co-constructed, circulated and deployed by "nomads" themselves, always involving a great deal of ambiguity and uncertainty, rather than the bombastic assertions typical of the guru literature itself.

7.6 Conclusion

The works of Hamel, Laloux, Robertson, and others are all part of a long history of a commercial industry of management training and education. But they also play crucial roles in centring, normalising and augmenting contemporary notions of the entrepreneur, the DIY capitalist, the job-hopper, the "plug and player". The zeitgeist rests on a mindset of embracing disruption, relying on self-determination, and expecting no continuity or security. The situation is contradictory – we manage ourselves yet members of a Teal or Holacratic organisation are still subject to sophisticated new forms of managerial control; amongst them ever increasing levels of precarity.

Stripping out managers so that "everyone" is a leader or micro-entrepreneur lends itself to a form of market fundamentalism in which the basis of any decision is ultimately one of market calculation. Teal and Holacracy create "a start-up mentality in which everyone is encouraged to ask, 'If this was my company, what would I do?'" (Robertson, 2015: 24–25). Rather than engagement with unions or staff associations, these systems emphasise the individual. The quest for personal realisation under Teal is to be understood through the mechanisms of market competition. It aligns with Robertson's discussion of the Holacracy "constitution" which sounds not unlike US right libertarian or neoconservative views of the virtues of "limited government"; "a legislative process has granted them [...] authority with due input and consideration" (Robertson, 2015: 25). The Koch brothers' "Market-Based Management" claims to encourage companies to succeed by "applying the principles that allow free societies to prosper. Just as upholding values as free speech, property rights, and progress is important to a healthy, growing society, it is also pivotal in fostering a healthy, growing organization."[15] In spite of the liberatory language that permeates the leadership literature of Laloux, Robertson, Collins, Hamel, Peters, Koch and others, what they ultimately lead to is the reduction of employees to a market-driven role in a "plug and play" model in which employment is vulnerable and precarious.

Throughout, this material lacks clarity and shows consistently weak use of evidence and argument. Near the opening of *Holacracy*, for example, Robertson discusses how he met Hsieh at a conference, where Hsieh explained to him that he wanted Zappos to be more like a city and less like a corporation (Robertson, 2015: 15–16, 21). He seemed to be implying that cities are somehow inherently open and innovative whereas corporations are conservative and restrictive. But this rhetorical claim, like so many in the no-managers literature, is extremely weak when subjected to minimal critical scrutiny. Robertson and Hsieh seem to be claiming that there is no need for authorisation in a city? Yet urban environments the world over feature extremely complicated, contested, and overlapping forms of authority, such as licences, registration, permits, bylaws, zoning orders, etc. They are also stratified by class, income and access to networks of power – hardly the archetype of a self-managed organisation.

More collective, institutional and statutory forms of workplace power dispersal barely feature. Laloux and Robertson do not discuss trade unions, professional associations, works councils or any other forms of employee advocacy, workplace democracy or staff representation. Of course, under their utopian model, these would never be needed. Instead we have the enlightened, "conscious" CEO and their direct connection to the staff, like a monarch and their people, with no government or civil service to get in the way. Not only is the no-managers literature faddish, it also contains a highly traditional right-libertarian argument in favour of markets and the reduction of regulation. Management itself is seen as something that gets in the way of market forces and should be diluted and eroded as far as possible. There are dangerously regressive arguments hidden within the "funky" and "woke" narrative of post-management and the destruction of hierarchy. This is yet another reason to recommend extreme scepticism when researching and discussing the nature and content of globalising business ideology. Libraries of new business ideology are created and circulated every day. There is no end of potential sources of textual research data for a critically informed and ideologically sensitive IB/M to engage with.

Notes

1. "Becoming Self-Managed: 2 Approaches, 100 Case Studies", *Corporate Rebels* website, https://corporate-rebels.com/k2k-update/ (retrieved 8 October 2020).
2. "Why the annual appraisal is going extinct", *Fast Company*, 20 October 2015; "Six companies that are redefining performance management", *Fast Company* 15 December 2015.
3. See https://conference.consciouscapitalism.org/ (retrieved 16 December 2019).
4. See https://corporate-rebels.com/ (retrieved 13 December 2019).
5. Holacracy Constitution, version 4.1, paragraph 2.2.1, https://static1.squarespace.com/static/5d1239a79c02150001db74d4/t/5d23a 0cb974b5f0001e989c7/1562616012223/Holacracy-Constitution-v4.1.pdf (retrieved 29 July 2020).
6. Holacracy Constitution, version 4.1, paragraph 1.1, https://static1.squarespace.com/static/5d1239a79c02150001db74d4/t/5d23a 0cb974b5f0001e989c7/1562616012223/Holacracy-Constitution-v4.1.pdf (retrieved 29 July 2020).
7. See https://www.glassfrog.com (retrieved 19 July 2020).
8. See https://www.holacracy.org/whos-practicing-holacracy (retrieved 19 July 2020).
9. There are several critical pieces of journalism on Zappos' difficult experiences of Holacracy. See, for example, a blog post by organisational consultant Julia Culen: https://juliaculen.com/2016/04/03/holacracy-not-safe-enough-to-try/ (retrieved 29 July 2020); also "Zappos says 18 percent of the company has left following its radical 'no bosses' approach", *The Washington Post*, 14 January 2016; and "How a radical shift left Zappos reeling", *Fortune*, 4 March 2016; and "Zappos CEO Tony Hsieh: Adopt Holacracy or Leave", *Fast Company*, 30 March 2015.
10. See https://www.enliveningedge.org/field-reports/gathering-of-evolutionaries-in -china-the-2nd-china-organizational-evolution-forum/ (retrieved 19 July 2020).
11. Tony Hsieh's email to Zappos staff about the need to adopt Holacracy in March 2015 also contained two lengthy articles by Laloux's writings on Teal. See "Zappos CEO Tony Hsieh: Adopt holacracy or leave", *Fast Company*, 30 March 2015.
12. "Mango Season: self-management in India", *Enspiral Tales*, https://medium .com/enspiral-tales/mango-season-self-management-in-india-bee4a254b5ab# .ugic2e8jk (retrieved 30 July 2020).
13. See https://www.yashpakka.com/ (retrieved 16 December 2019).
14. See https://www.holacracy.org/explore/why-practice-holacracy/ (retrieved 27 October 2020).
15. See https://www.charleskochinstitute.org/about-us/market-based-management/ (retrieved 19 July 2020).

References

Abrahamson, E. (1991). Management fads and fashions: The diffusion and rejection of innovations. *Academy of Management Review*, 16(3): 586–612.

Abrahamson, E. (1996). Management fashion. *Academy of Management Review*, 21(1): 254–285.

Abrahamson, E. and Fairchild, G. (1999). Management fashion: Lifecycles, triggers, and collective learning processes. *Administrative Science Quarterly*, 44(4): 708–740.

Alcadipani, R. and Caldas, M.P. (2012). Americanizing Brazilian management. *critical perspectives on international business*, 8(1): 37–56.

Appadurai, A. (1990). Disjuncture and difference in the global cultural economy. *Theory, Culture & Society*, 7(2–3): 295–310.

Aroles, J., Granter, E. and de Vaujany, F.-X. (2020). 'Becoming mainstream': The professionalisation and corporatisation of digital nomadism. *New Technology, Work and Employment*, 35(1): 114–129.

Aroles, J., Mitev, N. and de Vaujany, F.-X. (2019). Mapping themes in the study of new work practices. *New Technology, Work and Employment*, 34(3): 286–299.

Benders, J. and van Veen, K. (2001). What's in a fashion? Interpretative variability and management fashions. *Organization* 8(1): 33–53.

Bernstein, E., Bunch, J., Canner, N. and Lee, M. (2016). Beyond the Holacracy hype. *Harvard Business Review*, 94(7/8), 38–49.

Béteille, A. (2009). Sociology and ideology. *Sociological Bulletin*, 58(2): 196–211.

Beyes, T. (2017). Colour and organization studies. *Organization Studies*, 38(10): 1467–1482.

Birkinshaw, J., Brannen, M.Y. and Tung, R.L. (2011). From a distance and generalizable to up close and grounded: Reclaiming a place for qualitative methods in international business research. *Journal of International Business Studies*, 42: 573–581.

Birnbaum, R. (2000). The life cycle of academic management fads. *The Journal of Higher Education*, 71(1): 1–16.

Birnbaum, R. (2001). *Management Fads in Higher Education: Where They Come From, What They Do, Why They Fail*. New York: Jossey-Bass.

Boltanski, L. and Chiapello, E. (2005). *The New Spirit of Capitalism*. London: Verso.

Boussebaa, M. and Morgan, G. (2014). Pushing the frontiers of critical international business studies: The multinational as a neo-imperial space. *critical perspectives on international business*, 10(1/2): 96–106.

Boussebaa, M., Morgan G. and Sturdy, A. (2012). Constructing global firms? National, transnational and neocolonial effects in international management consultancies. *Organization Studies*, 33(4): 465–486.

Brunsson, N. (2006). *Mechanisms of Hope: Maintaining the Dream of the Rational Organization*. Copenhagen: Copenhagen Business School Press.

Burnham, J. (1941). *The Managerial Revolution*. New York: John Day.

Carney, B.M. and Getz, I. (2010). *Freedom, Inc: Free Your Employees and Let Them Lead Your Business to Higher Productivity, Profits and Growth*. New York: Crown Publishing Group.

Collins, J. (2001). *Good to Great: Why Some Companies Make the Leap … And Others Don't*. London: Random House.

Cooke, B. and Alcadipani, R. (2015). Toward a global history of management education: The Case of the Ford Foundation and the São Paulo School of Business

Administration, Brazil. *Academy of Management Learning and Education*, 14(4): 482–499.

David, E.M., Kim, T.-Y., Farh, J.-L., Lin, X. and Zhou, F. (2021). Is 'be yourself' always the best advice? The moderating effect of team ethical climate and mediating effects of vigor and demand–ability fit. *Human Relations*, 43(3): 437–462.

Delios, A. (2017). The death and rebirth (?) of international business research. *Journal of Management Studies*, 54(3), 391–397.

Dore, R. (2000). *Stock Market Capitalism: Welfare Capitalism. Japan and Germany versus the Anglo-Saxons*. Oxford: Oxford University Press.

Eagleton, T. (1991). *Ideology: An Introduction*. London: Verso.

Ekman, S. (2015). Win-win imageries in a soap bubble world: Personhood and norms in extreme work. *Organization*, 22(4): 588–605.

Fleming, P. and Sturdy, A. (2009). "Just be yourself!" Towards neo-normative control in organisations? *Employee Relations*, 31(6): 569–583.

Fleming, P. and Sturdy, A. (2010). 'Being yourself' in the electronic sweatshop: New forms of normative control. *Human Relations*, 64(2): 177–200.

Frenkel, M. (2005). The politics of translation: How state-level political relations affect the cross-national travel of management ideas. *Organization*, 12(2): 275–301.

Furnham, A. (2004). *Management and Myths: Challenging Business Fads, Fallacies and Fashions*. Basingstoke: Palgrave Macmillan.

Gantman, E.R. (2005). *Capitalism, Social Privilege, and Managerial Ideologies*. Aldershot: Ashgate.

Gould, J. (1964). Ideology. In J. Gould and W.L. Kolb (Eds), *A Dictionary of the Social Sciences*. Glencoe: Free Press.

Graham, L. (1995). *On the Line at Subaru-Isuzu*. Ithaca, NY: Cornell University Press.

Groth, A. (2017). *The Kingdom of Happiness: Inside Tony Hsieh's Zapponian Utopia*. New York: Touchstone.

Hall, P.A. and Soskice, D. (Eds) (2001). *Varieties of Capitalism: The Institutional Foundations of Comparative Advantage*. Oxford: Oxford University Press.

Hamel, G. (2009). Moon shots for management. *Harvard Business Review*, 87(2): 91–98.

Hamel, G. (2011). First, let's fire all the managers. *Harvard Business Review*, 19(12): 48–60.

Hamel, G. and Zanini, M. (2020). *Humanocracy: Creating Organizations as Amazing as the People Inside Them*. Boston, MA: Harvard Business Review Press.

Hassard, J., McCann, L. and Morris, J. (2007). At the sharp end of new organizational ideologies: Ethnography and the study of multinationals. *Ethnography*, 8(3): 324–344.

Hassard, J., McCann, L. and Morris, J. (2009). *Managing in the Modern Corporation: The Intensification of Managerial Work in the USA, UK and Japan*. Cambridge: Cambridge University Press.

Hsieh, T. (2010). *Delivering Happiness: A Path to Profits, Passion, and Purpose*. London: Hachette UK.

Kanter, R.M. (1990). *When Giants Learn to Dance*. New York: Free Press.

Klikauer, T. (2015). What is managerialism? *Critical Sociology*, 41(7–8): 1103–1119.

Koch, C.G. (2007). *The Science of Success: How Market Based Management Built the World's Largest Private Company*. New York: John Wiley & Sons.

Laloux, F. (2014). *Reinventing Organizations: A Guide to Creating Organizations Inspired by the Next Stage of Human Consciousness*. Brussels: Nelson Parker.

Laloux, F. (2015). The future of management is teal. *strategy+business*, Autumn.

Marens, R. (2010). Destroying the village to save it: Corporate social responsibility, labour relations, and the rise and fall of American hegemony. *Organization*, 17(6): 743–766.

McCann, L. (2016). From management to leadership. In S. Edgell, H. Gottfried and E. Granter (Eds), *The SAGE Handbook of the Sociology of Work and Employment*. London: Sage, 167–184.

McCann, L. (2020). Meaningless leadership. In T. Dundon and A. Wilkinson (Eds), *Case Studies in Work, Employment, and Human Resource Management*. Cheltenham, UK and Northampton, MA, USA: Edward Elgar Publishing, 184–190.

Mills, C.W. (1956/2000). *The Power Elite*. Oxford: Oxford University Press.

Mills, J.H., Dye, K. and Mills, A.J. (2009). *Understanding Organizational Change*. Abingdon: Routledge.

Murphy, P. (2016). *Auto-Industrialism: DIY Capitalism and the Rise of the Auto-Industrial Society*. London: Sage.

Nordstrom, K. and Ridderstrale, J. (2007). *Funky Business Forever: How to Enjoy Capitalism*. London: FT Prentice Hall.

Orfalea, P. and Marsh, A. (2005). *Copy This! Lessons from a Hyperactive Dyslexic Who Turned a Bright Idea into One of America's Best Companies*. New York: Workman.

Parker, M. (2018). *Shut Down the Business School*. London: Pluto.

Peters, T.J. (1992). *Liberation Management: Necessary Disorganization for the Nanosecond Nineties*. New York: Alfred A. Knopf.

Peters, T.J. and Waterman, R.H. (1982/2004). *In Search of Excellence: Lessons from America's Best-Run Companies*. London: Profile.

Piazza, A. and Abrahamson, E. (2020). Fads and fashions in management practices: Taking stock and looking forward. *International Journal of Management Reviews*, 22: 264–286.

Ralston, D.A., Holt, D.H., Terpstra, R.H. and Kai-Cheng, Y. (2008). The impact of national culture and economic ideology on managerial work values: A study of the United States, Russia, Japan, and China. *Journal of International Business Studies*, 39(1): 8–26.

Rhodes, C. and Parker, M. (2008). Images of organizing in popular culture. *Organization*, 15(5): 627–637.

Robertson, B.J. (2015). *Holacracy: The Revolutionary Management System That Abolishes Hierarchy*. London: Penguin.

Røvik, K.A. (2011). From fashion to virus: An alternative theory of organisations' handling of management ideas. *Organization Studies*, 32(5): 631–653.

Seeck, H., Sturdy, A., Boncori, A.-L. and Fougère, A. (2020). Ideology in management studies. *International Journal of Management Reviews*, 22(1): 53–74.

Semler, R. (1989). Managing without managers. *Harvard Business Review*, 67(5): 76–84.

Sennett, R. (2007). *The Culture of the New Capitalism*. New Haven, CT: Yale University Press.

Spicer, A. (2017). *Business Bullshit*. Abingdon: Routledge.

Sturdy, A. (2004). The adoption of management ideas and practices: Theoretical perspectives and possibilities. *Management Learning*, 35(2): 155–179.

Sturdy, A. and Gabriel, Y. (2002). Missionaries, mercenaries or car salesmen? MBA teaching in Malaysia. *Journal of Management Studies*, 37(7): 979–1002.

Suzaki, K. (2010). *Results from the Heart*. New York: Simon & Schuster.

Suzaki, K. (2012). *The New Manufacturing Challenge: Techniques for Continuous Improvement*. New York: Free Press.

Tourish, D. (2020). The triumph of nonsense in management studies. *Academy of Management Learning and Education*, 19(1): 99–109.

Trist, E.L. and Bamforth, K.W. (1951). Some social and psychological consequences of the longwall method of coal-getting. *Human Relations*, 4(1): 3–38.

Westwood, R. and Jack, G. (2007). Manifesto for a post-colonial international business and management studies: A provocation. *critical perspectives on international business*, 3(3): 246–265.

Westwood, R. and Jack, G. (2008). The US commercial-military-political complex and the emergence of international business and management studies. *critical perspectives on international business*, 4(4): 367–388.

Whitehead, G. and Halsall, R. (2016). Corporate global nomadism: The role of the transnational professional as consumer of management discourses. *Management Learning*, 48(3): 311–327.

8. Emerging economy MNCs and their geopolitical embeddedness

Ursula Mense-Petermann

8.1   Introduction

In a recent critical debate on the state and future of international business (IB) research, scholars called for a reorientation of IB studies towards "making sense of critical global phenomena" and addressing societies' "grand challenges" (Buckley et al., 2017: 1046). As Buckley et al. (2017: 1053) noted, "a weakness of contemporary IB research is the shift away from studies addressing questions that emerge from observations in the world economy, towards questions that arise from theoretical puzzles".

One of the most important "grand challenges" in the contemporary world economy is the advent of emerging economy multinational corporations (EMNCs),[1] particularly those from China. It challenges the established positions of the advanced economies and the business models of their MNCs in several respects. EMNC research has therefore gained considerable ground in IB in the past decade and "is converging on common themes and shared theoretical ideas" (Meyer and Peng, 2016: 3). Yet extant IB literature on EMNCs, particularly Chinese MNCs (CMNCs), has concentrated on the antecedents and patterns of EMNC internationalisation and whether established theoretical frameworks based on MNCs from advanced economies can explain them. The internal workings of EMNCs include the HQ–subsidiary relations EMNCs establish, subsidiary roles and mandates, post-merger integration (PMI) processes, and knowledge transfer and practices. These are all well-researched topics for mature MNCs headquartered in advanced economies, yet have to date rarely been scrutinised in IB studies with regard to EMNCs. Research that sheds light on these issues is underdeveloped, and specifically for CMNCs, far from exhaustive (Buckley et al., 2018; cf. Haasis et al., 2018; Lai et al., 2020; Mense-Petermann, 2020). Whereas public and political debates on EMNCs, particularly CMNCs, are dominated by geopolitical considerations, including the consequences of their ascendance for host countries and the global economy, the embeddedness of EMNCs in a wider geopolitical context has widely been ignored by IB scholars (cf. Buckley, 2020; Zhang et al., 2018).

Those strands of IB and management studies that have focused on MNC embeddedness in wider political and cultural contexts have referred primarily to country-specific national institutions and cultures impacting organisational practices. An important strand of this scholarship builds on Hofstede's (1991) conceptualisation of culture as a mental programme or a "software" of the mind. The respective literature is, however, based on an essentialist conception of culture (Ailon-Souday and Kunda, 2003; Ybema and Byun, 2011), and considers its impact on organisations deterministically.

This chapter first suggests that the *internal workings of EMNCs* should be foremost on the IB and management research agenda for the coming years. In-depth empirical case studies are required to tackle the question of whether EMNCs elicit the shifts in the geography and gravity centres of the world economy ascribed to them in public and political debates. These case studies must deliver primary data on their internationalisation *practices*: the kind of HQ–subsidiary relations they establish, and how subsidiary roles, PMI, and knowledge transfer are negotiated and with what effects. Second, the chapter advocates considering the *geopolitical embeddedness of EMNC internationalisation* as an important, but hitherto neglected, dimension of organisational environment impacting on the internal workings of EMNCs. Geopolitical context, however, is not seen as *determining* inner-organisational practices. Instead, it is seen as shaping actors' perceptions, interests, and symbolic power resources, but also as depending on being enacted by organisational actors. We therefore suggest, as a theoretical framework, a *sensemaking approach* (Clark and Geppert, 2011; Schlindwein and Geppert, 2020; Vaara, 2000, 2003; Weick, 1995; Ybema and Byun, 2011) combined with qualitative methodologies as best suited to shed light on the processes whereby geopolitical imaginaries and dominance patterns are enacted in these firms.

This chapter therefore proposes that the research agenda for IB must incorporate the delivery of primary empirical data on the *factual* realisation of EMNC internationalisation. Such an agenda concentrates on the empirically observable course of EMNC internationalisation processes, and on the consequences of these (1) for the EMNCs themselves, that is, the success or failure of their expansion, (2) for their subsidiaries, that is, subsidiary roles and mandates, (3) for host countries, and (4) for the global economy. The remainder of the chapter details this agenda in theoretical terms and methodological suggestions.

8.2   EMNCs in IB studies and remaining research gaps

EMNCs are a recent phenomenon. As Cuervo-Cazurra and Ramamurti (2014a: 1) put it: "EMNCs were rarely the object of researchers' attention, and their behaviour was not considered when the foundational models of the MNC were developed. EMNCs were [...] rare firms on the world stage until the 2000s". This has changed dramatically within the past twenty years.

As several edited volumes (Cuervo-Cazurra and Ramamurti, 2014c) and overview articles (Alon et al., 2018; Buckley et al., 2018; Deng, 2011; Gugler and Boie, 2009) taking stock of extant EMNC research have revealed, the antecedents and motivations, and the institutional contexts in which these firms are embedded have been studied extensively. However, it should be noted that the available databases are small and particularly for CMNCs, access problems to the organisations might be one important reason. Much of the literature refers to a few well-known examples, including Lenovo, Haier, or TCL, often not based on primary data but building on newspaper articles or publicly accessible information instead. Primary research to shed light on the management practices and internal workings of EMNCs is currently lacking (Alon et al., 2018; Buckley et al., 2018: 11; Rugman and Nguyen, 2014).

Another shortcoming of the mainstream IB literature is its overwhelming emphasis on strategy and firm-specific advantages (FSA) and country-specific advantages (CSA) (Rugman 2009). Potential problems in implementing strategies and exploiting FSA/CSA in processes of integrating overseas acquisitions are only mentioned in passing, if at all (cf. Haasis et al., 2018; Kang, 2009: 95; Shenkar, 2009). Extant IB literature on EMNCs is therefore characterised by a rationalistic and functionalistic stance. Such a view on internationalisation prevents scholars from thoroughly analysing their practices and detecting new and different practices that have not yet been observed in advanced economy MNCs. For example, EMNCs may display different HQ–subsidiary relationships and subsidiary roles (Mense-Petermann, 2020), and adopt different practices regarding knowledge transfer and organisational practices (Chung et al., 2020). Child and Marinova (2014: 348) stated "more attention has been given to the motives behind Chinese OFDI than to how it is negotiated and implemented in different host country contexts".

A pending research gap, therefore, lies in the ways that EMNCs adopt in integrating their overseas acquisitions, and for tapping the markets, resources and assets they seek. Hence, the PMI processes of EMNCs that have rarely been examined to date (Deng, 2011: 417; cf. Ailon-Souday and Kunda, 2003; Franz et al., 2017; Haasis et al., 2018; Liu and Woywode, 2012; Mense-Petermann, 2020) represent a major "blind spot" in current research on EMNCs' internationalisation and a central open research gap for future IB research (Meyer and Peng, 2016). Studies on these questions are all the more necessary since the existing literature points to difficulties that EMNCs face regarding merger and acquisitions (M&As) in advanced economies and in asset-seeking strategies (Gugler and Boie, 2009: 49; Li, 2009; Meyer and Peng, 2016; Shenkar, 2009; Wang, 2009). Peng (2012: 100), for example, observes that 70 per cent of CMNCs' M&As fail.

While assessing the most important context variables impacting EMNC internationalisation, the IB scholarship has considered the politico-economic environment in emerging economies (EEs), the role of the state and of government policies, the global competitive environment, and the latecomer status of EMNCs. What has been neglected, however, is their global geopolitical embeddedness. So far, the larger MNCs have been headquartered primarily in a few advanced economies in the West, whereas many of their subsidiaries have been located in peripheral developing countries (Boussebaa, 2020; Boussebaa and Morgan, 2014: 99; Rugman, 2009). EMNCs do not follow this pattern: originating from an EE, EMNCs engage in M&As not only in neighbouring EEs and countries with a similar politico-economic context, for instance, Africa, but increasingly also in advanced economies. This applies particularly to CMNCs. The takeover of highly innovative and technologically advanced economy firms by CMNCs has been met with suspicion and spurred critical political debate (cf. Cuervo-Cazurra, 2018) and public debate in the West (Brink, 2015; Child and Marinova, 2014; Cuervo-Cazurra, 2018). Presumably, such negative attitudes towards EMNCs and CMNCs also prevail within the acquired firms, among senior managers, and workforces. Some IB authors observe that EMNCs originating from formerly peripheral countries may evoke "negative connotations of their emerging-market roots in the mind of customers" (Cuervo-Cazurra and Ramamurti, 2014a: 4), and of target countries of their investments (Cuervo-Cazurra, 2018). Nonetheless, the geopolitical embeddedness of EMNCs has not been systematically investigated regarding either its impact on internationalisation strategies or the internal workings of EMNCs (see Cuervo-Cazurra and Ramamurti, 2014b: 294f.; cf. Chung et al., 2020).[2]

This chapter suggests that IB research ought to concentrate on EMNCs' internal workings, and on the question of how HQ–subsidiary relations and PMI processes, including knowledge transfer and capabilities, are negotiated. It advocates an approach to these issues that addresses the geopolitical context in which EMNC internationalisation is embedded, beyond the contexts of the political economy of home and host countries and of global competition, and the question of how the geopolitical context is enacted within EMNCs. Hence the sensemaking approach in analysing EMNCs developed in the next section.

8.3 How to approach EMNCs in theoretical terms

Pursuing these gaps in IB research requires a different conception of the MNC than the dominant mainstream scholarship. As scholars with a sociological and organisation theoretical background have shown (Becker-Ritterspach and Dörrenbächer, 2011; Becker-Ritterspach et al., 2016; Collinson and Morgan, 2009; Dörrenbächer and Geppert, 2006, 2011; Geppert et al., 2016; Mense-Petermann, 2013, 2018; Morgan, 2001), MNC managers do not simply implement "fitting" strategies following a universal economic rationale, as suggested in mainstream IB, nor do MNCs simply adopt structures institutionalised in their politico-economic environments, as some institutionalist approaches posit. These authors have advocated "bringing the actor back in" (Dörrenbächer and Geppert, 2006) and understanding strategies as resulting from negotiations between core actors within MNCs who, in these negotiations, put forward their perceptions and interpretations, as well as their own interests and draw on power and symbolic resources at hand. We suggest this theoretical approach to grasp the internal workings of EMNCs and their geopolitical embeddedness.

8.3.1 Sensemaking and the social construction of (E)MNC identities

Such an approach, the so-called sensemaking approach, has been developed by Karl Weick (1979, 1995; also Clark and Geppert, 2011; Gioia and Chittipeddi, 1991; Schlindwein and Geppert, 2020; Vaara, 2000, 2003; Ybema and Byun, 2011). As Vaara (2003: 862) explains, "The sensemaking perspective highlights the complex socio-psychological processes through which organizational actors interpret organizational phenomena and thus socially construct or enact their 'realities'".

The sensemaking approach is suited to integrating an understanding of actors' agency and organisational context by drawing on the concept of enactment. In this perspective, the context–agency nexus is not conceptualised in a deterministic way, that is, context does not predetermine MNC agency but actors enact their organisational context. They draw upon specific context elements to orientate and legitimise their agency (Lai et al., 2020). It is a constructivist approach that emphasises actors' perceptions and social constructions of their own organisation's identity and specific units thereof, and of their wider socio-economic and political environment. It highlights how organisational actors "infuse the social worlds they inhabit (and the identities of the actors) with meaning" (Ybema and Byun, 2011: 316).

Some organisation scholars have adopted the sensemaking approach to HQ–subsidiary relations in MNCs (Ailon-Sauday and Kunda, 2003; Clark and Geppert, 2011; Vaara, 2000, 2003; Ybema and Byun, 2011), concentrating on cultural sensemaking as opposed to political (Clark and Geppert, 2011) and emotional sensemaking (Schlindwein and Geppert, 2020). Vaara (2000: 81) explains that "[c]ultural differences are often used as explanations of organizational problems following mergers", and criticises the scholarship as building on Hofstede's (1991) conceptualisation of culture as a mental programme or a "software" of the mind. Similarly, other scholars criticise the literature as based on an essentialist conception of culture (Ailon-Souday and Kunda, 2003; Ybema and Byun, 2011). As Ybema and Byun (2011: 315) emphasise, "This type of cross-cultural organization research ignores identity and ethnicity theorists, who have put emphasis on the situational and relational character of social identification processes".

These criticisms show that an important aspect of sensemaking in post-merger situations is identity building, that is, how actors develop representations of the self in relation to others (Clark and Geppert, 2011; Risberg et al., 2003: 122f.; Vaara, 2000; Ybema and Byun, 2011). "Othering", therefore, is an important preoccupation of actors in (E)MNCs in post-merger situations and in HQ–subsidiary relations. As studies on knowledge transfer and organisational practices show, it impacts how these processes are organised (Chung et al., 2020; Frenkel, 2008).

Although identity building is a cultural process, the importance of power relations between actors and entities in (E)MNCs for processes of identification must not be ignored (Ybema and Byun, 2011: 316). As Ailon-Souday and Kunda (2003: 1074) argue, "in organizations undergoing globalization, national identity constitutes a symbolic resource that is actively mobilized by members for the social goals of resistance". Sensemaking, thus, is a process of enacting organisational realities, including the identities of oneself and organisational others, and of organisational context. Within this process, actors draw upon and enact symbolic resources, such as notions of national cultures and cultural differences, and mobilise them in micro-political negotiations (Ailon-Souday and Kunda, 2003; Clark and Geppert, 2011). What the theoretical arguments and empirical studies of scholars in the field of sensemaking and identity construction teach us is that (national) cultures and identities do not matter per se for the ways in which (E)MNCs operate internally, but for the modes in which and the purposes for which organisational actors enact them in processes of sensemaking (cf. Lai et al., 2020; Schlindwein and Geppert, 2020).

This chapter advocates such an approach for scrutinising EMNCs' internationalisation practices because it emphasises the importance of the othering processes for the internal workings of EMNCs. It also shifts scholarly attention away from contexts per se to the ways and modes in which organisational actors *enact* different dimensions of context.

8.3.2   Hierarchical orders and imperial dominance patterns in EMNC sensemaking processes

Understanding the internal workings of EMNCs, however, requires not to conceive of sensemaking and othering as a smooth and balanced process. Instead, it offers a lens that sheds light on hierarchised cultures and identities, that is, the social construction of *superior* and *inferior* cultures and identities.

The concept of "domination effects" provides such a lens on hierarchised cultures and identities. Together with "systems effects" exerted by the global capitalist system and industrial sectors as its sub-systems, and "societal effects" or the impact of nationally distinct institutions, they shape organisational structures and practices, as developed in 1995 by Smith and Meiksins from the perspective of organisation studies. Domination effects draw upon imaginations of the economic world as consisting of more or less developed, efficient, and reputed economies.

The early contribution by Smith and Meiksins (1995), however, has not resonated extensively in organisation studies or in mainstream IB studies; it is only a small stream of scholarship that tackles the issue of geopolitical embeddedness and domination: scholars adopting (neo-)imperial and post-colonial lenses on MNCs (Boussebaa, 2015, 2020; Frenkel, 2008, 2014; Jack and Westwood, 2006; Prasad, 2003; Risberg et al., 2003; Westwood et al., 2014). Yet these accounts have not become part of the IB mainstream. As Frenkel (2008: 938f.) elaborates, "the academic discourse itself is often blind to the importance of geopolitical power relations between the first and third worlds in shaping the activities of MNCs in general, and the process of knowledge transfer within the MNC in particular".

Post-colonial scholars stress that hierarchical geopolitical imaginaries shape which knowledge, practices, and capabilities are deemed worth transferring within MNCs (Frenkel, 2008; Chung et al., 2020). In MNCs, "capabilities such as skills and knowledge and the professional staff that carry them tend to flow from offices based in the largest Western economies into peripheral subsidiaries located in small Western nations and, importantly, the 'developing' world" (Boussebaa and Morgan, 2014: 100; see also Frenkel's (2008) detailed discussion of knowledge transfer within MNCs). The authors posit "an imperial dominance effect", that is, "some parts of the MNC are 'peripheral', acting mostly as recipients rather than producers of skills and knowledge, while others are 'central' to the firm, operating more as exporters than importers of such capabilities" (Boussebaa and Morgan, 2014: 100). This imperial dominance effect is backed materially and ideologically: it is not necessarily based on "superior" products, production models, and knowledge (i.e. FSA), but on ideology in the sense that the production model used in the dominant society is believed to be the "most efficient model available and, therefore, societies that claim to be modernising and competing are under normative pressure to adapt to the model and to train their managers" (Boussebaa and Morgan, 2014: 100; Chung et al., 2020).[3]

This argument is backed by Chung et al.'s (2020: 537) empirical case study that demonstrates that "a particular concern of MNEs from emerging economies [...] lies in the fact that [...] local actors can challenge head office policies on the basis of a claim to superior expertise in the dominant practices". Studies by Mense-Petermann (2020), Yan (2020), and Fuchs and Schalljo (2016), have revealed neo-colonial attitudes of managers of advanced economy subsidiaries towards their EE HQ. Ailon-Souday and Kunda (2003), in their empirical study on sensemaking and identity constructions in an Israeli EMNC that had acquired a US competitor, also shed light on how actors related to "some wider, global social hierarchy; the hierarchy which renders America and things American as superior and powerful ideals [...] in constructing [...] their own national identity, the Israeli identity, [...] as connoting an inferior social status" (Ailon-Souday and Kunda, 2003: 1087–1088). Chung et al. (2020) show how EMNCs react to this challenge by not transferring home country practices, but instead tending to "borrow" and transfer HRM policy sources from a dominant economy (Chung et al., 2020: 537). This is because of "legitimacy challenges" that go back to the imagination of emerging economies and EMNCs as being inferior (Chung et al., 2020).

Post-colonial scholars typically draw on advanced economy MNCs and their EE subsidiaries (Frenkel, 2008; Jack and Westwood, 2006). The dominance of MNCs headquartered in former colonialist countries is, however, increasingly challenged by the rise of EMNCs. The increasing importance and consolidation of EMNCs raises questions pertaining to the sensemaking processes and identity constructions that can be observed in this constellation, how post-colonial stances impact them, and the dominance effects involved. As Smith and Meiksins (1995: 258) have emphasised, "The effects of combined and uneven development means [sic] that the role of 'dominant' state, sector or company as standard-maker rotates between societies". The rise of EMNCs may induce changes of the patterns of domination at the global level (Boussebaa and Morgan, 2014).

How far, then, can a post-colonial or (neo-)imperial lens be applied to EMNC internationalisation? Most post-colonial scholars suggest not to restrict the post-colonial lens to the colonial empires of the eighteenth and nineteenth centuries, but to adopt it more broadly to "power relations between the dominating and dominated forces in the contemporary world order" (Frenkel, 2008: 925). Kamoche and Siebers (2015: 2723) argue, "that where ethnocentric practices with a neocolonial character are resisted or questioned, we can infer a post-colonial ethos in unravelling the nature of the business relationship irrespective of the pre-existence of a colonial political one". Thus, it is not obvious whether to consider China as a newly emerging "colonizer" or as "colonized". The rise of powerful EMNCs, particularly CMNCs, on the global stage challenges clear cut differentiations between dominant and dominated societies and organisations.

EMNCs, therefore, call for a more nuanced account of processes of sensemaking, identity construction, and domination to grasp the complexities of relational processes of othering and their impact on inner-organisational processes of negotiating order and decision-making in EMNCs. The questions of what kind of sensemaking and othering processes are being enacted, what kind of HQ–subsidiary relations are being established within EMNCs, and whether the rise and consolidation of EMNCs challenges the existing patterns of domination call for "much more extensive inquiry into EMNEs in different circumstances, building especially on the rapidly growing research on Chinese MNEs in both developed economies [...] and less developed economies" (Chung et al., 2020: 551).

In this section, we have drawn from different strands of theoretical work to develop a framework for grasping the complexities of EMNC internal workings, the intricacies of their internationalisation, and the impact of their geopolitical embeddedness. Whereas the geopolitical embeddedness of MNCs is prominently dealt with in post-colonial approaches, this research concentrates on advanced economy MNCs and their subsidiaries in formerly colonised countries. Recent studies which focus on current shifts of the geopolitical world order (Buckley, 2020; Witt, 2019; Zhang et al., 2018) discuss the role of China, Chinese government policies, and the role of CMNCs therein. However, they remain at the macro level, leaving open the question of how such political programmes and policies translate into organisational practice within MNCs. A geopolitical embeddedness lens along with a sensemaking approach allows the issue to be tackled, eventually addressing the existence of shifts in the global economy, and the role of (E)MNCs therein.

8.4   How to scrutinise internal workings and investigate sensemaking within EMNCs methodologically

How can such a research agenda be realised in terms of methodology and methods? IB studies are dominated vastly by their ever-more sophisticated quantitative methodological approach and the underlying epistemology (Moore, 2017; also Hassard et al., 2007). Delios (2017: 391), in his provocative critique of current IB research, posits that "a stifling fixation with quantitative methods has squeezed the life out of IB research".

This chapter advocates combining a focus on EMNCs through a sensemaking and geopolitical theoretical lens with qualitative methodologies and methods. A sensemaking approach inevitably aligns with qualitative methodologies as it aims at disclosing "native categories" (Buckley and Chapman, 1997; cited from Moore, 2017: 167), that is, the "cognitive systems" (Gregory, 1983: 367) or "social categories [...] which are continuously formulated [...] with reference both to external and internal discourses and concepts, and which are used as a means of organising and understanding their social world" (Moore, 2012: 627; cited from Moore, 2017: 167). Put differently, the constructivist approach advocated here is incompatible with the quantitative paradigm and "an economic modelling of MNC" (Delios, 2017: 396).

Suggesting qualitative methodologies means encouraging in-depth case studies and ethnographies. Case studies should be based on open-ended and narrative interviews not only with the upper echelons of management, but with many members of the organisation in different ranks and functions, representing different ways to make sense of their organisation and of themselves and others. Ideally, interviewees will be sampled by "theoretical sampling" until saturation, as suggested by Glaser and Strauss (1967), to ensure that all cognitive schemes, "native categories", and ways of sensemaking relevant for the respective research question are represented in the sample.

Ethnographies, besides narrative interviews and informal talks based on participation and observation, can dig even deeper into "the nuances of day-to-day interactions in organisations, making the connection with the organisations' embeddedness in wider social processes" (Moore, 2017: 165). In scrutinising sensemaking practices and processes in EMNCs, ethnographies promise the most powerful methodology. Extant literature tends to attribute problems experienced by EMNCs, specifically CMNCs, in exploiting assets in advanced economies to a lack of familiarity of executives with advanced economy institutional settings (Child and Marinova, 2014), or failing to learn quickly enough (Peng, 2012); methodologies with more nuanced understanding from inside organisations can reveal the impact of processes of othering and identity construction, and of enacting EMNC internal practices based on hierarchical imaginaries. Yet how can this geopolitical embeddedness of EMNCs be captured in empirical studies?

Our recent study on Chinese direct investments in Germany (cf. note 4) offers an example of how such a lens can be employed in terms of empirical methods, and of the insights that may be generated. In his comparative analysis of the PMI of two German acquisitions of CMNCs, drawing on in-depth case studies complemented by on-site observations, Yan (2020) explores how actors inside the organisation create meaning, the consequences of their actions, and the micro-politics of PMI (also Lai et al., 2020; Schlindwein and Geppert, 2020). He shows variability in the ways CMNCs respond to becoming a subsidiary of a CMNC in terms of identity construction, with important consequences for PMI. He observed that hierarchised imaginaries and neo-colonial stances of the German managers in one case led to mistrust and high levels of conflict, and to resistance to common HQ–subsidiary projects, whereas in another case the "undoing" of neo-colonial and hierarchised perceptions of the "Chinese other" was deliberately pursued towards creating a productive learning environment (also Mense-Petermann, 2020).

Through reconstructing sensemaking of the M&A situation in his first case, Yan (2020) shows how German subsidiary interviewees devaluated "Chinese culture" as lacking deep historical roots and rich traditions, which they ascribe to "European cultures". He also analyses the "naming practices" (Spivak, 1988) of interviewees showing how the "Chinese other" was named with pejorative terms such as "Hansel" (the German fairy tale "Hansel and Gretel") or "Häuptling" (chief of a tribe), indicating childishness or primitiveness, respectively. In the construction of their own identity and that of their acquirer, the German managers constructed a superior position for themselves, whereas their acquirer was seen as inferior regarding technological and organisational capabilities and management know-how. Here is a neo-imperial hierarchy enacted that deems the capabilities of the German subsidiary superior.

In his second case, by contrast, Yan observed a deliberate "undoing" of Eurocentric and neo-colonial stances by the subsidiary management, targeted towards a sense of belonging together and assuring social integration. One mode of such undoing was storytelling (Sole and Wilson, 2002), that is, presenting the takeover as a step for the acquired subsidiary towards becoming a "truly global" player, and discursively ascribing to it an active and recognisable role in the process of globalisation of the overall group. Regarding naming practices, in this case interviewees presented the acquirer as a "world market-leading company" (Yan, 2020: 27) that had managed to become a first-tier supplier of the world's leading automobile manufacturers. Aware of negative and neo-colonial stereotypes prevalent in media reports of Chinese acquisitions in Germany, and possibly resonating also within the workforce, the subsidiary management actively promoted sensemaking processes that enacted the "Chinese other" as an eye-level partner in a positive-sum game of globalisation.

This study demonstrates that the geopolitical embeddedness and its internal enactment in processes of sensemaking and othering represent a major impact on EMNCs' practices of internationalisation. As Yan (2020) and Mense-Petermann (2020) show, how actors in post-merger settings in EMNCs make sense of this constellation and draw distinctions between themselves and the acquirer impacts the HQ–subsidiary relations being established in PMI, the collaboration between the units, and the outcomes thereof.

Similarly, the single case study of a CMNC and its UK operations by Lai et al. (2020) shows how senior managers enacted Chinese national and organisational contexts to construct a set of identities for employees. Based on their case study, built on a range of in-depth interviews, participant observations, and extensive document analysis, they show how "managers are able to activate discourses and symbols available in the wider institutional context and make them meaningful in terms of the goals of the firm and the identity of the employees" (Lai et al., 2020: 662), and to theorise the links between the wider societal context, that is, dominant discourses and practices, and organisational and individual identities. In line with our suggestion for a future IB research agenda, the authors call for further research on questions of (hierarchically nested) organisational and individual identities and identity regulation, and how these are linked to dominant societal discourses and practices, specifically in the case of EMNCs.

Qualitative studies like the ones cited above (and, e.g. Ailon-Souday and Kunda, 2003; Ybema and Byun, 2011) can contribute substantively to theory building important for EMNCs and their internationalisation practices, and for pushing MNC theory towards a more complex and fully-fledged account. They address the question of "how the complexities of culture and the cultural framing of meanings affect MNCs' operations" (Moore, 2017: 168). This is the overarching question suggested here for a future IB research agenda.

Critics of such a qualitative, even ethnographic approach, may object that long-term participation in ethnographies is not an option for most scholars, and that access to MNCs for interviews in different units and at different levels of the MNC is hard to secure. Although this objection cannot be denied, ethnographies do not always necessitate long-term participation in the field. With "focused ethnographies" (Knoblauch, 2001; Spiegel et al., 2018), only a few days of participating observations in the field are required for MNC research where different localities may be visited (Hassard et al., 2007). Although scholars planning case studies cannot always reach full saturation, they can conduct interviews with a larger sample of members beyond upper-level management. The proposed methodology and methods are certainly demanding: obtaining access to organisations, conducting semi-structured or open-ended interviews, analytical skills in dealing with qualitative data, and not least the language skills required of the researchers. Setting up mixed teams including researchers originating from the respective EEs is imperative to successfully research the internal workings of EMNCs following the suggested methodological approach.

8.5   Discussion and conclusion

The rise of EEs and EMNCs changes the competitive environment for advanced economy MNCs and may lead to shifts in the global economy (Boussebaa and Morgan, 2014; Witt, 2019). This is most obvious for China and CMNCs. However, IB scholars have only just begun to consider the geopolitical dimensions of this development (Buckley, 2020). The "One Belt, One Road" Initiative launched by Xi Jinping in 2013, for example, has recently attracted some scholarly attention (Buckley, 2020; Zhang et al., 2018). Witt (2019) has discussed the question of the impact of current processes of "de-globalization" on the global economy and on strategies, structures, and behaviours in IB. Buckley's (2020) call on IB scholars to consider large-scale shifts in the global trade and investment regime, as represented by the Belt and Road Initiative, as a new factor in IB research aligns with our proposition for a future IB agenda.

However, we argue that a solely macro perspective is not sufficient to enhance our understanding of these issues. Global regimes and geopolitical contexts do not translate in a deterministic way into specific organisational practices. Hitherto, IB has not delivered sufficient insights into EMNCs' internationalisation practices and how they confront challenges, especially when entering advanced economies. The role of EMNCs in the global economy and possible shifts their advent might entail require much more attention than before.

A sensemaking and domination pattern perspective, as suggested herein, emphasises the embeddedness of MNCs in a wider geopolitical context; it sheds light on the socially constructed hierarchies in which organisational actors position their countries, organisations and themselves, and how they construct their identities vis-à-vis others. Complementing extant micro-political and sensemaking approaches by a post-colonial or neo-imperial dominance perspective helps to uncover an important and hitherto neglected factor impacting the course and outcomes of PMI in the case of EMNCs.

This approach to EMNCs allows for broadening the understanding of context by considering geopolitical imaginaries of hierarchically ranked countries and their enactment within processes of sensemaking; and connecting inner-organisational sensemaking with societal dominance patterns at the level of the world economy. It can, therefore, deliver regarding the call on IB to address "big questions" and shifts in the global economy. The approach suggested herein contributes to approaches that advocate the multiple embeddedness of MNCs (Meyer et al., 2011).

Given the rise of EMNCs, the question of how identities and positions are socially constructed and re-negotiated within MNCs, in both advanced and emerging economies, and if and how geopolitical imaginaries might change over time, represents a "grand challenge" but also a promising undertaking for IB. Future IB research should tackle the questions of what kind of HQ–subsidiary relations EMNCs establish and how these differ across host countries; what subsidiary roles and mandates EMNCs' subsidiaries take on in different host country settings, and how these are negotiated; how knowledge transfer, and "reverse knowledge transfer" (Ai and Tan, 2017) from advanced economies is organised and how hierarchised processes of othering impact these transfers; and lastly, how such hierarchised imaginaries and identities are the source of conflicts. Hitherto, the propositions of extant IB research on EMNCs, be they pessimistic or optimistic regarding EMNCs' capabilities, competitive advantages, and challenger status with regard to mature MNCs from advanced economies, have been hypothetical. Empirical research on the internal workings and internationalisation practices, therefore, is required. In sum, IB could, with such an agenda, "make real contributions by being at the forefront of learning about globalization and its influences on people, organizations, and societies" (Delios, 2017: 397).[4]

Notes

1. Meyer and Peng (2016: 5) have defined emerging economies "as mid- or low-income economies with growth potential that makes them attractive for IB".
2. Recent publications by Zhang et al. (2018) and Witt (2019) focus on geopolitical issues raised by the rise of EEs, and particularly China, and the respective EMNCs, but remain on the meso and macro levels of the economies and organisations.
3. Existing IB scholarship has addressed these questions using the concept of psychic or cultural distance (Meyer and Peng, 2016). Yet "distance" is a neutral term that does not reflect power asymmetries and hierarchies between countries. Meyer et al. (2011: 240f.), therefore, concede that "distance" may be too simplistic a concept (also Vaara, 2000). The same can be said of the concept of "liability-of-foreignness" (Zaheer, 1995; Luo and Mezias, 2002). This concept is deeply grounded in transaction cost economics, and it solely takes the perspective of HQ and its top management and a functionalist view asking how MNCs can overcome liabilities-of-foreignness.
4. This chapter has been developed in the context of the research project "Chinese direct investments in Germany", funded by the German Research Council (Deutsche Forschungsgemeinschaft), grant number ME 2008/7-1, of which the author was the principal investigator, with Junchen Yan and Christoph Seidel on the project team. The author is grateful for helpful feedback on an earlier draft of the chapter by the participants of an Authors' Workshop held in March 2020 at Friedrich-Schiller-University in Jena, and for comments by the editors of this volume and by Florian Becker-Ritterspach and Khaled Fourati, and by Alexander Funke.

References

Ai, Q. and Tan, H. (2017). Acquirers' prior related knowledge and post-acquisition integration: Evidences from four Chinese firms. *Journal of Organizational Change Management*, 30(4): 647–662.

Ailon-Souday, G. and Kunda, G. (2003). The local selves of global workers: The social construction of national identity in the face of organizational globalization. *Organization Studies*, 24(7): 1073–1096.

Alon, I., Anderson, J., Munim, Z.H. and Ho, H. (2018). A review of the internationalization of Chinese enterprises. *Asia Pacific Journal of Management*, 35(3): 573–605.

Becker-Ritterspach, F.A.A., Blazejewski, S., Dörrenbächer, C. and Geppert, M. (Eds) (2016). *Micropolitics in the Multinational Corporation: Foundations, Applications and New Directions*. Cambridge: Cambridge University Press.

Becker-Ritterspach, F.A.A. and Dörrenbächer, C. (2011). An organizational politics perspective on intra-firm competition in multinational corporations. *Management International Review*, 51(4): 533–559.

Boussebaa, M. (2015). Professional service firms, globalisation and the new imperialism. *Accounting, Auditing & Accountability Journal*, 28(8): 1217–1233.

Boussebaa, M. (2020). Identity regulation and globalization. In A.D. Brown (Ed.), *The Oxford Handbook of Identities in Organizations*. Oxford: Oxford University Press, 683–698.

Boussebaa, M. and Morgan, G. (2014). Pushing the frontiers of critical international business studies: The multinational as a neo-imperial space. *critical perspectives on international business*, 10(1/2): 96–106.

Brink, T. (2015). Chinese firms 'going global': Recent OFDI trends, policy support and international implications. *International Politics*, 52(6): 666–683.

Buckley, P.J. (2020). Book review: China's belt and road initiative: Changing the rules of globalization. *Journal of International Business Studies*, 51(2): 279–281.

Buckley, P.J. and Chapman, M. (1997). The use of native categories in management research. *British Journal of Management*, 8(4): 283–299.

Buckley, P.J., Clegg, J.L., Voss, H., Cross, A.R., Liu, X. and Zheng, P. (2018). A retrospective and agenda for future research on Chinese outward foreign direct investment. *Journal of International Business Studies*, 49(1): 4–23.

Buckley, P.J., Doh, J.P. and Benischke, M.H. (2017). Towards a renaissance in international business research? Big questions, grand challenges, and the future of IB scholarship. *Journal of International Business Studies*, 48(9): 1045–1064.

Child, J. and Marinova, S. (2014). The role of contextual combinations in the globalisation of Chinese firms. *Management and Organization Review*, 10(3): 347–371.

Chung, C., Brewster, C. and Bozkurt, Ö. (2020). The liability of mimicry: Implementing 'global human resource management standards' in United States and Indian subsidiaries of a South Korean multinational enterprise. *Human Resource Management*, 59(6): 537–553.

Clark, E. and Geppert, M. (2011). Subsidiary integration as identity construction and institution building: A political sensemaking approach. *Journal of Management Studies*, 48(2): 395–416.

Collinson, S. and Morgan, G. (Eds) (2009). *Images of the Multinational Firm*. Chichester: Wiley-Blackwell.

Cuervo-Cazurra, A. (2018). Thanks but no thanks: State-owned multinationals from emerging markets and host-country policies. *Journal of International Business Policy*, 1: 128–156.

Cuervo-Cazurra, A. and Ramamurti, R. (2014a). Introduction. In A. Cuervo-Cazurra and R. Ramamurti (Eds), *Understanding Multinationals from Emerging Markets*. Cambridge: Cambridge University Press, 1–12.

Cuervo-Cazurra, A. and Ramamurti, R. (2014b). Conclusion: An agenda for EMNC research. In A. Cuervo-Cazurra and R. Ramamurti (Eds), *Understanding Multinationals from Emerging Markets*. Cambridge: Cambridge University Press, 271–299.

Cuervo-Cazurra, A. and Ramamurti, R. (Eds) (2014c). *Understanding Multinationals from Emerging Markets*. Cambridge: Cambridge University Press.

Delios, A. (2017). The death and rebirth (?) of international business research. *Journal of Management Studies*, 54(3): 391–397.

Deng, P. (2011). The internationalization of Chinese firms: A critical review and future research. *International Journal of Management Reviews*, 14(4): 408–427.

Dörrenbächer, C. and Geppert, M. (2006). Micro-politics and conflicts in multinational corporations: Current debates, re-framing, and contributions of this special issue. *Journal of International Management*, 12(3): 251–265.

Dörrenbächer, C. and Geppert, M. (2011). Politics and power in the multinational corporation: An introduction. In C. Dörrenbächer and M. Geppert (Eds), *Politics and Power in the Multinational Corporation*. Cambridge: Cambridge University Press, 3–38.

Franz, M., Bollhorn, K. and Röhrig, R. (2017). Industrial relations and FDI from China and India in Germany. In M. Fuchs, S. Henn, M. Franz and R. Mudambi (Eds), *Managing Culture and Interspace in cross-Border Investments: Building a Global Company*. London: Routledge, 33–42.

Frenkel, M. (2008). The multinational corporation as a third space: Rethinking international management discourse on knowledge transfer through Homi Bhabha. *The Academy of Management Review*, 33(4): 924–942.

Frenkel, M. (2014). Can the periphery write back? Periphery-to-centre knowledge flows in multinationals based in developing and emerging economies. In R. Westwood, G. Jack, F.R. Khan and M. Frenkel (Eds), *Core-Periphery Relations and Organisation Studies*. Basingstoke: Palgrave Macmillan, 33–52.

Fuchs, M. and Schalljo, M. (2016). 'Western' professional ethics challenged by foreign acquisitions: German managers' patterns of interpretation surrounding Chinese and Indian investors. *Geoforum*, 75: 20–28.

Geppert, M., Becker-Ritterspach, F.A.A. and Mudambi, R. (2016). Politics and power in multinational companies: Integrating the international business and organization studies perspectives. *Organization Studies*, 37(9): 1209–1225.

Gioia, D.A. and Chittipeddi, K. (1991). Sensemaking and sensegiving in strategic change initiation. *Strategic Management Journal*, 12(6): 433–448.

Glaser, B.G. and Strauss, A.L. (1967). *The Discovery of Grounded Theory: Strategies for Qualitative Research*. New York: Aldine.

Gregory, K.L. (1983). Native-view paradigms: Multiple cultures and culture conflicts in organizations. *Administrative Science Quarterly*, 28(3): 359–376.

Gugler, P. and Boie, B. (2009). The rise of Chinese multinational enterprises. In J. Chaisse (Ed.), *Expansion of Trade and FDI in Asia: Strategic and Policy Challenges*. London: Routledge, 25–57.

Haasis, T.I., Liefner, I. and Garg, R. (2018). The organization of knowledge transfer in the context of Chinese cross-border acquisitions in developed countries. *Asian Business & Management*, 17(4): 286–311.

Hassard, J., McCann, L. and Morris, J. (2007). At the sharp end of new organizational ideologies: Ethnography and the study of multinationals. *Ethnography*, 8(3): 324–344.

Hofstede, G. (1991). *Cultures and Organizations: Software of the Mind*. New York: McGraw-Hill.

Jack, G. and Westwood, R. (2006). Postcolonialism and the politics of qualitative research in international business. *Management International Review*, 46(4): 481–501.

Kamoche, K. and Siebers, L.Q. (2015). Chinese management practices in Kenya: Toward a post-colonial critique. *The International Journal of Human Resource Management*, 26(21): 2718–2743.

Kang, R. (2009). The internationalization process of Chinese multinationals. In J.-P. Larçon and C. Liu (Eds), *Chinese Multinationals*. Singapore: World Scientific, 77–97.

Knoblauch, H. (2001). Fokussierte ethnographie: Soziologie, ethnologie und die neue Welle der ethnographie. *Sozialer Sinn*, 2(1): 123–141.

Lai, K., Morgan, G. and Morris, J. (2020). "Eating bitterness" in a Chinese multinational: Identity regulation in context. *Organization Studies*, 41(5): 661–680.

Li, D. (2009). Innovation & knowledge transfer in Chinese multinationals. In J.-P. Larçon and C. Liu (Eds), *Chinese Multinationals*. Singapore: World Scientific, 151–166.

Liu, Y. and Woywode, M. (2012). Chinese M&A in Germany. In I. Alon, M. Fetscherin and P. Gugler (Eds), *Chinese International Investments*. Basingstoke: Palgrave Macmillan, 212–233.

Luo, Y. and Mezias, J.M. (2002). Liabilities of foreignness: Concepts, constructs, and consequences. *Journal of International Management*, 8(3): 217–221.

Mense-Petermann, U. (2013). Expatriates as micro-political actors: Power resources and strategizing on global assignments. *Gazdasági élet és társa dalom (Economy and Society)*, 5(1–2): 44–73.

Mense-Petermann, U. (2018). Working in transnational social spaces: Expatriate managers in transnationally integrated MNCs. In A. Spiegel, U. Mense-Petermann and B. Bredenkötter (Eds), *Expatriate Managers: The Paradoxes of Working and Living Abroad*. New York: Routledge, 19–39.

Mense-Petermann, U. (2020). Post-merger integration and subsidiary roles in Chinese MNCs: The case of Chinese M&As in Germany. Manuscript under review.

Meyer, K.E., Mudambi, R. and Narula, R. (2011). Multinational enterprises and local contexts: The opportunities and challenges of multiple embeddedness. *Journal of Management Studies*, 48(2): 235–252.

Meyer, K.E. and Peng, M.W. (2016). Theoretical foundations of emerging economy business research. *Journal of International Business Studies*, 47(1): 3–22.

Moore, F. (2012). The diorama: Symbolism, interpretation and identity in the British plant of a transnational automobile manufacturer. *Management International Review*, 55: 619–642.

Moore, F. (2017). Altered states of consciousness: MNCs and ethnographic studies. In C. Dörrenbächer and M. Geppert (Eds), *Multinational Corporations and Organization Theory: Post Millennium Perspectives* (Research in the Sociology of Organizations, Volume 49). Bingley: Emerald Publishing, 161–189.

Morgan, G. (2001). The multinational firm: Organizing across institutional and national divides. In G. Morgan, P.H. Kristensen and R. Whitley (Eds), *The Multinational Firm: Organizing Across Institutional and National Divides*. New York: Oxford University Press, 1–24.

Peng, M.W. (2012). The global strategy of emerging multinationals from China. *Global Strategy Journal*, 2: 97–107.

Prasad, A. (Ed.) (2003). *Postcolonial Theory and Organizational Analysis: A Critical Engagement*. New York: Palgrave Macmillan.

Risberg, A., Tienari, J. and Vaara, E. (2003). Making sense of a transnational merger: Media texts and the (re)construction of power relations. *Culture and Organization*, 9(2): 121–137.

Rugman, A.M. (2009). Theoretical aspects of MNEs from emerging economies. In R. Ramamurti and J.V. Singh (Eds), *Emerging Multinationals in Emerging Markets*. Cambridge: Cambridge University Press, 42–63.

Rugman, A.M. and Nguyen, Q.T.K. (2014). Modern international business theory and emerging market multinational companies. In A. Cuervo-Cazurra and R. Ramamurti (Eds), *Understanding Multinationals from Emerging Markets*. Cambridge: Cambridge University Press, 53–80.

Schlindwein, E. and Geppert, M. (2020). Towards a process model of emotional sensemaking in post-merger integration: Linking cognitive and affective dimensions. *critical perspectives on international business*, DOI 10.1108/cpoib-02-2020-0008.

Shenkar, O. (2009). Becoming multinational: Challenges for Chinese firms. *Journal of Chinese Economic and Foreign Trade Studies*, 2(3): 149–162.

Smith, C. and Meiksins, P. (1995). System, society and dominance effects in cross-national organizational analysis. *Work, Employment & Society*, 9(2): 241–267.

Sole, D. and Wilson, D.G. (2002). Storytelling in organizations: The power and traps of using stories to share knowledge in organizations. Learning Innovation Laboratory (LILA). Harvard University. http://www.providersedge.com/docs/km_articles/Storytelling_in_Organizations.pdf.

Spiegel, A., Mense-Petermann, U. and Bredenkötter, B. (Eds) (2018). *Expatriate Managers: The Paradoxes of Working and Living Abroad*. New York: Routledge.

Spivak, G.C. (1988). Can the subaltern speak?, In C. Nelson and L. Grossberg (Eds), *Marxism and the Interpretation of Culture*. Urbana: University of Illinois Press, 66–111.

Vaara, E. (2000). Constructions of cultural differences in post-merger change processes: A sensemaking perspective on Finnish-Swedish cases. *Management*, 3(3): 81–110.

Vaara, E. (2003). Post-acquisition integration as sensemaking: Glimpses of ambiguity, confusion, hypocrisy, and politicization. *Journal of Management Studies*, 40(4): 859–894.

Wang, Y. (2009). Corporate culture and organization of Chinese multinationals. In J.-P. Larçon and C. Liu (Eds), *Chinese Multinationals*. Singapore: World Scientific, 167–191.

Weick, K.E. (1979). *The Social Psychology of Organizing*, 2nd edition. New York: McGraw-Hill.

Weick, K.E. (1995). *Sensemaking in Organizations*. Thousand Oaks, CA: Sage.

Westwood, R., Jack, G., Khan, F.R. and Frenkel, M. (Eds) (2014). *Core-Periphery Relations and Organisation Studies*. Basingstoke: Palgrave Macmillan.

Witt, M.A. (2019). De-globalization: Theories, predictions, and opportunities for international business research. *Journal of International Business Studies*, 50(7): 1053–1077.

Yan, J. (2020). Talking Chinese: Othering strategies in German companies acquired by Chinese multinational corporations. Bielefeld: unpublished manuscript.

Ybema, S. and Byun, H. (2011). Unequal power relations, identity discourse and cultural distinction drawing in MNCs. In C. Dörrenbächer and M. Geppert (Eds), *Politics and Power in the Multinational Corporation: The Role of Institutions, Interests and Identities*. Cambridge: Cambridge University Press, 315–345.

Zaheer, S. (1995). Overcoming the liability of foreignness. *Academy of Management Journal*, 38(2): 341–363.

Zhang, W., Alon, I. and Lattemann, C. (Eds) (2018). *China's Belt and Road Initiative: Changing the Rules of Globalization*. Cham: Palgrave Macmillan.

PART IV

Theorizing and studying new phenomena in IB/M: crisis, slavery and methodology

9. Managing the unavoidable: new avenues for research on MNEs and societal crises

Verena Girschik and Jasper Hotho

9.1 Introduction

Due to the proliferation and combination of health emergencies including the COVID-19 pandemic, violent conflicts, and climate change-related natural events, humanitarian needs reached unprecedented levels in 2020 (OCHA, 2020a, 2020b). Tending to the humanitarian needs arising from crises and emergencies has traditionally been considered the preserve of the public sector as well as non-governmental, international, and civil society organisations. However, as the global response to COVID-19 has demonstrated, societal crises and the humanitarian needs to which they give rise concern, affect, and involve businesses as well, including multinational enterprises (MNEs).

International business (IB) research has long recognised the economic impact of societal crises on the global activities of MNEs, as well as the efforts MNEs make to avoid and protect their operations against such effects (e.g. Getz and Oetzel, 2010; Henisz et al., 2010; Li and Vashchilko, 2010; Oetzel et al., 2007). In the process, the field has converged on a set of dominant theories and paradigms from which to study and understand these relations. However, over the past two decades, relations between MNEs and societal crises, including armed conflict and humanitarian emergencies, have become more complex and more intertwined (Hotho and Girschik, 2019). To ensure the timeliness and relevance of IB research on this important topic, we believe that now is the time to revisit the theoretical assumptions behind IB research in this area. Specifically, we see a need to consider whether dominant paradigms in this line of research still effectively serve our understanding of this complex topic, as well as whether the questions these paradigms inspire still capture the most pressing concerns of MNEs and societies affected by crisis. Our hope is that such a re-evaluation will help consolidate awareness of what has been achieved in this line of research over the past decades, and that it will encourage new, ambitious and relevant next-generation IB research on societal crises.

To this end, section 9.2 presents a brief review of IB research on societal crises. Partially due to our interest in business and humanitarianism, we focus our discussion on IB research in the context of crises that result in significant humanitarian needs, such as armed conflict, health emergencies and natural disasters. In section 9.3, we subsequently discuss three empirical realities that appear to challenge the theoretical assumptions and/or empirical focus of IB research on conflict and crisis. Building on these challenges, we use section 9.4 to introduce and discuss alternative theoretical lenses and methodological approaches as we sketch the potential contours of what we see as next-generation IB research in this increasingly relevant area. We hope that doing so provides inspiration for IB researchers interested in pursuing meaningful research on business, conflict and crisis, and that it will push both authors and reviewers to be appropriately demanding of the scope and depth of such research over the next decade.

9.2   Societal crises and IB research: crises as risks

Societal crises are dramatic events that severely disrupt economic and social life and often result in significant human suffering. Examples include natural disasters, intra-state conflict, and health emergencies such as the COVID-19 pandemic. Because societal crises come in various forms that may affect IB activity in different ways, IB research distinguishes between different crisis types (Getz and Oetzel, 2010). A first distinction concerns the *origin* of crises and whether crises are man-made, as with technological disasters and violent conflict, or considered natural events (e.g. Oh and Oetzel, 2011; Oetzel and Oh, 2014). Among others, this distinction has implications for the degree of politicisation of a crisis (Hotho and Girschik, 2019). A second distinction is between crises that constitute *discontinuous* events and crises that are *continuous*, as this may have implications for the extent that MNEs can anticipate and prepare for them (Oetzel and Oh, 2014; Witte et al., 2017). For example, violence can consist of short-lived events such as terrorist attacks or constitute protracted events such as civil war and inter-state conflict (Getz and Oetzel, 2010). Similarly, health emergencies may be relatively acute events, or, as with COVID-19, take on a protracted character. A final distinction recognised in the literature concerns the *intensity* of crises and whether the economic impact on IB activity is high or low (Getz and Oetzel, 2010; Witte et al., 2017).

IB research on societal crises has examined the effects of crises and the risks they present for a variety of conventional IB outcomes. Examples are the effects of crises on location and investment decisions (Driffield et al., 2013; Li and Vashchilko, 2010; Oetzel and Oh, 2014; Witte et al., 2017) and the post-entry effects of societal crises on subsidiary performance (Chen, 2017), expansion (Oh and Oetzel, 2011; Oetzel and Oh, 2014) and survival (Dai et al., 2013, 2017). In the process, IB scholars often draw on theoretical frameworks that emphasise or enable them to theorise the impact of societal disruptions on the cost of doing business, such as new institutional economics (Oh and Oetzel, 2011) or the OLI paradigm (Dai et al., 2013; Driffield et al., 2013; Skovoroda et al., 2019). Correspondingly, the literature tends to characterise MNEs as responding to the costs and risks of crises reactively and through avoidance (John and Lawton, 2018). With the notable exception of Oetzel and Getz (2012), who examine MNE engagement with violent conflict, less attention has been paid to how MNEs cope and engage with crises rather than their economic consequences.

IB research has examined various moderating factors that may shift the balance between the costs and benefits of operating in crisis contexts. A first factor is the governance quality of crisis-affected countries. For example, Oh and Oetzel (2011) draw on new institutional economics to develop the compelling argument that the quality of host country governance will moderate the relationship between the risk of disaster and subsidiary investments, insofar as governance quality reflects and shapes countries' willingness and ability to respond to disasters and to rebound from them. However, their empirical results indicate that reality is more complicated: the positive moderating effect of governance quality on subsidiary investments only appears to hold for crises caused by terrorist attacks. The authors also find that voice and accountability tend to *increase* the likelihood of subsidiary divestments after technological disasters, possibly because such accidents may result in political upheaval. Hence, the authors' results suggest that the relation between the type of crisis and country governance may warrant more nuanced theorising.

A second factor linked to variation in the impact of societal crises on IB activity is the firm's actual level of exposure to crisis events. As Dai et al. (2013, 2017) point out, differences in their proximity to conflict mean that MNEs operating in countries riven by war do not necessarily exhibit equal vulnerability levels. In addition to considering the vulnerability and substitutability of the assets that firms hold in crisis-hit locations (see also Skovoroda et al., 2019), therefore, the authors emphasise and show the need to consider sub-national geographic determinants to estimate the actual threat that crises pose to MNEs (Dai et al., 2013, 2017). Witte et al.'s (2017) finding, that political violence has a more substantial impact on greenfield FDI when political violence is nation-wide than when it is localised, resonates with this call.

In line with earlier work in political economy and related fields in the relations between conflict and natural resource extraction (e.g. Collier and Hoeffler, 1998; Le Billon, 2001), IB research also acknowledges the relevance of sectoral differences and associated investment motives for understanding the relationship between conflict and IB activity. In particular, IB research acknowledges and highlights that natural resource-seeking FDI may be less sensitive to conflict as such investments may be subject to particularly strong first-mover advantages and location constraints (Driffield et al., 2013; Witte et al., 2017). Skovoroda et al. (2019) even find intra-state war and some forms of political instability to be positively associated with US FDI investments in oil and gas. The authors link this finding to the reduced risk that unstable or incapacitated states will expropriate non-lootable assets. Rather than *minimise* their exposure to crises, such studies suggest that for some MNEs the location-specific advantages of crisis contexts may outweigh the increased risks.

A fourth factor linked to variation in the relationship between crises and IB activity is MNE experience with crisis events (Oetzel and Oh, 2014; Oh and Oetzel, 2017). However, this relationship is not straightforward, as findings suggest that the transferability of crisis experience is highly contingent on the type of crisis. For example, Oetzel and Oh (2014) find that experience with high-impact disasters is related more to expansion than new entry. This finding suggests that MNEs find it easier to leverage disaster experience *within* host countries where the disaster was experienced rather than in new countries experiencing similar disasters. Similarly, while Oh and Oetzel (2017) find that MNEs with country-specific experience are more likely to expand in countries facing armed conflict and one-sided conflicts, the impact on MNEs' ability to expand into countries experiencing similar conflicts is "not economically meaningful" (2017: 727). A persistent theme in the authors' learning-related work, therefore, is that those crises that are discontinuous events, and therefore difficult to anticipate, likely require context-specific knowledge for MNEs to respond to them. A potential explanation is that country-specific experience, such as political and social ties, renders companies better positioned to cope as well as participate in and benefit from recovery efforts (Oh and Oetzel, 2017). However, thus far, quantitative analyses have revealed relatively little about such complex local dynamics.

In sum, existing IB research demonstrates that the relationship between crises and MNE activity is complex and requires considerable contextual sensitivity. The focus on traditional IB dependent variables and emphasis on risk avoidance also means that we still know relatively little about how MNEs practically cope and engage with crisis events. Capturing such complex dynamics and relations requires a rethink of the theoretical perspectives and research methods used in IB research on societal crises. To this end, we proceed by presenting three empirical challenges to encourage readers to reconsider how MNE managers think about crises, how MNEs engage with crises, as well as the roles that MNEs may play as crises unfold. We then propose new theoretical directions that take up these challenges and consider alternative research designs that may enrich our understanding of MNEs' engagement with complex societal challenges.

9.3   International business research on conflict and crises: three empirical challenges

Theory shapes and structures our understanding of the world through the provision of concepts, relationships and vocabulary. As a result, theory not only affects how we see and what we notice about a phenomenon of interest but also the kinds of questions we ask and consider worthy of scholarly attention within a given research field. Because all theory is bounded in terms of explanatory scope (Bacharach, 1989), dominant theoretical perspectives inevitably contain "blind spots": aspects, tensions, or dynamics of a phenomenon of interest that are relevant to a given research field but fall outside the scope of a field's dominant theoretical perspective or are difficult to grasp with the concepts or vocabulary this perspective provides.

In this section, we highlight several aspects of IB activity in crisis contexts that are difficult to describe and explain (to notice, even) from theoretical perspectives emphasising cost minimisation or risk avoidance, or that run counter to what such perspectives would predict. In doing so, we draw on the case of the shipping industry's involvement in the context of the Mediterranean migration crisis as well as examples taken from the private sector's response to the COVID-19 pandemic. Our understanding of the shipping industry's involvement in the Mediterranean migration crisis is grounded in data collected within the scope of a broader research agenda on corporate engagement with humanitarian crises initiated in 2015. The data include interviews with significant players in Mediterranean search and rescue operations, including the shipping industry (shipping companies, national and international shipping associations), NGOs, intergovernmental organisations such as UNHCR, and the national coast guard of Italy, as well as secondary sources.

Challenge 1: MNEs may engage with crises for a variety of motives

As discussed in section 9.2, IB research tends to view conflict and crisis as forms of non-market risk that negatively affect the cost of doing business as well as the returns that MNEs are able to realise on their activities. This perspective suggests that MNEs and their managers will seek to minimise their exposure to such risks. However, while conceptualising *crises as risk* indeed reflects some of the key concerns of managers operating in conflict and crisis zones, in practice MNEs and their managers may also enact a variety of *other* lenses through which to understand crisis situations and formulate context-appropriate courses of action. In such instances, theoretical perspectives emphasising cost and risk minimisation may have reduced explanatory power.

One reason is that crisis contexts may offer a variety of opportunities for value creation (Hotho and Girschik, 2019). Examples are MNEs in the security sector or MNEs supplying emergency supplies for which conflicts and crises may offer attractive market opportunities. But crises also offer opportunities for MNEs whose business is not directly related to emergency response. Examples of such benefits include reputational and motivational benefits resulting from contributions to emergency response efforts, as well as opportunities for relationship-building with international organisations, societal actors and governments (OCHA, 2017). Such considerations may, for example, have contributed to the much-publicised decision by car manufacturers such as Tesla and other firms to produce makeshift ventilators in response to the COVID-19 pandemic (BBC, 2020). During crises, MNEs may also perceive opportunities to learn about and start building potential new markets. For example, its humanitarian partnerships provide MasterCard the opportunity to learn about untapped markets in countries that are currently in crisis but which may prove attractive in the future, such as Yemen (OCHA, 2017). Such motivations highlight that MNEs may consider crises instrumentally or strategically, rather than or in addition to viewing them as risky events to be avoided.

MNEs may also adopt a *moral lens* on crises when they are confronted with human needs and suffering. An example of a crisis where MNEs have exhibited a sense of moral duty is the Mediterranean migration crisis, where shipping companies have played vital roles in search and rescue operations and have been actively called upon by Maritime Rescue Coordination Centres. While the duty to provide assistance in distress situations at sea is technically a legal requirement (see e.g. The International Convention for the Safety of Life at Sea [SOLAS] Reg. 33), most seafarers view this duty as a cornerstone of their professional work ethic – a moral obligation which many seafarers take to extend to boat refugees as well. As one of our interviewees from the shipping industry phrased it: "When you see someone in distress at sea, then it is in your DNA as a seafarer to help them." Even when MNEs have not internalised such moral obligations, they may still be compelled to act accordingly by local stakeholders (Oetzel and Getz, 2012). For example, the activities of resource-seeking firms such as mining enterprises often require a "social licence to operate" from the local communities where they operate (Gifford and Kestler, 2008; Shapiro et al., 2018). Under such conditions, MNEs may seek to secure their legitimacy by engaging in courses of action that are considered morally appropriate.

This is not to say that MNEs exposed to crises privilege opportunities for value creation and moral obligations over cost considerations. Yet be it for strategic or moral reasons or, most likely, a combination of these two, MNEs increasingly choose to actively respond to human needs and suffering in crisis contexts. Well-documented examples include Wal-Mart's 2005 response to Hurricane Katrina (e.g. Horwitz, 2009), and the contributions by UPS, A.P. Møller-Mærsk and other logistics providers to the UN World Food Programme's Logistics Cluster. In each of these cases, MNEs opted to (further) expose themselves to the inherent risks that come with crises rather than avoid such costs and risks altogether. Such examples suggest that a singular reliance on perspectives emphasising risks and cost–benefit analyses may, increasingly, be inadequate to explain how MNEs respond to crises. Accordingly, next-generation IB research on conflict and crisis needs to draw on a broader set of theoretical perspectives; a set that is more in line with the mixed motives and considerations that MNEs face when deciding whether and how to engage with crises.

Challenge 2: MNEs respond to crises in a variety of ways

Whereas Challenge 1 relates to the theories in use in IB research on conflict and crises, the second set of challenges relates to the dependent variables this line of research has considered. IB research on conflict and crises commonly starts from the assumption that crises increase costs and hence decrease returns on investment. Correspondingly, MNEs' *responses* to conflict and crises are often modelled in terms of location, investment and exit decisions. As others have emphasised (Oetzel et al., 2007), however, research into the effects of conflict and crises on MNE activity currently provides little guidance for MNEs already operating in crisis-hit locations. Focusing on conventional dependent variables thus leaves our understanding of how MNEs respond to crises incomplete.

One limitation is that location and entry mode decisions may only represent a limited part of the multifaceted, variegated, and multilevel ways in which MNEs engage with the challenges emanating from crises in daily practice.

As an illustration, consider again the shipping industry's response to the Mediterranean migration crisis. At the height of the crisis, in 2016, over 180,000 people arrived in Italy through the Central Mediterranean Route and an estimated 5,000 died trying (International Organization for Migration [IOM], 2020). As part of our ongoing research on corporate responses to humanitarian crises, we found that shipping companies relied upon a variety of measures to handle the reality of shipping in a humanitarian crisis during this time. Some of these measures were primarily operational, and designed to limit the effects of the crisis on daily operations as well as the firm's exposures to such risks. For example, some companies altered their shipping routes to minimise the delays, costs, and considerable safety threats involved in search and rescue operations. Moreover, there are also persistent rumours that some vessels illegally chose to "go dark" by switching off their Automatic Identification Signals (AIS) transponder, the device Maritime Rescue Coordination Centres rely upon to identify vessels to be called upon to assist with search and rescue operations. Seeking to avoid exposure to crises and the associated costs, MNEs may thus adapt their operations to crises in ways that are not reflected in investment patterns.

What is more, shipping companies rely upon more than avoidance strategies alone. A significant part of the response by shipping companies from the Nordics, for example, involved the proactive preparation to engage with crisis situations at sea. To illustrate, the guidelines developed by the Norwegian Shipowners' Association, which were partially adopted by the International Chamber of Shipping, encouraged shipping companies to be prepared to run "a medium sized refugee camp at sea" (Norwegian Shipowners Association, 2015: 4). Recommended activities included educating staff in camp management and crowd control, exploration of different scenarios, and the pre-storing of tarps, toilets, medical kits and blankets. While other national shipowners' associations were more hesitant to recommend such far-reaching preparations, and not all shipping companies adhered to these recommendations, their relevance is reflected in statistics by the Italian Coast Guard which show that, between 2013 and 2016, merchant vessels saved around 80,000 people on the Central Mediterranean Route alone (Italian Coast Guard, 2016).

In addition to illustrating some of the operational measures that firms may take to cope with crises, the Mediterranean migration crisis is noteworthy because of the variety of strategies the shipping industry employed to call political attention to its systematic role in search and rescue operations and incite others into action. In particular, shipping companies used political strategies at a variety of levels to call on the EU and its member states to invest more effort and resources into relieving the burden carried by the shipping industry and to address factors at the root of the migration crisis more profoundly and more systematically. Among others, shipping companies engaged in targeted information and constituency-building strategies (Hillman and Hitt, 1999) to convince the EU and its member states to step up their search and rescue capabilities. These strategies were pursued by shipping companies individually, such as the public appeal by logistics conglomerate A.P. Møller-Mærsk in a Danish business daily (Østergaard and Keller, 2015), as well as through interest organisations at national and international level such as the International Chamber of Shipping.

The shipping industry's response to the Mediterranean refugee crisis illustrates the multifaceted, variegated and multilevel ways in which companies may handle societal crises. Indeed, MNEs may be forced to draw on such a broad repertoire of responses whenever leaving is not a viable option and MNEs have to find ways to actively cope with a crisis instead (Getz and Oetzel, 2010). For example, both mining companies in Ebola-affected areas in Africa (Bermúdez-Lugo and Menzie, 2015; Reuters, 2019) and the now disgraced French cement company Lafarge AS in civil war-struck Syria (Alderman, 2018) needed to find ways to respond to crises that would allow them to carry on their business activities. The Mediterranean refugee crisis also highlights that MNEs' crisis response not only shapes the extent to which crises affect MNEs' operations but may also directly affect people's suffering. We therefore encourage next-generation IB research on societal crises to expand the scope of inquiry beyond entry, expansion and exit decisions.

Challenge 3: MNEs play active roles in how crises unfold

In line with its focus on location and investment decisions, IB research tends to view crises as resulting from the external environment and, therefore, as exogenous to MNE activity (Buckley et al., 2020). Yet viewing crises as exogenous to IB activity is less appropriate when we expand the scope of IB research beyond traditional variables. As we pointed out above, MNEs engage in and manage societal crises through a broad set of responses. As they do so, MNEs may proactively or inadvertently influence how crises unfold (Oetzel and Getz, 2012). For example, previous research on business and peace has shown that MNEs may incite or perpetuate crises when they are complicit in promoting their underlying causes, such as when they fuel conflict by increasing inequality across ethnic divides or by exacerbating environmental degradation (Hotho and Girschik, 2019; Idahosa, 2002; Westermann-Behaylo, 2009). Thus far, IB research has largely ignored this potential co-evolution of societal crises and MNE activity.

One reason why this oversight is problematic is that it obscures the fact that crises often entail the collapse of normal structures and the formation of new relations and ways of organising to cope with new practical demands (Hällgren et al., 2018). To illustrate, the Mediterranean migration crisis represents a case where business is widely recognised to have borne a disproportionately large responsibility for humanitarian action. The shipping industry's extensive presence in the Mediterranean, coupled with moral and legal obligations, makes it this crisis's actor of last resort: when collective action fails to materialise and others fail to act, it inevitably falls upon the shipping industry to provide assistance to migrants at sea. Apart from the challenge to fulfil its social responsibilities in the face of intense commercial pressure, a key challenge for the shipping industry is therefore to negotiate its engagement in the Mediterranean migration crisis and guard against having to take on even greater responsibility.

Viewing crises as exogenous to MNE activity may also lead us to overlook critical legitimacy concerns. There has been growing recognition that companies are expected by both international and local stakeholders to respond to crises (Chen et al., 2019; Oetzel and Getz, 2012). When they do so and thereby become an integral part of the crisis, however, they may risk being viewed as complicit in perpetuating human suffering. In the case of the Mediterranean migration crisis, for example, concerns have been raised that the shipping industry's involvement may encourage rather than hamper the activities of human traffickers and thereby reinforce the crisis rather than alleviate it. Shipping MNEs thus find themselves between a rock and a hard place, where both withdrawal and continued engagement are seen as morally problematic. As a result, the shipping industry, the EU and humanitarian organisations have sought to renegotiate the division of roles and responsibilities in the handling of the crisis in an attempt to arrive at a solution that is both effective and sustainable.

Only rarely do shipping companies publicise their engagement in the Mediterranean migration crisis or promote it under the corporate social responsibility (CSR) banner. Most shipping companies have avoided such communications because of concerns around their complicity in perpetuating the crisis as well as on the grounds that it is inappropriate to boast about fulfilling a moral obligation. Indeed, when companies do communicate about their engagement in crises, they risk being perceived as self-serving (Chen et al., 2019). Thus, while companies are often expected to respond to crises (Oetzel and Getz, 2012), their engagement is under close scrutiny and may in fact jeopardise their legitimacy. In order to appreciate and understand these complex legitimacy dynamics, we encourage next-generation IB research on crises to consider the engagement of MNEs and their impact on crises over time.

9.4   New avenues for IB research on societal crises: four recommendations

The previous section highlighted three empirical blind spots in IB's understanding of the relation between societal crises and IB activity: MNEs' various motives for proactively engaging with crises, the broad variety of MNE responses to crises, and MNEs' active role in how crises unfold. Our hope is that next-generation IB research on societal crises will address these gaps. To encourage such a move towards a more comprehensive IB agenda on this topic, we conclude this chapter with a number of recommendations. In doing so we aim to inspire greater theoretical and methodological pluralism in IB research on MNEs and crises as well as to create greater awareness and recognition of the interconnectedness between MNE responses to crises and their consequences for firms, crises and crisis-hit societies.

9.4.1   Complementing risk-management with value-creation and organisational institutionalist perspectives

Our first recommendation is for IB research on conflict and crisis to draw on a broader range of theoretical lenses to explain the effects of crises on conventional IB outcomes, including entry, expansion and exit decisions. Current research explaining these outcomes from a risk-avoidance perspective often builds on arguments derived from transaction cost economics or the related new institutional economics. As illustrated in section 9.2, both approaches have been taken to suggest that MNEs will seek to minimise the possible risks and costs they incur as a result of conflict and crises as well as MNEs' exposure to such risks. In practice, however, MNEs and their managers may employ a variety of considerations when exposed to conflict and crises. As highlighted in section 9.3, opportunities for value creation as well as moral values and social expectations may all shape MNE managers' thinking as to the appropriate corporate response to a crisis, in addition to cost considerations.

We suggest two alternative theoretical paradigms that may help advance explanations of IB activity in crisis contexts. The first, epitomised by the resource-based view (RBV; e.g. Barney, 1991; Wernerfelt, 1984), foregrounds the opportunities for value creation afforded by crisis contexts. In contrast to perspectives emphasising cost minimisation, an RBV perspective suggests that

MNEs select entry modes which allow them to maximise opportunities for value creation (Meyer et al., 2009). Applied to crisis contexts, this perspective suggests that market-seeking MNEs with geographically fungible ownership advantages in the area of emergency response may seek out crisis-hit locations rather than avoid them and that such MNEs may prefer relatively resource-intensive entry modes, even if this comes at the cost of higher risk exposure. Similarly, knowledge-based and learning perspectives (e.g. Barkema and Vermeulen, 1998; Sapienza et al., 2006) provide theoretical support for the observation that, for businesses whose business is not directly related to emergency response, crisis contexts may offer opportunities to develop and enhance knowledge and capabilities that may be relevant elsewhere in the organisation, or at a later time. Answering to the first challenge above, such arguments may help explain theoretically why some MNEs actively seek to engage with crises.

The second complementary paradigm with direct relevance to MNE decision-making towards crisis contexts consists of organisational institutionalist perspectives (Hotho and Pedersen, 2012). In contrast to new institutional economics, which pays particular attention to the stability and effectiveness of formal institutions and governance structures and the resulting costs and uncertainty, organisational institutionalist perspectives such as the institutional logics and "orders of worth" perspectives devote deliberate attention to the managerial relevance of social conformity and cognition as well as the extent to which different domains of social life are characterised by distinct decision-making logics (e.g. Boltanski and Thévenot, 2006; Cloutier and Langley, 2013; Thornton et al., 2012). In doing so, the organisational institutionalist perspective privileges considerations around the appropriateness of various courses of action over cost–benefit calculations. In the context of MNEs and societal crises, organisational institutionalist perspectives draw attention to issues and questions about the roles of morality and social expectations in MNEs' decision to engage with rather than avoid crisis contexts. Organisational institutionalist perspectives also support lines of inquiry into how MNEs practically handle the plurality of often conflicting social expectations they are exposed to when operating in crisis-hit locations, both external and internal to the firm.

9.4.2   Understanding a broader variety of MNE responses

Our second recommendation for next-generation IB research on MNEs and crises pertains to the IB activities and outcomes to be explained. Previous research has mainly focused on how crises affect entry, expansion and exit decisions. Yet MNEs respond to crises in a variety of ways that are not necessarily reflected in investment patterns. Echoing earlier calls to focus on

MNEs' innovative responses to crises (e.g. Oetzel and Oh, 2015), we therefore encourage research into how MNEs handle and may most effectively deal with the challenges and opportunities they encounter in crisis contexts.

As we have argued and illustrated above, companies often proactively engage with societal crises to attain various benefits afforded by the environment in which they operate. Such motivations are not surprising in light of non-market strategy (NMS) research that has linked companies' non-market strategies to positive organisational outcomes, such as financial performance (Baron, 1995; Mellahi et al., 2016). For example, through proactive non-market strategies, companies may shape their environments to foster competitive advantages vis-à-vis their competitors (Doh et al., 2012; Oliver and Holzinger, 2008). Taking the RBV as starting point, IB research may ask questions about the bundles of resources and dynamic capabilities that firms can develop and utilise in and across crisis contexts.

Previous research on MNEs and crises has suggested that MNEs' relational embeddedness renders them better positioned to cope with as well as participate in and benefit from recovery efforts (Oh and Oetzel, 2017). What is more, relations with the right groups of stakeholders may aid subsidiary survival by positioning the MNE's presence in a crisis context as socially valuable (Darendeli and Hill, 2016). To further explore such relational dynamics, next-generation IB research on societal crises may take inspiration from NMS research on relational strategies. Relational strategies entail that companies cultivate and manage dependency relations with non-market actors, thereby establishing their institutional influence (Doh et al., 2012; Hillman and Hitt, 1999; Marquis and Raynard, 2015; Oliver and Holzinger, 2008). Future research may usefully ask what kinds of relations, and with whom, enable companies' responses and resilience in crisis contexts.

9.4.3 Embracing endogeneity

Acknowledging the broad range of responses through which MNEs engage with crises also draws attention to the potential role of MNEs in how crises unfold. Given that companies assume active roles and responsibilities in and for crises, theorising and modelling crises as exogenous explanations of MNE activity does not seem to do justice to the complexity of the empirical phenomenon. Hence, endogeneity renders traditional ways of modelling the relation between crises and MNE activity less fitting. We therefore encourage next-generation IB research on conflict and crisis to embrace endogeneity by considering the complex interplay of IB activity and crises over time.

In doing so, we encourage IB research to consider insights from the literature on political CSR and corporate citizenship (Matten and Crane, 2005; Scherer et al., 2016; Scherer and Palazzo, 2011), which has long emphasised the fluidity of business–society relations and the renegotiation of companies' responsibilities for social problems. One key insight from this literature is that it is often the inability of governments to act that propels companies to fill governance gaps. Indeed, weak governance or lack of capacity or resources may prevent governments from responding appropriately to crises, thus shifting part of the burden of solving acute problems to companies (Oh and Oetzel, 2011). Moreover, the resource constraints of humanitarian actors may put companies into the position of being the most powerful actors in local crisis contexts and thereby confer to them a humanitarian role. Again, the Mediterranean migration crisis vividly illustrates such dynamics, as the shipping industry's extensive presence in the Mediterranean, coupled with moral and legal obligations, makes it this crisis's actor of last resort: when collective action fails to materialise and others fail to act, it inevitably falls upon the shipping industry to provide assistance to migrants at sea. Apart from fulfilling its social responsibilities in the face of intense competitive pressure, a key challenge for the shipping industry is therefore to negotiate its engagement in the crisis and guard against having to take on even greater responsibility. Relevant questions for IB research to address are therefore: How do MNEs negotiate their role in societal crises and to what effects on business and society?

Examining the roles and responsibilities of MNEs in crisis contexts may also contribute new insights as to how companies manage their legitimacy. Both locally and internationally, companies confront ever-stronger expectations from stakeholders demanding that they become involved and navigate such acute situations responsibly (Oetzel and Getz, 2012). One important question for further research is whether and how legitimacy is grounded in social impact (see also Miklian, 2019). Perhaps equally importantly, legitimacy also hinges on whether and how companies communicate their roles and responsibilities (e.g. Carlos and Lewis, 2018; Girschik 2020). Given that their involvement is under increased scrutiny insofar as it is covered by social media, companies need to ensure that their responses to societal crises are not perceived as profit-driven (Chen et al., 2019). An exciting avenue for further research is therefore to examine how companies manage their legitimacy as they engage with crises over time.

9.4.4 Methodological implications

Methodologically, we encourage complementing large-n analyses with in-depth qualitative research, including case studies (Welch et al., 2011). Such research lends itself well to attempts to more accurately capture the varied ways in which MNEs respond to and manage crises, as well as the challenges that arise when MNEs engage with such events (Oh and Oetzel, 2017). Specifically, to understand MNEs' role in how crises unfold over time, next-generation IB research may employ qualitative process research (Langley, 1999; see also Chapter 11). As such, qualitative studies may be one of the ways in which IB research on crises may acknowledge and account for the fact that societal crises are often partially endogenous to IB activity and shed light on MNE activities that may perpetuate or alleviate crises.

We also encourage IB research on conflict and crisis to consider multiple levels of analysis. As illustrated with reference to the Mediterranean migration crisis, MNEs' attempts to respond to and manage societal crises may play out across a variety of levels, including the subsidiary level, the level of the MNE, and the industry level at which much corporate interest representation takes place. The migration crisis also illustrates the relevance of considering the connections between these different levels, since what is negotiated at the level of industry representation may have implications for the responses that MNEs and their referent audiences find acceptable and legitimate at country or subsidiary level. In addition to qualitative process studies, we therefore also recommend qualitative and quantitative studies that examine the interdependencies between MNE responses and the factors enabling these across multiple levels of analysis. For example, future research may usefully explain how an MNE's corporate political activity and engagement in public discourse interacts with how the company handles the practical challenges of the crisis situation.

While we see great value in the development of a more qualitative understanding of the various relationships between MNEs and crisis contexts, it is important to recognise the challenges of qualitative research in crisis-hit locations. Apart from the practical challenges involved in negotiating access to and maintaining a viable working relationship with MNEs operating in crisis contexts and securing access to such locations, there are important safety and ethical concerns to consider. While the potential risks to personal safety may be relatively apparent, the ethical challenges involved in fieldwork on MNEs in crisis areas may not: some of these concerns arise from the fact that fieldwork often requires time and resources from participating MNEs and other actors that could have been used to tend to the needs of people in distress. Similarly, when not managed carefully, fieldwork in crisis areas may consume resources such as accommodation, security, transportation and translation services that are vital to aid workers and/or people affected by crises. As Barber (2019) highlights, the burden of participation in research activities is often particularly high for already vulnerable individuals. In addition to emphasising the regular ethical standards for field research and the need for close attention to safety, we therefore echo Barber's recommendation for researchers to carefully consider whether field research in crisis areas passes the justificatory threshold, in the sense that the expected benefits of the research justify the risk of harm to researchers and participants, and to take diligent care to assess the vulnerability of research informants.

Acknowledgement

We thank Tania Grønbæk and Thomas Oostheim for excellent research assistance. Tania contributed to the data collection for the ongoing project on the role of the shipping industry in the Mediterranean migration crisis referred to in the chapter. Thomas assisted with the literature review and analysis.

References

Alderman, L. (2018). French cement giant Lafarge indicted on terror financing charge in Syria. *The New York Times*, 28 June. https://www.nytimes.com/2018/06/28/business/lafarge-holcim- syria-terrorist-financing.html (retrieved 16 March 2019).

Bacharach, S.B. (1989). Organizational theories: Some criteria for evaluation. *Academy of Management Review*, 14: 496–515.

Barber, R. (2019). The ethics of research in humanitarian action. In V. Harris (Ed.), *Ethics in a Crowded World: Globalisation, Human Movement and Professional Ethics* (Research in Ethical Issues in Organizations, Vol. 22). Bingley: Emerald Publishing, 69–85.

Barkema, H.G. and Vermeulen, F. (1998). International expansion through start-up or acquisition: A learning perspective. *Academy of Management Journal*, 41(1): 7–26.

Barney, J. (1991). Firm resources and sustained competitive advantage. *Journal of Management*, 17(1): 99–120.

Baron, D.P. (1995). Integrated strategy: Market and nonmarket components. *California Management Review*, 37(2): 47–65.

BBC (2020). Coronavirus: Tesla donates hundreds of ventilators to New York. https://www.bbc.com/news/technology-52071314 (retrieved 27 March 2020).

Bermúdez-Lugo, O. and Menzie, W.D. (2015). *The Ebola Virus Disease Outbreak and the Mineral Sectors of Guinea, Liberia, and Sierra Leone*. US Geological Survey, Fact Sheet 2015-3033, April. https://pubs.usgs.gov/fs/2015/3033/pdf/fs2015-3033.pdf (retrieved 27 March 2020).

Boltanski, L. and Thévenot, L. (2006 [1991]). *On Justification: Economies of Worth*. Princeton, NJ: Princeton University Press.

Buckley, P.J., Chen, L., Clegg, L.J. and Voss, H. (2020). The role of endogenous and exogenous risk in FDI entry choices. *Journal of World Business*, 55(1): 101040.

Carlos, W.C. and Lewis, B.W. (2018). Strategic silence: Withholding certification status as a hypocrisy avoidance tactic. *Administrative Science Quarterly*, 63: 130–169.

Chen, S. (2017). Profiting from FDI in conflict zones. *Journal of World Business*, 52(6): 760–768.

Chen, Y.R.R., Cheng, Y., Hung-Baesecke, C.J.F. and Jin, Y. (2019). Engaging international publics via mobile-enhanced CSR (mCSR): A cross-national study on stakeholder reactions to corporate disaster relief efforts. *American Behavioral Scientist*, 63(12): 1603–1623.

Cloutier, C. and Langley, A. (2013). The logic of institutional logics: Insights from French pragmatist sociology. *Journal of Management Inquiry*, 22(4): 360–380.

Collier, P. and Hoeffler, A. (1998). On economic causes of civil war. *Oxford Economic Papers*, 50(4): 563–573.

Dai, L., Eden, L. and Beamish, P.W. (2013). Place, space, and geographical exposure: Foreign subsidiary survival in conflict zones. *Journal of International Business Studies*, 44(6): 554–578.

Dai, L., Eden, L. and Beamish, P.W. (2017). Caught in the crossfire: Dimensions of vulnerability and foreign multinationals' exit from war-afflicted countries. *Strategic Management Journal*, 38(7): 1478–1498.

Darendeli, I.S. and Hill, T.L. (2016). Uncovering the complex relationships between political risk and MNE firm legitimacy: Insights from Libya. *Journal of International Business Studies*, 47(1): 68–92.

Doh, J.P., Lawton, T.C. and Rajwani, T. (2012). Advancing nonmarket strategy research: Institutional perspectives in a changing world. *Academy of Management Perspectives*, 26(3): 22–39.

Driffield, N., Jones, C. and Crotty, J. (2013). International business research and risky investments, an analysis of FDI in conflict zones. *International Business Review*, 22(1): 140–155.

Getz, K.A. and Oetzel, J. (2010). MNE strategic intervention in violent conflict: Variations based on conflict characteristics. *Journal of Business Ethics*, 89(4): 375–386.

Gifford, B. and Kestler, A. (2008). Toward a theory of local legitimacy by MNEs in developing nations: Newmont mining and health sustainable development in Peru. *Journal of International Management*, 14(4): 340–352.

Girschik, V. (2020). Managing legitimacy in business-driven social change: The role of relational work. *Journal of Management Studies*, 57(4): 775–804.

Hällgren, M., Rouleau, L. and De Rond, M. (2018). A matter of life or death: How extreme context research matters for management and organization studies. *Academy of Management Annals*, 12(1): 111–153.

Henisz, W.J., Mansfield, E.D. and Von Glinow, M.A. (2010). Conflict, security, and political risk: International business in challenging times. *Journal of International Business Studies*, 41(5): 759–764.

Hillman, A.J. and Hitt, M.A. (1999). Corporate political strategy formulation: A model of approach, participation, and strategy decisions. *Academy of Management Review*, 24(4): 825–842.

Horwitz, S. (2009). Wal-Mart to the rescue: Private enterprise's response to hurricane Katrina. *The Independent Review*, 13: 511–528.

Hotho, J.J. and Girschik, V. (2019). Corporate engagement in humanitarian action: Concepts, challenges, and areas for international business research. *critical perspectives on international business*, 15: 201–218.

Hotho, J.J. and Pedersen, T. (2012). Beyond the 'rules of the game': Three institutional approaches and how they matter for international business. In M. Demirbag and G. Wood (Eds), *Handbook of Institutional Approaches to International Business*. Cheltenham, UK and Northampton, MA, USA: Edward Elgar Publishing, 236–273.

Idahosa, P. (2002). Business ethics and development in conflict (zones): The case of Talisman Oil. *Journal of Business Ethics*, 39(3): 227–246.

International Organization for Migration (2020). *Tracking Deaths Along Migration Routes*. https://missingmigrants.iom.int/ (retrieved 7 September 2020).

Italian Coast Guard (2016). *Italian Maritime Rescue Coordination Centre: Search and Rescue Activity and Migratory Flows in Central Mediterranean Sea*. https://www.guardiacostiera.gov.it/en/Documents/search-and-rescue-activity/search-and-rescue-activity-and-migratory-flows-in-central-mediterranean-sea.pdf (retrieved 27 March 2020).

John, A. and Lawton, T.C. (2018). International political risk management: Perspectives, approaches and emerging agendas. *International Journal of Management Reviews*, 20: 847–879.

Langley, A. (1999). Strategies for theorizing from process data. *Academy of Management Review*, 24(4): 691–710.

Le Billon, P. (2001). The political ecology of war: Natural resources and armed conflicts. *Political Geography*, 20(5): 561–584.

Li, Q. and Vashchilko, T. (2010). Dyadic military conflict, security alliances, and bilateral FDI flows. *Journal of International Business Studies*, 41(5): 765–782.

Marquis, C. and Raynard, M. (2015). Institutional strategies in emerging markets. *Academy of Management Annals*, 9(1): 291–335.

Matten, D. and Crane, A. (2005). Corporate citizenship: Toward an extended theoretical conceptualization. *Academy of Management Review*, 30: 166–179.

Mellahi, K., Frynas, J.G., Sun, P. and Siegel, D. (2016). A review of the nonmarket strategy literature: Toward a multi-theoretical integration. *Journal of Management*, 42(1): 143–173.

Meyer, K.E., Wright, M. and Pruthi, S. (2009). Managing knowledge in foreign entry strategies: A resource-based analysis. *Strategic Management Journal*, 30(5): 557–574.

Miklian, J. (2019). Contextualising and theorising economic development, local business and ethnic cleansing in Myanmar. *Conflict, Security & Development*, 19(1): 55–78.

Norwegian Shipowners' Association (2015). *Migrants at Sea: Large Scale SAR Operations. Updated NSA Advice, Suggested Procedures, Debrief/Checklists*. https://rederi.no/en/DownloadFile/?file=63311 (retrieved 27 March 2020).

OCHA (2017). *The Business Case: A Study of Private Sector Engagement in Humanitarian Action*. https://www.unocha.org/sites/unocha/files/PSS-BusinessCase-FINAL_0.pdf (retrieved 21 November 2019).

OCHA (2020a). *Global Humanitarian Response Plan: COVID-19 – July Update*. https://reliefweb.int/sites/reliefweb.int/files/resources/GHRP-COVID19_July_update_0 .pdf (retrieved 9 September 2020).

OCHA (2020b). *Global Humanitarian Overview 2020 – Monthly Funding Update*. https://www.unocha.org/sites/unocha/files/GHO_Monthly_Update_31JUL2020 .pdf (retrieved 9 September 2020).

Oetzel, J. and Getz, K. (2012). Why and how might firms respond strategically to violent conflict. *Journal of International Business Studies*, 43: 166–186.

Oetzel, J., Getz, K. and Ladek, S. (2007). The role of multinational enterprises in responding to violent conflict: A conceptual model and framework for research. *American Business Law Journal*, 44: 331–358.

Oetzel, J. and Oh, C.H. (2014). Learning to carry the cat by the tail: Firm experience, disasters, and multinational subsidiary entry and expansion. *Organization Science*, 25: 732–756.

Oetzel, J. and Oh, C.H. (2015). Managing non-market risk: Is it possible to manage the seemingly unmanageable? In T.C. Lawton and T.S. Rajwani (Eds), *The Routledge Companion to Non-Market Strategy*. London: Routledge, 263–278.

Oh, C.H. and Oetzel, J. (2011). Multinationals' response to major disasters: How does subsidiary investment vary in response to the type of disaster and the quality of country governance? *Strategic Management Journal*, 32: 659–681.

Oh, C.H. and Oetzel, J. (2017). Once bitten twice shy? Experience managing violent conflict risk and MNC subsidiary-level investment and expansion. *Strategic Management Journal*, 38: 714–731.

Oliver, C. and Holzinger, I. (2008). The effectiveness of strategic political management: A dynamic capabilities framework. *Academy of Management Review*, 33(2): 496–520.

Østergaard, N. and Keller, T. (2015). *Maersk Line: Flygtlingekrise er en tragedie uden sidestykke*. Børsen, 21 April.

Reuters (2019). Ebola concentrated in Congo mining area, still an emergency: WHO. 18 October. https://www.reuters.com/article/us-health-ebola/ebola-concentrated -in-congo-mining-area-still-an-emergency-who-idUSKBN1WX2ED (retrieved 27 March 2020).

Sapienza, H.J., Autio, E., George, G. and Zahra, S.A. (2006). A capabilities perspective on the effects of early internationalization on firm survival and growth. *Academy of Management Review*, 31(4): 914–933.

Scherer, A.G. and Palazzo, G. (2011). The new political role of business in a globalized world: A review of a new perspective on CSR and its implications for the firm, governance, and democracy. *Journal of Management Studies*, 48: 899–931.

Scherer, A.G., Rasche, A., Palazzo, G. and Spicer, A. (2016). Managing for political corporate social responsibility: New challenges and directions for PCSR 2.0. *Journal of Management Studies*, 53: 273–298.

Shapiro, D., Hobdari, B., Oh, C.H., Kolk, A. and Peng, M. (2018). Multinational enterprises and sustainable development in the extractive and natural resource sectors. *Journal of World Business*, 53(1): 1–14.

Skovoroda, R., Goldfinch, S., DeRouen, K., and Buck, T. (2019). The attraction of FDI to conflicted states: The counter-intuitive case of US oil and gas. *Management International Review*, 59(2): 229–251.

Thornton, P.H., Ocasio, W. and Lounsbury, M. (2012). *The Institutional Logics Perspective: Foundations, Research, and Theoretical Elaboration*. Oxford: Oxford University Press.

Welch, C., Piekkari, R., Plakoyiannaki, E. and Paavilainen-Mäntymäki, E. (2011). Theorising from case studies: Towards a pluralist future for international business research. *Journal of International Business Studies*, 42(5): 740–762.

Wernerfelt, B. (1984). A resource-based view of the firm. *Strategic Management Journal*, 5(2): 171–180.

Westermann-Behaylo, M. (2009). Institutionalizing peace through commerce: Engagement or divestment in South African and Sudan. *Journal of Business Ethics*, 89(4): 417–434.

Witte, C.T., Burger, M.J., Ianchovichina, E.I. and Pennings, E. (2017). Dodging bullets: The heterogeneous effect of political violence on greenfield FDI. *Journal of International Business Studies*, 48: 862–892.

10. Developing parameters for the occurrence of modern slavery: towards an empirical validation of Crane's (2013) theory of modern slavery

Christoph Dörrenbächer and Lukas Ellermann

10.1 Introduction

Modern slavery is among the most evil phenomena in international business (IB). It is part of the illicit economy and a crime similar to trafficking migrants or smuggling drugs. Following recent statistics of the ILO, for every 1,000 people in the world there are 5.4 victims of modern slavery, with children and women disproportionately affected (ILO and Walk Free Foundation, 2017). Modern slavery can take various forms including the archaic form of chattel slavery, debt bondage slavery or contract slavery. Unlike other academic fields such as organisation and management studies (Cooke, 2003; Mena et al., 2016), IB research has shown little interest in dealing with modern slavery, even though it is beyond doubt that multinational corporations (MNCs) are often contributors to the persistence of modern slavery due to insufficient oversight of their global supply chains (Bales, 2012; Stringer and Michailova, 2018). While it is clear that MNCs have failed to take full responsibility for their value chains and do less than they could to seriously fight modern slavery (Burmester et al., 2019), the occurrence of modern slavery is influenced by a number of factors that lie beyond the reach of MNCs.

In order to understand why modern slavery occurs, some theoretical models of enabling conditions for the practice of modern slavery have been proposed. These show both similarities and differences in the conditions considered. Discussing these models, we focus in this chapter on Crane (2013), one of the most heavily cited academic papers on the subject matter of modern slavery. Following Crane, enabling conditions for modern slavery lie in the following five macro-institutional contexts: the regulatory, the socioeconomic, the industry, the geographical and the cultural context. While Crane supports his claim and five associated hypotheses by anecdotal evidence, an empirical validation of his theory and by that of the deeper reasons for the occurrence of modern slavery is missing. This chapter aims to contribute by addressing the next step towards an empirical validation of Crane's theory, namely, to develop appropriate parameters for the five contexts that are able to assess the propensity for modern slavery to occur. In essence, the chapter will discuss different measurement approaches, also taking into consideration the availability of robust national and international data sets. Going beyond this, one context, the cultural context, is statistically validated. Here, Hofstede's taxonomy of cultural dimensions is used, as comparative data is available for a large number of countries, covering many countries where modern slavery is widespread. It should be noted right from the outset that this chapter is not meant to discredit existing approaches that operate with somewhat different enabling conditions such as the vulnerability approach adopted by the World Slavery Index (Walk Free Foundation, 2018). Rather the aim of this chapter is to operationalise Crane's (2013) model in order to create the basis for a systematic comparison of approaches that explain the occurrence of modern slavery in further research. The chapter closes by assessing the contribution of the operationalised model to better map the likelihood of modern slavery to occur. It also shows some avenues for societally engaged IB research regarding modern slavery (Dörrenbächer and Michailova, 2019; see Chapter 11).

10.2   Literature review

One of the first (if not the first) mention of the term "modern slavery" is by the 1906 book entitled *A Modern Slavery* by Henry Woodd Nevinson, a British journalist and political commentator (Nevinson, 1906). It is a travel ethnography based on Nevinson's 1904/5 trip to the Portuguese overseas colonies Angola and the neighbouring islands of Sao Tomé and Principe. In his book, Nevinson describes how despite the legal abolition of slavery in its colonies in 1836, Portugal allowed slave trading and servitude through labour contracts and other formally legal employer relationships. It is these more subtle forms of slavery, Nevinson called "modern slavery". He writes: "I am aware that … the whole question of slavery is still before us. It has reappeared under the more pleasing names of 'indentured labor', 'contract labor', or compulsory labor ..." (Nevinson, 1906: 209).

Today, more than 100 years later, we know how right Nevinson was and is. Firstly, most recent data estimates that in 2016 a total of 40.3 million people were still living in modern slavery over a period of five years, and 89 million people experienced some form of slavery over a period of a few days up to several years (ILO and Walk Free Foundation, 2017: 25). Secondly, modern slavery has many faces. It includes a large variety of practices with not all practices being illegal everywhere or seriously prosecuted where they occur. Finally, abolishing modern slavery seems to be a herculean task today, as it was a hundred years ago. In 2015, government leaders around the world agreed to the Sustainable Development Goals (SDGs), among them SDG 8.7 to end forced labour, modern slavery, and human trafficking, as well as child labour in all its forms by 2030. Taking stock, four years later the Walk Free Foundation (2019: 5) concludes "progress made toward ending these abhorrent practices has been disgracefully marginal".

What is modern slavery?

There is no single definition of modern slavery, nor a common understanding of whether it is useful at all to separate slavery practices from other forms of exploitation and/or inhuman and degrading working and living conditions. Leaving the latter discussion aside here (for a treatment see Mende, 2019), there are three elements that characterise modern slavery practices: (1) the control of one person over another, (2) the involuntary aspect of this relationship including the use of structural power and/or physical violence and (3) the motivation to economically exploit the dominated person. In the words of Bales (2012: 6), modern slavery is "the total control of one person by another for the purpose of economic exploitation". There are numerous practices where the three elements come together: human trafficking, contract slavery, debt bondage, compulsory labour, chattel slavery, forced marriage, domestic slavery in private households, forced prostitution, war slavery, work in sweatshops, mining and brick lanes, cult and ritual slavery in religious shrines and sects, the selling of organs and so on (Mende, 2019).

Following Bales and Trodd (2013: 7), these practices can be subsumed under three main categories of slavery: (1) Chattel slavery, in which people are born, captured or sold into permanent slavery. This form resembles the historic form of slavery. Overall, it represents a small fraction of modern slavery and it is found most often in Northern and Western Africa. (2) Debt bondage slavery, in which people pledge themselves against loans for an undefined length of time but their work does not diminish the debt due to exorbitant interest rates or false accounting. This is the most common form of modern slavery but often overlooked. It is most often found in South Asia and appears in a large variety of industries. (3) Contract slavery, where fake employment contracts lure workers into the trafficking and enslavement process. This is the second largest form of modern slavery and rapidly growing. It is found in many countries, for instance in South-East Asia, Brazil, India and some Arab states, but also in the United States and Europe.

A different categorisation, including an estimate of their prevalence, is given by the ILO (ILO and Walk Free Foundation, 2017: 21f.). Here a distinction is made between forced labour and forced marriage. The report estimates that 24.9 million people (equals 62 per cent of a total of 40.3 million enslaved people) are subject to private or state imposed forced labour or forced sexual exploitation; and 15.4 million people (equals 38 per cent of a total of 40.3 million enslaved people) are living in a forced marriage, involving the loss of their freedom to move and their sexual autonomy as well as being subject to forced work within the context of marriage.

Modern slavery is by no means an issue involving only developing or emerging economy countries. No country in the world is exempt from modern slavery. Even in high GDP countries such as Germany there are a notable number of victims. According to the German Federal Criminal Police Office, there have been 356 legal proceedings with 430 identified victims of forced positions and 21 proceedings with 60 victims of forced work in 2018 (Bundeskriminalamt, 2019). In both cases the Federal Criminal Police Office assumes a very high number of unreported victims, next to victims of forced marriage that are not reported officially. The Global Slavery Index estimates that on any given day in 2016 there were 167,000 people in conditions of modern slavery in Germany (Walk Free Foundation, 2018).

In addition to modern slavery within their own borders, high GDP countries are involved in it through the import and consumption of products that are at a particular risk of modern slavery such as electronic devices (mobile phones, laptops, computers), garments, fish, cocoa and sugarcane (Walk Free Foundation, 2018). In most cases, the focal firms in the global value chains, dealing in these and other products that incorporate slave work, are headquartered in high GDP countries.

Conditions enabling modern slavery

To the best of our knowledge, the first systematic approach to theorise the enabling conditions for modern slavery was by Bales (2006). His paper entitled "Testing a theory of modern slavery" starts out with the general hypothesis that there is an unprecedented fall in the prices for slaves to a current all-time low, leading to an all-time high of the absolute number of people enslaved (2006: 4). According to Bales, this is due to three interrelated factors supporting the occurrence of slavery: (1) population growth, (2) impoverishment and (3) governmental corruption. To the first point: there is a steep growth in the worldwide population in particular in developing countries, leading to more supply of potential slaves as resources are not sufficient to support the increased population. To the second point: there is an impoverishment of large populations in the Global South due to civil wars, the looting of resources by dictators, failed reforms, migration to the cities and so on, leading to an increased vulnerability of individuals to be enslaved. To the third point: the collapse of the rule of law and a dilution of the state's monopoly for violence in many countries supports enslavement, as slaveholders may use violence to enslave people without facing sanctions from the government.

An empirical test by Bales (using UN and primary statistical data) showed that these general assumptions also hold true for explaining the prevalence of slavery at a country level. A number of significant indicators could be found for the three causal factors. Moreover, a second empirical test by Bales with an enhanced data set brought more indicators as well as a fourth causal factor that drives the occurrence of slavery in a country, that is, the presence of conflict and social unrest in the country (see Table 10.1).

To a considerable extent Bales' (2006) theory is represented in the 2018 Vulnerability Model of the Walk Free Foundation (2018: Appendix 2), the next approach to be discussed here. The Vulnerability Model underlies the Global Slavery Index, which is today's most elaborated empirical data source on modern slavery. In line with the theory of Bales, the model starts out with the assumption that systemic factors such as corruption, conflict and adverse environmental conditions are basic predictors as to where modern slavery is most likely to occur. Based on statistical analyses of existing data sources, the Vulnerability Model comes up with 23 individual risk variables in five major dimensions (see Table 10.1). A strong similarity to the approach of Bales (2006) shows in regard to the following three dimensions: "Governance issues" ("governmental corruption" in Bales, 2006), "lack of basic needs" ("impoverishment" in Bales, 2006) and "effects of conflicts" ("conflict and social unrest" in Bales, 2006), with the former two dimensions seen as those with the highest

Table 10.1   Factors/indicators for the prevalence of modern slavery in a country

Bales (2006): Theory of Modern Slavery

Governmental corruption	Impoverishment	Population growth	Conflict and social unrest
Level of corruption (Corruption Index)	Infant mortality	% of the population under the age of 14	Presence of conflict and social unrest
	Low food production	Population density	
	GDP per capita		
	Human Development Index		
	International indebtedness		

Walk Free Foundation (2018): Global Slavery Index/Vulnerability Model

Governance issues	Lack of basic needs	Inequality	Disenfranchised groups	Effects of conflict
Political instability	Cell phone users	Ability to obtain emergency funds	Acceptance of immigrants	Impact of terrorism
GSI government response	Undernourishment	Violent crime	Acceptance of minorities	Internal conflicts fought
Women's physical security	Social safety net	GINI coefficient	Same-sex rights	Internally displaced persons
Political rights	Ability to borrow money	Confidence in judicial proceedings		

Bales (2006): Theory of Modern Slavery

Regulatory quality	Tuberculosis
Disabled rights	Access to clean water
Weapons access	

Crane (2013): Theory of Modern Slavery/Conditions Enabling Slavery

Regulatory context	Socioeconomic context	Industry context	Geographic context	Cultural context
Strength of governance	Poverty and relative poverty	Labour intensity	Geographic isolation	Traditions
Issue attention	Education and awareness	Value distribution	Physical / political / psychological distance	Entrenched inequalities
	Unemployment	Elasticity of demand		Religious beliefs
		Legitimacy		
		Regional clustering		

Sources: Bales (2006); Crane (2013); Walk Free Foundation (2018).

explanatory power in the Vulnerability Model. Two dimensions, however, can be seen as an extension to Bales' theory. Following the Vulnerability Model, the level of inequality a country harbours as well as the treatment of disenfranchised groups, that is groups of people that are stripped of their power are predictors for the existence of modern slavery in a country.

The last approach to systematically understand enabling conditions for the existence of modern slavery discussed here is Crane (2013). Unlike the two previous approaches that emanate from civil society movements against modern slavery, the approach by Crane is rather inspired by academic research in business and management. This, for one, explains Crane's interest in a scientific understanding of "slavery management capabilities", which goes beyond the scope of the two previous approaches. It also explains why the approach of Crane assumes very different explanatory factors when assessing the enabling conditions for the occurrence of modern slavery in a country. Unlike the approaches of Bales (2006) and the Walk Free Foundation (2018), Crane (2013) claims that industry, geographic and cultural contexts have an impact on the occurrence of modern slavery. These contexts are standard variables considered in (international) business and management, when addressing the external environment of the firm.

10.3 Towards an operationalisation of Crane's (2013) theory of modern slavery

As laid out in the introduction, the aim of this chapter is to find ways of measuring the different conditions that according to Crane (2013) enable modern slavery. Thus, this chapter is not a critique of Crane's model, nor does it discuss its full application. It rather aims at providing suitable parameters/measurements for the various factors of the five contexts that according to Crane enable modern slavery.

To this end, we check for the existence of suitable data sets for each factor, with public availability and reliability being important conditions for their selection. Most data sources found are published by the World Bank, the Walk Free Foundation and the United Nations Development Programme. However, in a number of cases only proxies are available. In other cases, it is necessary to deconstruct factors in place in order to find suitable data to measure them. An example here is "population density" that is adjusted by the specifics of the geographical environment (deserts, mountains, islands) to measure geographic isolation. In a second step, the measurements chosen for the various factors of a slavery enabling context are combined. A problem, for instance, was the combination of factors where high values indicate a positive development (Education Index), with factors where high values indicate a negative development (Poverty Index), such as in Crane's "socioeconomic context". Subtracting the Education Index from a maximum Education Index of 1 resulted in a normalised parameter with higher numbers, indicating a negative development.

In the remainder of this section, the factors of the five slavery enabling contexts, as proposed by Crane, are introduced and parameters with measurements are proposed.

Regulatory context

Slavery is legally banned through international agreements in almost every country. A problem in a number of countries, including high GDP countries, however, is anti-slavery law enforcement. Anti-slavery law enforcement depends on the strength of governance in a country, with governance comprising "government effectiveness, regulatory quality, rule of law, political stability, control of corruption and voice and accountability to citizens" (Crane, 2013: 57). Weak governance increases the likelihood of modern slavery. Civil regulation through corporations, NGOs or the media can play a moderating role. NGOs and the media are crucial for issue attention and investigations into cases of modern slavery. As they do not have the power to execute the laws, they are mostly a supporting factor in banning modern slavery, through, for instance, scandalising cases and organising consumer boycotts. The activities of corporations can work in opposite directions. They may contribute to banning modern slavery, for instance through appropriate provisions in supplier contracts, but they may also contribute to a weak governance by bribery, corruption and direct use of modern slavery.

Measuring Crane's regulatory context is relatively straightforward as Crane's concept for the regulatory context is directly derived from the "Worldwide Governance Indicators" data set of the World Bank. These indicators collate information from a broad set of informants (households, companies, commercial business information providers, non-governmental organisations, public sector organisations; World Bank, 2018) and comprise the following indicators:

- Voice and Accountability (VA) – capturing perceptions of the extent to which a country's citizens are able to participate in selecting their government, as well as freedom of expression, freedom of association, and a free media.

- Political Stability and Absence of Violence/Terrorism (PV) – capturing perceptions of the likelihood of political instability and/or politically motivated violence, including terrorism.
- Government Effectiveness (GE) – capturing perceptions of the quality of public services, the quality of the civil service and the degree of its independence from political pressures, the quality of policy formulation and implementation, and the credibility of the government's commitment to such policies.
- Regulatory Quality (RQ) – capturing perceptions of the ability of the government to formulate and implement sound policies and regulations that permit and promote private sector development.
- Rule of Law (RL) – capturing perceptions of the extent to which agents have confidence in and abide by the rules of society, and in particular the quality of contract enforcement, property rights, the police and the courts, as well as the likelihood of crime and violence.
- Control of Corruption (CC) – capturing perceptions of the extent to which public power is exercised for private gain, including both petty and grand forms of corruption, as well as "capture" of the state by elites and private interests (World Bank, 2018).

Each individual indicator has a range from -2.5 to 2.5 with higher scores corresponding with a better governance. For example, in 2017 Afghanistan scored 1.33 for Government Effectiveness while Germany scored higher at 1.72 (World Bank, 2018). As the individual indicators are already standardised, it is possible to add them together and rank them:

VA Indicator + PV Indicator + GE Indicator + RQ Indicator + RL Indicator + CC Indicator = Governance Strength Indicator (-15 to 15)

Socioeconomic context

The socioeconomic context is crucial to understand the fundamental reasons behind modern slavery. Poverty is assumed to be the most relevant factor here since it creates a "fertile context for the worst kinds of labour exploitation" (Crane, 2013: 55). This relates not only to absolute poverty but also to relative poverty when different poverty levels trigger migration that involves intermediaries, trafficking people. Closely connected to poverty is unemployment. The absence of legal employment opportunities turns slave holders' offers into an alternative to safeguard economic survival. Finally, the level of education and the level of local awareness are important factors that drive modern slavery. Low levels of education support an understanding of slave work as being without alternatives. Low adult literacy limits workers' opportunity to avoid contract slavery (Andrees, 2008; Crane, 2013). Moreover, a low level of education inhibits the reporting of slavery incidents.

In order to measure the impact of the socioeconomic context of a country on the occurrence of modern slavery, we propose an average indicator made up of a country's relative poverty rate in per cent, a country's unemployment rate in per cent and the difference of the maximum United Nations Education Index (1) and the Education Index of the chosen country:

((Relative Poverty Rate + Unemployment Rate) + (1 - Education Index of chosen country)) / 3 = Parameter for the socioeconomic context

Numerical data to calculate the impact of the socioeconomic context is available from the UN Development Programme and the World Bank. Relative poverty in per cent is defined as "the percentage of the population living below the national poverty line" (World Bank, 2018), with the national poverty line being defined by the World Bank as the line below which a person's minimum nutritional, clothing, and shelter needs cannot be met. The unemployment rate is defined as "the share of the labour force that is without work but available for and seeking employment" (World Bank, 2018). The Education Index of the UN is part of the Human Development Index (HDI). It is calculated as the mean years of schooling and expected years of schooling (UNDP, 2018). The mean years of schooling is defined as the "average number of years of education received by people aged 25 and older" (UNDP, 2018: 25). The expected years of schooling is defined as the "number of years of schooling that a child of school entrance age can expect to receive if prevailing patterns of age-specific enrolment rates persist throughout the child's life" (UNDP, 2018: 25).

Industry context

Although modern slavery occurs in all industries, it tends to thrive in specific sectors. Following Crane, modern slavery is most prevalent in industries like agriculture, mining, basic manufacturing and poorly regulated service industries (for instance domestic work) (Crane, 2013). There are several interconnected factors that determine the attractiveness of an industry for slave work. One factor considered by Crane is labour intensity. In labour intensive industries, labour cost represents a large part of the overall costs for companies with high incentives to cut down labour costs through slave work. This is aggravated in industries that exhibit a low profit margin. The same goes for industries with a high elasticity of demand and a low elasticity of labour supply. Another factor relevant for the occurrence of modern slavery is the legitimacy of an industry. Crane proposes that low legitimacy industries, such as unauthorised mining, facilitate the use of modern slavery as those industries are already operating beyond the law, with no government oversight of labour conditions and mechanisms to escape state oversight already in place. In addition, the characteristics of slave industries (hidden-trailing is not easily done; incompatibility with social norms) leads to some level of regional clustering as "slaveholding skills" are transferred through personal connections in criminal networks (Crane, 2013).

One possibility to measure the industry context of modern slavery would be to analyse the industries of a country according to the well-known "three-sector model" of Fisher (1939). Due to modern slavery being most prevalent in primary industries, the first measurement needed would be the amount of people working in the primary industry. Next, it is necessary to define which service industries (tertiary sector) in a specific country are poorly regulated and which basic manufacturing industries (secondary sector) are in place. Employment figures for those secondary and tertiary industries need to be added to the number of workers in the primary industry. The total then needs to be divided by the overall working population of a country to get a relational parameter:

P = Amount of people working in the primary sector
Tpr = Amount of people working in poorly regulated industries in the tertiary sector
Sbm = Amount of people working in basic manufacturing (secondary sector)
WP = Overall working population of a country

((P + Tpr + Sbm)) / WP = Parameter for the industry context

A more fine-grained measurement of the industry context would require that specific industry conditions such as labour intensity, profit margins and demand elasticity are taken into consideration. While statistical data about labour intensity of subsectors might be available for some countries, data about profit margins and demand elasticity might be more difficult to obtain. For instance, to address the problem of low profit margins, the analysis could take the power and number of strong buyers and intermediary traders into consideration. High power of those groups can lead to a stronger pressure on prices and profit margins. However, translating such empirical findings into a numerical assessment of margins is difficult in itself. Moreover, carrying out such an analysis in multiple sub-industries in a large number of countries is possible but laborious.

Geographical context

According to Crane (2013), geographical isolation leads to a greater likelihood of slavery. This is due to three factors. Firstly, geographically isolated economic activity potentially faces a mismatch between labour demand and supply. High demand for labour (for instance in mining) is confronted with a small supply of labour due to the geographical location of the activity (such as in mountainous areas). This creates a high incentive to recruit labour either through forced migration or contract slavery with the workers transferred often being locked-in, lacking any means to return home. Secondly, geographical isolation shelters slaveholders from law enforcement, governmental oversight and trade union activity. While most countries in the world have officially abolished modern slavery (in the realm of international agreements such as article four of the Universal Declaration of Human Rights; New, 2015) law enforcement is particularly difficult in isolated areas. Similarly, trade union activity for better working conditions and human rights is more difficult to sustain in isolated areas. Thirdly, workers enslaved in isolated areas are easier to control as their actual possibility to escape is weak or non-existent. An extreme example is the case of slave workers in the fishing industry who literally have been imprisoned in ships for years (Stringer and Simmons, 2013; Tickler et al., 2018). Moreover, the isolation of enslaved workers due to language barriers (in case of forced migration over language borders) and due to limiting or not allowing communication with their homes creates a psychological distance that strengthens the dependence of the enslaved workers and reduces their force of resistance.

Measuring geographical isolation is a challenge as there is neither a generally agreed parameter, nor data. Hence, an appropriate parameter needs to be constructed. To this end, we take "population density" as a basis as it gives a rough indication about the number of people in an area. This parameter, however, fails in countries with an uneven spread of population. The Heihe–Tengchong line in China is an illustration of this phenomenon (see Figure 10.1). This imaginary line is used to divide China into an Eastern and a Western region. Despite the Western region covering 57.2 per cent of the landscape in 2015, it had only 6.1 per cent of the population. The Eastern region harboured 93.9 per cent of the population with only 42.8 per cent of the landscape covered (Li et al., 2018). Hence, while the overall population density of China would suggest a rather small potential for isolated areas, the uneven distribution speaks for a substantial potential of isolated areas in the Western part of China.

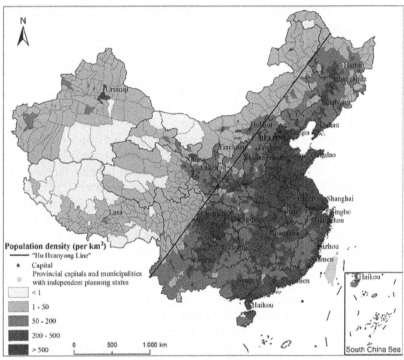

Source: Li et al. (2018: 5).

Figure 10.1   Population density in China in 2015

To cope with this problem, we propose a parameter that subtracts the population of highly populated areas from the overall population density. Our proposed parameter to cover the geographic context reads as follows:

((Population - population of high population areas)) / ((square kilometres - square kilometres of high population areas)) = Potential for Isolated Areas (PIA)

One challenge associated with the parameter is to define a threshold for highly populated areas. Another challenge is the granularity of data available. Is data only available for major regions (such as federal countries) or is there more fine-grained data for smaller regions and/or the divide between rural areas and agglomerations? Moreover, our proposed parameter would gain in precision if it could incorporate the distance from isolated regions to regions with a high population, as it can be argued that a sparsely populated area far away from every population hub is more isolated than an area bordering a population hub.

Another way of getting a more precise parameter would be to add geographical characteristics of the terrain such as mountainous regions, deserts, swamps and islands that all have a high isolation potential. This is especially important when our parameter PIA (Potential for Isolated Areas) shows similar results across countries. This, however, would require a detailed qualitative assessment for each country.

Cultural context

According to Crane (2013), cultural traditions, entrenched inequalities and religious beliefs that lead to discrimination against minorities and ethnic groups enhance the likelihood for modern slavery. Cultural traditions may provide a fertile breeding ground for modern slavery when the local population for reasons of customs and cultural tradition does not object a minority to be enslaved. An example for this is the lowest caste in the Indian caste system. Approximately 80 per cent of slaves in India are part of the Dalit caste, the lowest caste described as the untouchables (Crane, 2013). Religious beliefs may have a similar effect. They might provide some legitimacy for slave practices. According to Bales (2012), sex slavery in Thailand might be enabled by Thai Buddhism's belief in Karma and suffering.

Unlike the Vulnerability Model that indirectly studies cultural impacts through the presence of disenfranchised groups, in the remainder of this section we directly explore culture's impact on modern slavery. In order to do so we make use of Hofstede's theory of cultural dimensions as a predictor for modern slavery. Going beyond our elaborations on the previous contexts above, we will not only propose a parameter here, but exemplarily validate its usefulness by statistical analyses.

Despite criticism,[1] Hofstede's theory of cultural dimensions fulfils a number of criteria that are relevant for the attempt to directly uncover cultural predictors for modern slavery. It is not only that Hofstede's theory of cultural dimensions is still among the most often used taxonomies in IB research, but the theory also defines a number of distinct cultural dimensions/characteristics and quantifies these on a national or regional basis. Most importantly, data is available for a large number of countries/regions including those where modern slavery is widespread.

According to Hofstede, national culture or culture-based behaviour of national citizens can be characterised by the interplay of six distinct characteristics: Power Distance Index (PDI), Individualism vs. Collectivism (IDV), Masculinity vs. Femininity (MAS), Uncertainty Avoidance (UAI), Long-term vs. Short-term Normative Orientation (LTO) and Indulgence vs. Restraint (IVR). The Power Distance Index (PDI) indicates the extent to which unequal power distribution and hierarchical differences are accepted in a society. Individualism vs. Collectivism (IDV) describes the extent to which the self or the group constitutes the centre point of identification for the individual. Masculinity vs. Femininity (MAS) specifies the extent to which traditional masculine values like aggressiveness and assertiveness are valued. Uncertainty Avoidance (UAI) is defined as the extent to which uncertainty and ambiguity are tolerated/avoided. Societies with a Long-term Orientation (LTO) are described as societies that value traditions, virtues and behaviours that prepare for success in the future. Indulgence vs. Restraint (IVR) defines the degree of freedom that a society grants its citizens in fulfilling their desires. For example, according to Hofstede, Germans on average show a low to medium PDI (35) and IVR (40) while they display a medium to high level of IDV (67), MAS (66) and UAI (65) and score high on LTO (83).[2]

Below we correlate the actual data available for Hofstede's six cultural dimensions[3] with country data for the occurrence of modern slavery from the 2018 Global Slavery Index.[4] Given the missing linearity of the data sets, we use Spearman's rank correlation coefficient (Spearman's r) and check for significance. The effect size is measured according to Cohen (1988) with $r = 0.10$ being considered as a weak correlation, $r = 0.30$ being considered as a medium correlation, and $r = 0.50$ being considered as a strong correlation. The correlation analysis was carried out with the help of the IBM SPSS Statistics tool.

Hofstede's data is available for a large number of countries (such as Angola, Brazil, Germany) and three world regions (the Arab region, East and West Africa, each comprising several countries). Therefore, we run two different correlation analyses. In a first correlation analysis, we omitted all countries for which only regional data is available. In a second correlation analysis, we integrated Hofstede's regions and correlated them with the average value for the occurrence of modern slavery which the World Slavery Index reports for the countries of the region in question. Hofstede's cultural dimension scores vary between 0 and 100; the occurrence of modern slavery is calculated as slavery victims per 1,000 inhabitants of a country/region.

Correlation analyses

Table 10.2 shows the data pairs available (countries with information on the specific cultural dimension and information on the number of slavery victims per 1,000 inhabitants) and the results of our first correlation analysis, that is, omitting countries for which only regional data is available.

Table 10.2   Correlation analysis 1

	PDI	IDV	MAS	UAI	LTO	IVR
Data pairs	68	68	68	68	90	90
Spearman's r	0.490	0.342	0.026	0.038	0.056	0.452
Significance at the 0.01 level	Yes	Yes	No	No	No	Yes

The correlation analysis shows that Spearman's r is the highest with regard to the Power Distance Index (PDI), Indulgence (IVR) and Individualism (IDV). Moreover, these all exhibit a significance level of 0.01. Following Cohen, the r level for Power Distance of 0.490 represents a close to high correlation (threshold = 0.500) between the Power Distance Index (PDI) of a country and the relative number of victims of modern slavery in that country. The values for Indulgence (IVR) and Individualism (IDV) are between 0.3 and 0.5 and hence display a medium correlation according to Cohen. The values for Masculinity (MAS), Uncertainty Avoidance (UAI) and Long-term Orientation (LTO) are below 0.1 and hence do not show statistical correlation.

Table 10.3 shows the results of the second correlation analysis that has a slightly extended database now including three more data pairs with regional data on the Arab region, East and West Africa.

The results are pretty similar. Again Power Distance (PDI) shows the highest correlation with the relative number of victims of modern slavery (r = 0.496, now very close to a strong correlation) followed by Indulgence (IVR) (r = 0.420, medium correlation) and Individualism (IDV) (r = 0.347, medium correlation). Again, these results are significant at the 0.01 level. What is different to the results of the first correlation analysis is that the results for Long-term Orientation (LTO) now surpass the threshold of 0.100 (0.103) which indicates a weak correlation. However, this result is not significant at the 0.01 level.

Table 10.3   Correlation analysis 2

	PDI	IDV	MAS	UAI	LTO	IVR
Data pairs	71	71	71	71	93	93
Spearman's r	0.496	0.347	0.026	0.003	0.103	0.420
Significance at the 0.01 level	Yes	Yes	No	No	No	Yes

Direction of the observed correlations

A look at the scatterplots for the three significant results of the more encompassing correlation Analysis 2 (PD, IDV, IVR), informs about the direction of the observed correlations. We assume that a value ≥ 50 of a cultural dimension equals a high dimension value and respectively a value <50 a low dimension value. Moreover, given a global occurrence of 6.5 victims of modern slavery per 1,000 inhabitants, a corridor of 0.0 to 5.0 victims per 1,000 inhabitants in a particular county/region is defined as low incidence of modern slavery.

Figure 10.2 shows the data points for the relationship between a country's/region's Power Distance Index (PDI) and the relative number of victims of modern slavery in this country/region.

The trendline indicates that the relative number of victims of modern slavery increases with an increasing value of the PDI. Among the countries/regions with a low power distance (<50), Lithuania (PDI = 42) displays the highest relative number of victims, that is 5.8 victims of per 1,000 inhabitants. This number is still well below the global average of 6.5. All other countries/regions with a low power distance score between 0.0 and 5.0 victims per 1,000 inhabitants; defined here as low incidence of modern slavery.

Figure 10.3 shows the data points for the relationship between a country's/region's value for Individualism (IDV) and the relative number of victims of modern slavery in this country/region.

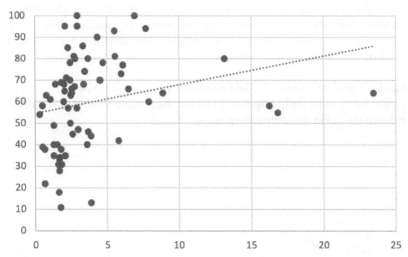

Note: x-axis: estimated number of victims per 1,000 inhabitants / y-axis: PDI values.

Figure 10.2   PDI / victims per 1,000 inhabitants

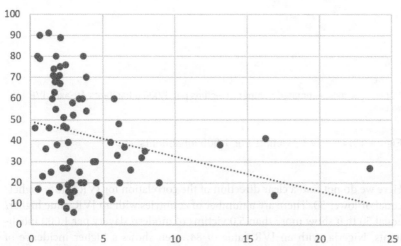

Note: x-axis: estimated number of victims per 1,000 inhabitants / y-axis: IDV values.

Figure 10.3   IDV / victims per 1,000 inhabitants

Here, the trendline indicates that countries/regions with a high value of Individualism (IDV ≥50) show a low incidence of modern slavery. An exception is Lithuania with a value for Individualism of 60 and 5.8 victims of modern slavery per 1,000 inhabitants.

Finally, Figure 10.4 shows the data points for the relationship between a country's/region's value for Indulgence (IVR) and the relative number of victims of modern slavery in this country/region.

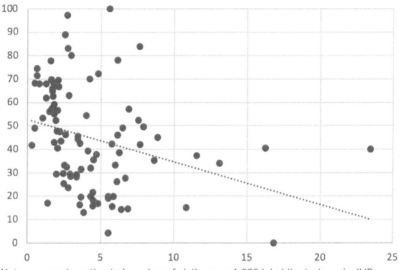

Note: x-axis: estimated number of victims per 1,000 inhabitants / y-axis: IVR values.

Figure 10.4   IVR / victims per 1,000 inhabitants

Here we do not find a clear direction of the correlation for IVR values higher/equal or lower 50. There are a number of countries with an IVR value higher/equal 50 that show more than 5.0 victims of modern slavery per 1,000 inhabitants. Nigeria, with an IVR value of 84, even shows a higher incidence of modern slavery than the global average with 7.7 victims of modern slavery per 1,000 inhabitants.

10.4 Discussion

The high to medium correlations we found in our analysis regarding the cultural dimensions of PDI and IDV with the occurrence of modern slavery suggest two conclusions.

Firstly, a high power distance supports modern slavery. This can be sustained by the following arguments. According to Hofstede, a high power distance goes hand in hand with a high acceptance of hierarchical differences in a society. A high acceptance of hierarchical differences lowers the perception in society that enslavement is extremely unfair and hence lowers political resistance. For the same reason, external initiatives to abolish modern slavery might find little support. Finally, similar to some religious beliefs that support modern slavery, an internalised acceptance of even extreme hierarchical differences might ease the enslavement of individuals. In such a setting even slave holders with weak "slave management capabilities" (Crane, 2013: 52) might feel inclined and be able to engage in modern slaveholding.

Secondly, high values for Individualism hamper modern slavery. A high value for Individualism and hence a low value for Collectivism exhibit a lower number of victims of modern slavery. Following Hofstede, "Individualism is the extent to which people feel independent" as opposed to Collectivism where people "know their place" in life, which is determined socially.[5] Hence, Individualism might trigger a stronger individual resistance to being enslaved. Moreover, Individualism creates a political and societal disinclination to accept slavery practices, including an openness to accept external initiatives to abolish modern slavery.

Overall, our analysis shows that Hofstede's theory of cultural dimensions offers some explanation for the impact of the cultural context on the occurrence of modern slavery. However, the fact that we only found close to strong respectively medium statistical correlations for two dimensions (PDI and IDV) as well as the abundant critique of Hofstede's theory in general rather suggests a careful use of these indicators.

10.5 Conclusion

Modern slavery persists despite a broad consensus that it is one of the most evil of contemporary crimes (Enderwick, 2019). Understanding the reasons for why, when and where modern slavery occurs is a key prerequisite to fight modern slavery. This too is the background of approaches that aim to come up with sets of indicators for the occurrence of modern slavery. While Bales' (2006) Theory of Modern Slavery and the Vulnerability Model that underlies the Global Slavery Index (Walk Free Foundation, 2018) show a strong similarity regarding the proposed indicators, Crane's (2013) model of Slavery Enabling Conditions is somewhat different. Unlike the two other models, Crane's model is not inspired by an abolitionist perspective but rather represents an academic's view. This explains the selection of indicators that are standard variables used in (international) business and management research to conceptualise the business environment. Given the publication context, and the fact that Crane (2013) did not operationalise his constructs, the purpose of this chapter was to propose parameters for the five enabling contexts that drive modern slavery according to Crane: the regulatory, the socioeconomic, the industry, the geographical, and the cultural context. Moreover, as an example, we engaged in an empirical validation of the parameter we proposed for the cultural context.

In the remainder, we will assess the potential contribution of Crane's model to a better understanding of why modern slavery occurs. Our frame of reference is the Vulnerability Model that underlies the Global Slavery Index (Walk Free Foundation, 2018), which is today's most elaborated empirical data source on modern slavery. Despite its wide use and its practical relevance to understand and predict where modern slavery is most likely to occur, the Walk Free Foundation (2018) itself maintains that its Vulnerability Model is still "in the early stages of development and, as such, it should be viewed as iterative" (2018: 142).

Our operationalisation of Crane's model only brought slight differences to the operationalisation of the Vulnerability Model regarding the socioeconomic and the regulatory context (called: "lack of basic needs/inequality" and "governance issues" in the Vulnerability Model). However, we also proposed new parameters for the three (international) business and management specific factors in Crane's (2013) model, that is for the industry, the geographical and the cultural context. An exemplary empirical test of Crane's model for the cultural context using Hofstede's theory of cultural dimensions brought some evidence that a high Power Distance Index supports modern slavery while high scores for Individualism hamper modern slavery. Further research is needed to empirically validate the remaining new parameters we proposed for the industry and the geographical context. Here in-depth search and harmonisation of incommensurate national data sets and laborious qualitative analysis are needed, which goes beyond the scope of this chapter. Moreover, once all parameters are validated, the interaction of parameters needs to be studied in-depth, too, in order to realise the full explanatory power of the model.

It is obvious that estimating modern slavery with statistical means has limitations. Estimating modern slavery creates a need to define what is and what is not considered as modern slavery, with the boundaries being blurred in many cases. Moreover, in order to detect actual cases of modern slavery, it might be necessary to scale down parameters from a national to a regional or even local level, where data availability is even more of an issue than it is for the national level. These limitations call for both further conceptual work as well as the collection of new, more appropriate primary data. While such work is far from developing a "grand theory", it is an area where societally engaged IB scholars can meaningfully contribute.

Acknowledgement

The authors thank Snejina Michailova, Brent Burmester, Niina Nummela, Peter Zettinig, Julia Thielemann and the editors of the volume for their very useful comments on an earlier draft of this chapter.

Notes

1. There are numerous concerns regarding Hofstede's theory of cultural dimensions. For instance, Schwartz (1999) maintained that surveys (as applied by Hofstede) are not an appropriate instrument to measure culture. Søndergaard (1994) criticised that almost all data gathering for Hofstede's theory of cultural dimensions took place in the subsidiaries of one MNC (IBM). McSweeney (2002) argued that countries/nations are inappropriate frames of reference for culture as many cultures cut across nations/countries and almost all countries exhibit distinct subcultures.
2. See https://www.hofstede-insights.com/country-comparison/germany/ (accessed 24 June 2020).
3. See https://www.hofstede-insights.com/ (accessed 1 May 2020).
4. See https://www.globalslaveryindex.org/2018/findings/ (accessed 1 May 2020).
5. See https://geerthofstede.com/culture-geert-hofstede-gert-jan-hofstede/6d-model -of-national-culture/ (accessed 26 June 2020).

References

Andrees, B. (2008). Forced labour and trafficking in Europe: How people are trapped in, live through and come out. ILO Working Paper 57. Geneva: International Labour Office.

Bales, K. (2006). Testing a theory of modern slavery. http://freetheslaves.net/f/Testing-a-Theory-of-Modern-Slavery.pdf (retrieved 10 October 2019).

Bales, K. (Ed.) (2012). *Disposable People: New Slavery in the Global Economy*. Berkeley, CA: University of California Press.

Bales, K. and Trodd, Z. (Eds) (2013). *To Plead Our Own Cause: Personal Stories by Today's Slaves*. Ithaca, NY: Cornell University Press.

Bundeskriminalamt (2019). *Menschenhandel und Ausbeutung*. Bundeslagebild 2018, Wiesbaden.

Burmester, B., Michailova, S. and Stringer, C. (2019). Modern slavery and international business scholarship: The governance nexus. *critical perspectives on international business*, 15(2/3): 139–157.

Cohen, J. (1988). *Statistical Power Analysis for the Behavioral Sciences*. New York: Routledge.

Cooke, B. (2003). The denial of slavery in management studies. *Journal of Management Studies*, 40(8): 1895–1918.

Crane, A. (2013). Modern slavery as a management practice: Exploring the conditions and capabilities for human exploitation. *Academy of Management Review*, 38(1): 49–69.

Dörrenbächer, C. and Michailova, S. (2019). Editorial: Societally engaged, critical international business research: A programmatic view on the role and contribution of *cpoib*. *critical perspectives on international business*, 15(2/3): 110–118.

Enderwick, P. (2019). Understanding cross-border crime: The value of international business research. *critical perspectives on international business*, 15(2/3): 119–138.

Fisher, A. G. B. (1939). Production, primary, secondary and tertiary. *Economic Record*, 15(1): 24–38.

ILO and Walk Free Foundation (2017). *Global Estimates of Modern Slavery: Forced Labour and Forced Marriage*. Geneva: International Labour Office.

Li, M., He, B., Guo, R., Li, Y., Chen, Y. and Fan, Y. (2018). Study on population distribution pattern at the county level of China. *Sustainability*, 10, 3598.

McSweeney, B. (2002). Hofstede's model of national cultural differences and their consequences: A triumph of faith – a failure of analysis. *Human Relations*, 55(1): 89–118.

Mena, S., Rintamäki, J., Fleming, P. and Spicer, A. (2016). On the forgetting of corporate irresponsibility. *Academy of Management Review*, 41(4), 720–738.

Mende, J. (2019). The concept of modern slavery: Definition, critique, and the human rights frame. *Human Rights Review*, 20(2): 229–248.

Nevinson, H.W. (1906). *A Modern Slavery*. London and New York: Harper and Brothers.

New, S. (2015). Modern slavery and the supply chain: The limits of corporate social responsibility? *Supply Chain Management: An International Journal*, 20(6): 697–707.

Schwartz, S.H. (1999). A theory of cultural values and some implications for work. *Applied Psychology*, 48(1): 23–47.

Søndergaard, M. (1994). Hofstede's consequences: A study of reviews, citations and replications. *Organization Studies*, 15(3): 447–456.

Stringer, C. and Michailova, S. (2018). Why modern slavery thrives in multinational corporations' global value chains. *Multinational Business Review*, 26(3): 194–206.

Stringer, C. and Simmons, G. (2013). Forced into slavery. *Samudra Report*, 65, 8–13.

Tickler, D., Meeuwig, J.J., Bryant, K., David, F., Forrest, J.A.H., Gordon, E., Joudo Larsen, J., Oh, B., Pauly, D., Sumaila., U.R. and Zeller, D. (2018). Modern slavery and the race to fish. *Nature Communications*, 9(1): 1–9.

UNDP (2018). *Education Index*. http://hdr.undp.org/en/content/education-index (retrieved 19 February 2019).

Walk Free Foundation (2018). *Global Slavery Index 2019*. https://www.globalslaveryindex .org/ (retrieved 10 October 2019).

Walk Free Foundation (2019). *Measurement, Action, Freedom 2019. An independent assessment of government progress towards achieving UN Sustainable Development Goal 8.7*. https://www.globalslaveryindex.org/ (retrieved 17 September 2019).

World Bank (2018). *The Worldwide Governance Indicators*. https://www.govindicators .org (retrieved 23 February 2019).

11. The future of international business research: theorising on unfolding phenomena in a complex, dynamic world

Peter Zettinig and Niina Nummela

11.1   Introduction

According to Delios' (2017: 391–393) assessment of the international business (IB) research community's activities, "In strict counterpoint to the real world of IB, contemporary research in IB is outdated, staid and boring […] the interesting in IB is to be found in non-quantifiable phenomena". This evaluation is painful and stimulates reflections. IB is an enormously dynamic and fruitful field of inquiry (Pitelis and Teece, 2018), with complexly intertwined and exciting empirical phenomena. From the beginnings of the young field, empirical observations have given reason to ask why the world is how it is. For instance, economist John Dunning (1958), an early and influential contributor to IB, observed that US-owned manufacturing firms in Britain achieve higher productivity than domestically owned producers did. This triggered exploration and actions, leading to explanations for originally counterintuitive facts as a starting point for a phenomenon-driven field of inquiry. The purpose of this chapter is to outline and discuss a *futures-oriented perspective* of IB research to enhance its relevance and practical utility. Our use of the plural *futures* is intentional, as we subscribe to the view that the *Future* is not determined; contrary to the present and the past, it contains no facts. Instead, it consists of possible trajectories and outcomes, many of which can and are influenced by our actions.

To start, we should look at the surrounding changes, take notes, ponder the connections between unfolding events and wonder how they will affect the thinking and actions of students and practitioners of IB. We need to confront the world of concepts and explanations with the empirical (cf. Piekkari et al., 2009) and changing world around us. We should seek the statistical outliers and ask whether this is a "talking pig" (Siggelkow, 2007: 20) – a phenomenal occurrence observed in a single case that challenges our generalised assumptions. However, where should we start?

Students of IB often appreciate the holistic phenomenal richness and dynamics. They are passionate about challenging ethical phenomena at the fringe of our mainstream consciousness, for instance, in dealing with issues like modern slavery (see Chapter 10), global structural violence, international money laundering or organised crime, corruption and ruthless opportunistic behaviours and "neglected crises"; despite their enormous importance, such issues are mostly treated as niche topics (Ahen and Zettinig, 2015; Dörrenbächer and Gammelgaard, 2019). At the same time, the mainstream IB research community favours reductionist examinations, often eliminating the surprising elements. We need to ask *what emerging phenomena* are important, interesting and awake our curiosity. Do we need to rethink the ontological and epistemological traditions of IB and widen rather than narrowing the scope of research (cf. Buckley et al., 2017)? *How* do we study important emerging phenomena when they are still in the making? What *theorising approaches* do we need for dealing with the time, dynamics, richness and uncertainties involved when interested in ongoing change? What *value* can IB research provide for a broad variety of constituencies? How do we take the *future* into account?

11.2 Emerging phenomena

IB as a research field has a healthy tendency to question its relevance and debate what the big research questions are that shape our disciplinary curiosity (e.g. Buckley et al., 2017; Delios, 2017). One example of a potentially rising research question is the role of multinational enterprises (MNEs) in the future. According to an article in *The Economist* (2017), although MNEs dominate many industries, global firms are starting to retreat. Interestingly, as Eleanor Westney (2019) notes, the same magazine published a survey in 1972 stating that MNEs are facing a period of decline. Westney (2019) states that the reasons given in both articles are remarkably similar and can be attributed to three sets of factors, which are as follows: (1) growing internal complexity is challenging effective control in MNEs, (2) national governments are threatening the openness of the global business environment and (3) MNEs' advantages are diminishing in terms of their scale economies and geographic dispersion due to technological advances. The analysis (The Economist, 2017) is considering a downward trend in the share of exports that participate in cross-border supply chains and a decline in total foreign direct investment (FDI) flows as a percentage of global gross domestic product since the 2008 crisis. Moreover, the article takes note of the falling rate of return of FDIs by MNEs over the past thirty years and illustrates the developments from 2016 to 2017 because MNEs' overall return on equity (ROE) is increasingly resembling local firms' ROE levels.

The outlined explanations are conclusive within the chosen timeframes, evidencing less room overall for arbitrage in globally integrated business models. Rising incomes in major transition economies like China are decreasing their attractiveness as production locations but increasing their attractiveness as markets. Further, due to the development of transition economies' institutions, other previous arbitrage advantages are diminishing for MNEs. Yet, this perspective underemphasises the changes MNEs are undergoing. The MNE as an organisational form is not passively waiting for evolutionary selection to take its toll; rather, it is a highly adaptable entity. As such, it develops new strategies and sources of competitive advantages and generates structures that reap the benefits provided by environmental changes (Pitelis and Teece, 2018).

A recent report from the McKinsey Global Institute (Bughin et al., 2019) describes changes in value chains between 2007 and 2017 and finds that global trade intensity has decreased by 5.6 percentage points (from 28.1 per cent to 22.5 per cent, while growing in absolute terms). Simultaneously, services trade has grown 60 per cent faster than goods trade. According to the report, this is due to the following factors: (1) the rising share of emerging markets of global consumption, (2) reduced cross-border transfers because of the self-sufficiency of emerging markets and (3) the increasing importance of cross-border data flows and new technologies (i.e. digital platforms, automation, artificial intelligence [AI], Internet of Things). These documented changes mean that *MNEs are not only adapting to a global transition but are also part of driving it* as they shift to more localised operations (resulting in similar performance to domestic actors), as research on emerging economies' MNEs is showing (e.g. Buckley et al., 2018).

MNE global activities have changed, locations are evolving, and at the same time, new business models and technological advances are generating new means for creating value. Moreover, some cross-border activities may go undetected due to a lack of measures for identifying when immaterial value flows are transferred across borders. Complex value-creation setups have emerged, and knowledge, capabilities and technology are developed at multiple locations and transferred within MNEs and to strategic partners. Many of these flows are currently not seen as MNEs' cross-border activities; they appear to be local generation of value. This also implies that less of the value creation deployed by MNEs is to reap labour-cost arbitrage because the realisation of value uses high local input by locally collaborating firms. These changes have resulted from the interactions between dynamics of developments in the macro-environment (institutional and non-institutional) and actions by MNEs and their stakeholders. They have produced a fast-paced global business environment in which traditional strategic planning is challenged and proactive or reactive behaviour is increasingly rewarded (Wiltbank et al., 2006), making local or regional value creation in collaborative settings more important. However, this has led to an environment in which uncertainties are growing and where alertness, flexibility and resilience are key capabilities. Therefore, according to Bughin et al. (2019), firms are more selective of the positions along the value chain at which they want to compete, including geographic locations.

To respond to changes, MNEs favour localised value chains with collaborating partners rather than transactional relationships, which has far-reaching implications for MNE structure and suppliers' strategies. It also partially explains why the ROEs of MNEs and local firms may increasingly align (The Economist, 2017) in several industries. The increasing intertwining of firms' value-creating activities in collaborative arrangements also suggests the need to gain new understandings of governance models between them (e.g. Strange and Zucchella, 2017; see Chapter 2) and how international cooperation is coordinated and controlled through alternative modes. In sum, these trends favour advanced economies and firms with strengths in knowledge-intensive industries that are driven by technology innovations and service-based market approaches, which require a highly skilled workforce. Developing economies that may benefit from these changes are those near large consumer markets because responsive production systems seek to move closer to consumer demand (Bughin et al., 2019).

The MNE as an organisational form is adaptable, but the capability to shape the environment does not mean that all firms thrive as some have better fit with the changing environment. A PWC (2018) publication comparing the *Global Top 100 Companies by Market Capitalization* 2009–2018 gives some indication of this (see Table 11.1).

Table 11.1   Global top 10 by market capitalisation

March 2018

Technology Firms	Country	Number in Ranking
Apple	USA	1
Alphabet	USA	2
Microsoft	USA	3
Tencent	CHINA	5
Facebook	USA	8

Consumer Services	Country	Number in Ranking
Amazon	USA	4
Alibaba	CHINA	7

Financial Services	Country	Number in Ranking
Berkshire Hathaway	USA	6

March 2009

Natural Resources	Country	Number in Ranking
Exxon Mobile	USA	1
PetroChina	CHINA	2
Royal Dutch Shell	UK	9

Telecommunication	Country	Number in Ranking
AT&T	USA	7
China Mobile	CHINA/HK	5

Retail	Country	Number in Ranking
Walmart	USA	3

Financial Services	Country	Number in Ranking

March 2018

	Country	Number in Ranking
JPMoean Chase	USA	9
Healthcare	**Country**	**Number in Ranking**
Johnson&Johnson	USA	10

March 2009

	Country	Number in Ranking
ICBC	CHINA	4
Consumer Goods	**Country**	**Number in Ranking**
P&G	USA	10
Technology Firms	**Country**	**Number in Ranking**
Microsoft	USA	6
Healthcare	**Country**	**Number in Ranking**
Johnson&Johnson	USA	8

Source: Adapted from PWC (2018).

In 2018, only Microsoft and Johnson & Johnson remained on the list, with four current firms not being among the top 100 a decade earlier. While we accept that such listings are selective[1] and indicative of changes, this finding supports the idea of transforming business landscapes. Knowledge- and technology-intensive service MNEs (i.e. building business platforms; Van Alstyne et al., 2016), which are less focused on labour-cost arbitrage and more focused on intra-regional geographies (Bughin et al., 2019), have been on the rise. Yet, MNEs with a focus on goods trade and globally integrated value chains have become less appreciated, including from an investor-centric perspective.

The value-creation models of MNEs deserve our attention. The firms that enjoyed investors' future confidence a decade ago integrated asset-heavy operations at a global level. In particular, firms in natural resource production and distribution were proportionally overrepresented. These firms – in the words of Van Alstyne et al. (2016) – deployed a linear *pipeline value chain* that relied heavily on scale economies' effects on the unit cost, resource-seeking activities on the supply and market-seeking activities on the demand side. However, investors' affection has shifted to firms that employ ecosystem-centred business models relying on highly scalable technologies that create economies with often negligible variable unit cost and build the bulk of their value by utilising network economies. These models produce increasing returns exponentially through growing network membership. These changes at the business model level have altered the bases of MNEs' competitive advantages and influenced strategy; consequently, they have modified the organisational forms and relational governance modes (Kano, 2018) required to reap benefits from the business.

According to Westney (2019: 5), what has remained the same can be expressed as follows:

> What the 21st century IB models [i.e. developed through IB research] have in common with 20th century models is the assumption of convergence from variety towards a single "ideal type" (in both the Weberian and the normative sense) of the MNE.

In her view, this aspect stems from the strong economist tradition in IB aiming to develop "the theory of the firm" as one general model, and maybe empirically, the assumed shared global institutional and competitive pressures, which may lead to convergence over time. Another aspect that may influence this in IB is the aim to uncover universal knowledge, which assumes generalisations across contexts (Meyer, 2007; Tsui, 2004), and ironically, has been accused of mostly ignoring context or being context-free (Michailova, 2011; Oesterle and Wolf, 2011), along with a wide neglect of *time* (and implicitly, change).

After pondering these empirical changes in the world of IB and MNE in this *setting the scene section*, which purposefully leans on analysis by consultants and other practitioners of IB, in the next section of this chapter, we reflect on two exemplary conceptual approaches in mainstream IB research. These provide shared reference points for a discussion on theorising approaches that may be able to take time, changes and multiple perspectives into account.

11.3   Theorising with envelopes

We start this section with initial considerations on the question of relevance, which is a tricky item. While calls to become more relevant are frequent, and the IB community's greater influence on decision-makers is desirable (e.g. Collinson, 2017; Corley and Gioia, 2011), relevance is not a generalisable characteristic. Rather, it depends on the audience, which has idiosyncratic interests and concerns. Stakeholders are biased by at least their situational, geographic, political and temporal contexts. Their meaning is created within organisational and social communities and relies on their experiences with questions on "what is happening" or "what to do next" (Wiltbank et al., 2006). However, relevance-as-perspective is a sensitive issue. When researchers *take* perspective, we may also be prone to biases or neglect of others' perspectives, often deeming managerial relevance to be inferior to scholarly interests, where it is added as an afterthought in the final discussion section of papers. However, as for many research disciplines dealing with complex social phenomena, this is a well-known problem and part of the decisions that needs to be weighted when balancing theorising between parsimony and comprehensiveness and to clearly establish boundaries and discuss limitations.

Inspired by Dunning's (2000) reflections on the "envelope", our discussion focuses on central IB theories and frameworks as widely shared references in the community of IB scholars. Here, envelopes serve as organising vehicles to investigate complex phenomena, and we utilise them as integrative categories for a variety of extant and future explanations developed within IB or other disciplines. This approach has the advantage of analysing emerging phenomena commencing from established explanations, but instead of establishing a theoretical paradigm, remaining open for extensions to consider inclusion of new theoretical explanations that emerge and develop over time. In early stages of a new theoretical development, the focus is often less on rigour and more concerned with the constructive potential of theorising, which can also generate novel relevance. Dunning suggested that O, L and I of the eclectic framework can be used as envelopes for emerging theories to contribute to explanations about MNEs. An envelope approach can be used to form probing questions that engage curiosity and frame the complications seen by practitioners in a stated *relevance-as-perspective* problem setting, depending on whose point of view we take. It serves to interpret and define phenomenal challenges *sufficiently* while being theoretically *loose* enough to provide plasticity that depends on a perspective purpose.

Dunning's (2000) envelope discussion engaged in questioning how the Eclectic Paradigm relates to some context-specific economic and business theories, allowing the framework to be agile for adopting new theoretical insights and appropriate for identifying and understanding newly emerging phenomena. The three-part paradigm (consisting of ownership [O]-specific advantages, location [L]-specific advantages and attractions of places and regions and the internalisation [I] choices of organisational modalities) was originally developed to analyse the complex constellations of competitive advantages of enterprises vis-à-vis their peers seeking to engage or expand their foreign direct investments. For our purpose, each of the three factor sets serves as *categories* of explanations to pay attention to what contributing factors *may* matter than a simple reductionist model. Claims of a universal reductionist model have been a major source of criticism of the paradigm (e.g. Itaki, 1991), due to the inseparability of ownership and location advantages or issues of modelling related to balancing *parsimony and comprehensiveness* (see Whetten, 1989). However, when envisioning it as a sufficiently framing and necessarily theoretically loose framework, it can be a source of inspiration on how to progress new research questions for emerging phenomena and a ground for potential relevance. In a similar vein, and exemplary for the strategic, organisational and managerial trajectories treated in IB/M, the *global integration* (GI) and *local responsiveness* (LR) dimensions (e.g. Bartlett and Ghoshal, 1987, 1991; Prahalad and Doz, 1987) can be seen as envelopes. The framework focuses on core strategic dimensions and the choices formed by sources of efficiency and differentiation. The two dimensions form conceptual ideal types, defining possible strategic positions. These ideal types are immensely useful because they are not limited by empirical occurrences, but instead, are open to positions that may emerge in the future, providing a range of possibilities and choices regarding the strategic journey on which to bet. Furthermore, the subsequent requirements of a selected strategic direction can be defined by outlining the implications organisational solutions can deliver and how to manage them.

The framework is an outcome of a long-term research project in which scholars and practitioners worked in close collaboration to better understand how MNEs *should* operate (Westney, 2019). During the framework's development, it could capture pioneering MNEs' choices and even foresee, or influence, the strategies MNE would develop subsequently in the *then* future.

The framework was a response to the rise of Japanese MNEs in Western countries. At the time of framework development, Japanese MNEs were conquering the world, and Western MNEs were desperate to understand how they did it, for instance, by investigating the nexus between strategic imperatives that could explain how organisational heritages influence organisational choices. This allowed decision-makers to define the features of organisational models that are necessary to deliver the benefits of strategy. The GI dimension, seeking to generate efficiencies based on standardisation, diverse sets of economies and advantages found in different locations, is a way of establishing where certain MNEs' competitive advantages originate when comprehending the international playing field as one market. The LR dimension contrasts how certain MNEs produce viability by adapting their models to specific market settings that require, for diverse institutional reasons, a differentiated approach that relies on local integration of productive factors. The research community working on this conceptual *ideal typology* established that the result of MNE gradually engaged in both dimensions, unifying the benefits of global efficiencies with LR, envisioned early and predicted largely before the fact, that most MNEs would aspire to transnational solutions realised by corresponding organisational structures. The interactions between scholars and practitioners during the development of the conceptual typology assured practical relevance because it was directly useful for managers to base their decisions regarding the future on a logical set of rationales. In return, it created the conceptual basis to engage in empirical work and generated shared schemata that allowed new research questions to emerge (e.g. the emergence of the neo-global corporation; Mees-Buss et al., 2019). The GI/LR framework is still considered by many as "the model" in the field of international management, and it has had an enormous effect on subsequent research, practice and education (Kostova et al., 2016). As recent examples, it has been used by Banerjee et al. (2019) to investigate the non-market corporate political strategies of MNC subsidiaries and by Venaik and Midgley (2019) to identify the archetypes of marketing mix standardisation-adaptation in MNC subsidiaries.

Both envelope frameworks, OLI and GI/LR, can serve as *examples* when pondering how to focus on relevance, producing dynamic explanations in changing environments and serving as the engines to generate research questions that put the IB community in a proactive role, establishing legitimacy for important stakeholders. This is not only important for MNEs but also for policymakers, civil society leaders and others who have gained important roles in the unfolding of IB. While these are central, "blockbuster" theories in IB, we use them here, due to their fame, to illustrate how envelopes could be useful for integrating theoretical advances and practical perspectives. Similarly, other real-world problems, such as the increasing influence of the platform business model-based MNE discussed in the previous section, could be served by organising them through different theoretical envelopes. For instance, one problem taken from a critical perspective on MNE management is the question of power in organisations and management of precarious work practices, often discussed in platform models, which create different forms of organisational realities in different institutional settings (cf. Geppert, 2015).

Table 11.2 constitutes an outline of categories that could be developed for an envelope approach to design an IB research programme. The envelope categories are anchor points for questions concerning *emerging phenomena* that are unfolding. The envelope categories are organising frameworks to structure abstract problems in complex dynamic settings, which are intertwined and often require decision-making under uncertainty. Envelope categories inspire practical questions about unfolding phenomena and may provoke perspectives on the relevant level of engagement with the phenomenon leading to pre-research questions. These questions aim to identify which levels of analysis are concerned in the explanation of phenomena in the making. These pre-research questions help in determining what parsimonious explanations may be useful, which aspects to consider and what boundary conditions to set. However, before engaging in forming research questions, this approach suggests instituting a relevance test asking, "Who cares?"

The exemplary framework presented in Table 11.2 leans on Whetten's (1989) list of valuable questions to work towards making a theoretical contribution. However, instead of the initial focus on theoretical reduction (what, why and how), we may initially consider the relevance perspective and the question of "Who cares?" before determining final research questions. This helps avoid leaving the "practical implications" section to degrade into an ex post addition. Instead of being initially focused on the research communities who will find theoretical work useful, we should aspire to ask *who the stakeholders are* within the unfolding phenomena. Whose angle do we take (or not take)? Who is our theorising creating value for? What provides real-world meaning to our work? Framing theorising perspectives to provide answers for someone has an *explicit quality* to generate relevance and value. It considers idiosyncratic viewpoints, situational and temporal features and even assignments of meaning and experience.

Table 11.2   Theorising through envelopes

Unfolding phenomena (illustrative examples[a])	Exemplary envelope categories	Pre-research questions (→ following)	Who cares? (Relevance-as-perspective[b])	What? How? Why?
MNEs with fewer assets appear to grow bigger, dominate own markets	Ownership-specific advantages	What drivers for internal advantages reshape the competitiveness of MNEs?	Which perspectives create utility and for whom? How do these perspectives relate/contradict?	Which concepts allow us to explain certain aspects? How do these concepts anchor in our frameworks and interrelate?
Knowledge and capabilities types of resources are more effective than location-bound assets	Location-specific advantages	How are location advantages shaping in ecosystems?	What vested interests create which biases? How are future interests shaped by current actions?	Which are necessary and sufficient? Are the resulting frameworks holistic enough? Do they
Roles in value chains and nets are more defined, partners are kept closer, cooperation is more critical	Internalisation choices	What governance models gear value creation? How do value-creation models influence governance choices?	What are the relevant constituencies that shape our purpose?	consider situational and temporal contexts?
MNEs' internal GI models are less favoured by current changes that shape globalisation	Global integration	What contextual factors drive value creation on global, local and ecosystem levels?	How do we maintain integrity and independence?	Are they providing useful working explanations for exploring futures
MNEs define their competitive positions based on internal resources/capabilities and those they access through their partners locally	Local responsiveness			and determining meaningful actions?

Notes: a Compare this with the section on emerging phenomena.
b Stakeholders' perspectives include those of owners, managers, employees, governments, government agencies, society at large, non-governmental organisations and future generations.

It may also allow us to build new bridges between economic perspectives dominating much of the IB discourse on MNEs' success and failure and the human agency perspectives that fundamentally wonder about "what people do" in the context in which they find themselves (Dörrenbächer and Geppert, 2017). Once we take a stance on *who we create value for with our explanations*, we can commence asking what constructs may be useful and how they are intertwined and complement other explanations. This will help to answer why these constructs generate value, considering parsimony and comprehensiveness, and how they anchor in larger theoretical organising frameworks that allow specific explanations to contribute to more complex and dynamic phenomena. To constitute a disciplinary core requires a fundamental theoretical platform on which to build the quest for theoretical development. This platform is concerned with particular types of phenomena. In the case of IB, these are systemic, dynamic and highly contextual in space and time.

There is one element missing that practitioners who are in roles of determining the fate of MNE are interested in. Where are we going? How do unfolding phenomena create the situations we will need to deal with in future, and what do we need to do now to set a positive trajectory? These kinds of concerns deal with questions of *agency* and *foresight* (e.g. Wiltbank et al., 2006), and the implicit nature of what knowledge we are certain about allows us to plan what actions we need to take to shape our understanding, and at the same time, influences how the environment in which we can succeed changes. The future orientation of research is implicitly assumed and as inherent in our theories as it is for natural sciences. Theories' function is to explain, and at least in a strict view, predict future instances. Newton's apple is subject to gravity. However, our research does not build natural science theories. The intertwined political, social, economic, technological and other systems create complexity and interdependencies. All these systems are driven by human agency, and they do not integrate into one inescapable outcome that can be readily predicted, and this is even less the case the further into the future we are looking. How can we bring this future orientation to a relevant research programme and approaches to carry out research?

11.4 An epistemology for theorising

We like to suggest, besides being attentive to ongoing changes and unfolding phenomena, strengthening a *futures* orientation in developing our field. The plural *futures* refers to the view that the future is not determined; it is in the making. Beyond the present and the past, no facts exist.

In the context of ice hockey, Wayne Gretzky is said to have commented, "Skate to where the puck is going, not where it has been". To increase relevance and influence, we need to entertain the implications for the field of IB when reflecting on the utility function of a theoretical contribution. The scope of utility, scientific or practical, is one dimension when assessing a theoretical contribution; the other is originality, whether incremental or revelatory (Corley and Gioia, 2011). Corley and Gioia (2011) ponder the question of how to increase the scope of utility by suggesting a *prescience* approach, leaning on Kuhn's (1962) terminology related to the post-positivist ideas of *Scientific Revolutions*, to fulfil "our scholarly role of facilitating organisational and societal adaptiveness" (Corley and Gioia, 2011: 12), applying that knowledge to the practice of management (Van de Ven, 1989).

According to Kuhn (1962), prescience is the first stage in the development of a disciplinary field, where paradigmatic pluralism prevails without dominating theories, practices or even a shared understanding of the key issues that would form a common or unifying direction for theoretical work. Corley and Gioia (2011) use numerous instances showing that organisational scholarship has become excessively distanced from practice such that language – and subsequently, understanding – has been divorced from the real-world context; it is to the point where practitioners have lost interest in academic papers due to missing value propositions. This is not concerning if we think that these are parallel worlds that do not need to be interacting. However, if our research activities should produce value beyond justifying the own existence, something needs to be done. As already discussed, the value of a theory and its relevance is perspective-based, idiosyncratic, situational and contextually and temporally inclined – a position we term *relevance-as-perspective*. How can we develop an approach to gain relevance and be more influential? What needs to be done to be part of the solution for important problems in significant organisational areas?

Our suggested trajectory is to acquire a *futures research orientation* that, rather than claiming possession of a crystal ball, develops and deploys potent epistemology about events and trajectories in the future, where no facts are yet available. It is a quest for truth-in-the-making. The foundation of an epistemology for future studies has been compellingly discussed in great detail, reviewing the major philosophical schools of thought of the last century, by Wendell Bell (2009). Spanning from the received view of positivism to post-positivist thought, including ideas of scientific revolutions, Bell (2009) derives the agreeable position that the future can be studied scientifically with the effect of pragmatically aligning scientific and practical utility. The philosophical stance generating this approach is *critical realism* (CR),[2] in which Bell (2009) articulates a post-Kuhnian theory of knowledge (Bell, 2009: 207). This philosophical perspective has been used by different researchers in IB (for a review, see Welch et al., 2011) and discussed by some who share similar concerns and agree that CR "offers an ontological position suited to illuminating organizations which operate at multiple levels, as exemplified by the MNC" (Rees and Smith, 2017: 267). This allows creating bridges between different perspectives on the MNE, cross-fertilising and integrating research interests in IB and International Management (see Dörrenbächer and Geppert, 2017).

It is fair to ask why CR is a useful approach for producing utility in futures-oriented research. The response is that it assumes ontological realism or the idea that reality exists independent from human constructions and knowledge of it (Skagestad, 1981). This perspective rests on the assumption that senses, and devices used for inquiry, are a source of "reasonable beliefs" (Bell, 2009: 211) rather than certain (and justified) knowledge. Reasonable beliefs imply that valid evidence exists in support of the belief. It differs from a positivist stance, which requires certainty of evidence, and shifts the criterion to the investigator who establishes valid evidence. While this alone is not a strong reason to assert trustworthiness, it assigns the responsibility of assessment to the scientific community to *critically* evaluate claims, and if validity is *reasonably questioned* and if needed based on evidence, to refute them, for instance, by applying a strategy of falsification. Thus, in CR, science is a collective effort to gradually improve an explanation through corrective means, producing a pragmatic quest for unveiling truth (Archer et al., 2013).

In our view, the philosophy of science described above is well suited for application in futures-oriented research. The future contains no facts but shares similarities to inquiry respecting uncertainties when studying the present and the past. Even if a proposition cannot be justified as being true, the belief in it "can be justified as being reasonable" (Bell, 2009: 221). The assessment of the proposition is an evolutionary, "fit-increasing process" (Bell, 2009: 213) driven by scrutiny of the scientific community. The mechanisms of selection, adaptation and retention increase the value of a proposition over time as the justified beliefs about the future in the past are compared with the emerging facts of the present. Yesterday's predictions, which are speculations, can be compared with and tested against today's facts.

This procedure eliminates far-reaching negative consequences in the quest for knowledge as it avoids what Popper (1957) termed historicism, or falling victim to the assumption that past trends or historic stages *as such* are valid foundations for predictions. Instead, they should be considered as facts that need to be understood in their situational, contextual and temporal setting; it should be recalled that they were produced by complex idiosyncratic *conditions*, and therefore, cannot be considered to imply a universal law. A stance well suited for IB research's knowledge about the future, however, is different compared to knowledge about the present and past because we only know the truth about future events after they occur, and at this stage, our knowledge will have become knowledge of the present or past.

The general idea of this application of CR towards futures research is that it "is reasonable to believe unrefuted rather than refuted hypotheses" (Musgrave, 1993: 172). It is pragmatic to *tentatively* accept them, even if they are unjustified in a strict sense, as in a view of certainty of truth, because they survived critical examinations up to that point. They provide the best available basis for deciding "what to do next" (cf. Wiltbank et al., 2006: 981), while acknowledging implicit uncertainties, which are treated with a collective corrective, as facts emerge and are subjected to critical examination. Thus, predictions that are based on reasonable beliefs are understood as reasonable because practitioners need to make decisions today that concern the uncertain future. Managers need to make plans from their own contextual understanding and carry them out with their best available knowledge and beliefs; in this way, they can adapt, control or alter the futures through their actions.

What is different here from most research undertaken in IB to date is the concern for this important function of research (to be useful in the real world) and becoming part of the active, exploratory sensemaking that goes into the process of understanding what is happening. We have many specific explanations that can be useful if we relate them to other specific explanations we know and we anchor them into larger organising frameworks, as illustrated above.

If we can accept this philosophy of science, then the next step is to think of methodological means that allow us to develop reasonable beliefs about possible futures. A useful concept for this futures research endeavour has been the concept of *posits*, developed by Reichenbach (1951). Posits can be used as statements about the future and treated *as if* or asking *what if* they were true, without knowing to what extent they will be true (Bell, 2009: 224). In principle, all posits are useful irrespective of their origin if they contain an imaginable possible future for which we can assign an estimate of the probability of their occurrence.[3]

The critical-realist scrutiny applied to posits and serious attempts at falsification sorts out those which constitute conjectural knowledge under the given initial conditions, and they remain as hypotheses that are adjusted and subject to revision while conditions change and phenomena unfold. Therefore, this approach constitutes an ongoing judgement of the reasonability of belief in a proposition about the future while events occur. This procedure acknowledges the additional threats to their validity due to greater uncertainty about the future than what we find in explanations about the past and present. The result is surrogate knowledge, as the posits contain the surviving propositions about the future after serious falsification attempts.

The result is also a wide range of *possible future outcomes* with diverse sets of probabilities assumed for them (Patomäki, 2006). In futures studies, not only are the most probable futures valuable, but quite improbable posits are also important to prepare for the unknown contingencies of the future. As practitioners act on these posits, some important effects come into play. The justified belief in future proposition may produce self-fulfilling prophecies for desirable future states, or alternatively, self-altering prophecies for negative outcomes because the projected negative outcomes produce reasons for changing the initial conditions under which posits were created. For instance, if we draw posits with the justified beliefs of negative outcomes of climate change, we might change the validity of the prophecy as such through the constitution of the prophecy. This is because human actors create actions to avoid such negative outcomes. At least, this remains what we should hope for, and ultimately, it shows the potential of futures research.[4]

To return to the question of utility of knowledge in our field, a futures research epistemology, with its many methods and techniques (e.g. Heinonen et al., 2017), opens up new possibilities for creating relevance and regaining voice for the IB research community. In light of the challenges humankind is facing, there should be no shortage of applications, if we consider the powerful role MNEs are playing in the world. The approach allows us to assist in the development of reasonable justified beliefs and theories about the future with posits of possible, probable and desirable outcomes and to establish how initial conditions, from a particular stakeholder's perspective, may create self-altering prophecies that set in motion the actions to avoid some of the most undesirable of these propositions and hypotheses. This would allow us to define what, how, why and for whom we develop knowledge, as illustrated in Table 11.2.

The strength of this approach is its inherent quest for self-correction of posits, when surprising outcomes emerge (Lawson, 2003). It allows us to return to the initial assumptions and reconsider how the contextual understanding might have changed, creating alternative causes of effects (cf. Welch et al., 2011) and altering conceptualisations when new facts emerge. This approach is different from mainstream IB research[5] because it takes situational, spatial and temporal contexts and ongoing changes seriously; it does not rely only on the given empirical observations but accepts that new evidence, including non-confirming evidence, will surface and allow us to change our best understanding, and subsequently, alter our explanations. This meshes with the theorising through envelopes idea outlined above, an approach that we accept as being as enabling as it is limiting due to initial choices based on relevance perspectives. Envelopes and the relationships between them are open for theorising in the sense that they give room to consider adding new theoretical ideas, which emerge as useful explanations when the world is changing in unexpected ways.

11.5 Concluding remarks

Closing the loop from this epistemological excursion back to the IB research thematic, we discuss the suggestions made in this chapter by presenting our overall thesis, which has the ambition for IB to regain influence on important stakeholders (who might find they cannot afford not to listen to us), respecting the question of the scholarly and practical utility of theorising. We prefer, as the previous section may have revealed, the idea of theorising (Weick, 1995) as a process of developing our understanding, and subsequently our explanations, over the end product of a theory; this is because social systems are open, not operating in isolated, recurring or stationary systems, as Popper (1957) characterised, for instance, the solar system and physicists trying to understand the underlying laws of how it functions.

In conclusion, our chapter commenced with a view that the world of IB is continuously changing, and these changes have far-reaching consequences. Changes generate systems level effects through human agency (and its reactions to changes in the natural world) in political, economic, social and technological systems' interactions and based on interdependencies, which can create unforeseeable consequences and new developmental trajectories. Against this backdrop, it is apparent that even our theoretical knowledge is rich; it cannot be complete for all possible occurrences that may emerge in the future. Therefore, it must be open for revision, refutations, extensions and repurposing.

Theoretical knowledge is dispersed, and at the same time, focused on specific and partial phenomena. However, our discipline is arguably based on two main interests. First, it deals with the complexities of organisations and their international activities, across many variants of externally intertwined systems;

second, it is about business, taking a stance to serve as integrator, among other related disciplines, to understand how partial and specific explanations relate to each other and the bigger picture. In this way, it puts forth the criteria for choices that have to be parsimonious and comprehensive.

IB is an integrative field of investigation dealing with complex phenomena, such as globalisation, and activities of complex types of organisations, such as MNEs and their responses to the environments that enable or limit them in often uncertain ways. Exploring in this context is critical because it drives us to gain a better understanding when conditions change. As Bateson (1972: xvi) notes, "An explorer can never know what he is exploring until it has been explored". Therefore, we see theorising as an action that allows us to make assumptions about the future, which has not yet happened, and base our actions on them to later see, once facts emerge, which assumptions have turned out to be useful and which have not.

Theorising requires a perspective; otherwise, relevance – as well as parsimony – is difficult to achieve. There is no theory of everything. If we make choices regarding which envelope frameworks serve a perspective, then we will have anchor points that allow us to establish new integrated theoretical posits that are linked to international and business phenomena, rather than theorising in a vacuum. Instead of becoming political, in the form of fiercely defended paradigms, these frameworks need to remain open and inclusive for new ideas that may explain how the world is changing; they need to be proactive but critical when the future of yesterday produces the facts of today.

Notes

1. Share prices are constantly changing for numerous reasons and therefore such comparisons provide limited information.
2. This philosophical point of view has been discussed under a number of terms, including *fallibilist realism*, *critical rationalism* and *critical empiricism*.
3. In 1916, Albert Einstein predicted the existence of gravitational waves based on his general theory of relativity; in 2016, they could be observed for the first time due to technological advances made over the past 100 years.
4. See the Club of Rome predictions of 1972 and the possible self-altering effects they may have had on policymakers to avoid the dark scenarios the report was drawing (Meadows et al., 1972).
5. Welch et al. (2011: 12) showed that this type of research constitutes a clear minority of articles in the highest ranked journals publishing IB research (i.e. case studies in *AMJ*, *JIBS* and *JMS*, 1999–2008).

References

Ahen, F. and Zettinig, P. (2015). What is the biggest question in CSR research? *Foresight*, 17(3): 274–290.

Archer, M., Bhaskar, R., Collier, A., Lawson, T. and Norrie, A. (Eds) (2013). *Critical Realism: Essential Readings*. London: Routledge.

Banerjee, S., Venaik, S. and Brewer, P. (2019). Analysing corporate political activity in MNC subsidiaries through the integration-responsiveness framework. *International Business Review*, 28(5): 101498.

Bartlett, C.A. and Ghoshal, S. (1987). Managing across borders: New strategic requirements. *Sloan Management Review*, 28(4): 7–17.

Bartlett, C.A. and Ghoshal, S. (1991). Global strategic management: Impact on the new frontiers of strategy research. *Strategic Management Journal*, 12(S1): 5–16.

Bateson, G. (1972). *Steps to an Ecology of Mind*. New York: Ballantine.

Bell, W. (2009). *Foundations of Futures Studies: History, Purposes, Knowledge. Volume I: Human Science for a New Era*. Piscataway, NJ: Transaction Publishers.

Buckley, P.J., Clegg, L.J., Voss, H., Cross, A.R., Liu, X. and Zheng, P. (2018). A retrospective and agenda for future research on Chinese outward foreign direct investment. *Journal of International Business Studies*, 49(1): 4–23.

Buckley, P.J., Doh, J.P. and Benischke, M.H. (2017). Towards a renaissance in international business research? Big questions, grand challenges, and the future of IB scholarship. *Journal of International Business Studies*, 48(9): 1045–1064.

Bughin, J., Manyika, J. and Woetzel, J. (2019). *Globalization in Transition: The Future of Trade and Value Chains*. New York: McKinsey Global Institute.

Collinson, S. (2017). The declining relevance and legitimacy of IB scholarship in a world that really needs it. *AIB Insights*, 17(2): 7–10.

Corley, K.G. and Gioia, D.A. (2011). Building theory about theory building: What constitutes a theoretical contribution? *Academy of Management Review*, 36(1): 12–32.

Delios, A. (2017). The death and rebirth (?) of international business research. *Journal of Management Studies*, 54(3): 391–397.

Dörrenbächer, C. and Gammelgaard, J. (2019). Critical and mainstream international business research. *Critical Perspectives on International Business*, 15(2/3): 239–261.

Dörrenbächer, C. and Geppert, M. (Eds) (2017). *Multinational Corporations and Organization Theory: Post Millennium Perspectives*. Bingley: Emerald Group Publishing.

Dunning, J.H. (1958). *American Investment in British Manufacturing Industry*. London: Routledge.

Dunning, J.H. (2000). The eclectic paradigm as an envelope for economic and business theories of MNE activity. *International Business Review*, 9(2): 163–190.

Geppert, M. (2015). Reflections on the methods of how we present and compare the political contents of our research: A prerequisite for critical institutional research. *Journal of Management Inquiry*, 24(1): 100–104.

Heinonen, S., Kuusi, O. and Salminen, H. (Eds) (2017). *How to Explore Our Futures? Acta Futura Fennica 10*. Helsinki: Finnish Society for Futures Studies.

Itaki, M. (1991). A critical assessment of the eclectic theory of the multinational enterprise. *Journal of International Business Studies*, 22(3): 445–460.

Kano, L. (2018). Global value chain governance: A relational perspective. *Journal of International Business Studies*, 49(6): 684–705.

Kostova, T., Marano, V. and Tallman, S. (2016). Headquarters–subsidiary relationships in MNCs: Fifty years of evolving research. *Journal of World Business*, 51(1): 176–184.

Kuhn, T.S. (1962). *The Structure of Scientific Revolutions*. Chicago: University of Chicago Press.

Lawson, T. (2003). *Reorienting Economics*. London: Routledge.

Meadows, D.H., Meadows, D.L., Randers, J. and Behrens, W.W. (1972). *The Limits to Growth: A Report to the Club of Rome*. New York: Universe Books.

Mees-Buss, J., Welch, C. and Westney, D.E. (2019). What happened to the transnational? The emergence of the neo-global corporation. *Journal of International Business Studies*, 50(9): 1513–1543.

Meyer, K.E. (2007). Contextualising organisational learning: Lyles and Salk in the context of their research. *Journal of International Business Studies*, 38(1): 27–37.

Michailova, S. (2011). Contextualizing in international business research: Why do we need more of it and how can we be better at it? *Scandinavian Journal of Management*, 27(1): 129–139.

Musgrave, A. (1993). *Common Sense, Science and Scepticism: A Historical Introduction to the Theory of Knowledge*. Cambridge: Cambridge University Press.

Oesterle, M.J. and Wolf, J. (2011). 50 years of management international review and IB/IM research. *Management International Review*, 51(6): 735–754.

Patomäki, H. (2006). Realist ontology for futures studies. *Journal of Critical Realism*, 5(1): 1–31.

Piekkari, R., Welch, C. and Paavilainen, E. (2009). The case study as disciplinary convention: Evidence from international business journals. *Organizational Research Methods*, 12(3): 567–589.

Pitelis, C.N. and Teece, D.J. (2018). The new MNE: 'Orchestration' theory as envelope of 'internalisation' theory. *Management International Review*, 58(4): 523–539.

Popper, K. (1957). *The Poverty of Historicism*. London: Routledge & Kegan Paul.

Prahalad, C.K. and Doz, Y.L. (1987). *The Multinational Mission: Balancing Local Demands and Global Vision*. New York: Simon & Schuster.

PWC (2018). *Global Top 100 Companies by Market Capitalization*. https://www.pwc.com/gx/en/audit-services/assets/pdf/global-top-100-companies-2018-report.pdf (retrieved 8 October 2019).

Rees, C. and Smith, C. (2017). Applying critical realism to the MNC: Exploring new realities in staffing and expatriation. In C. Dörrenbächer and M. Geppert (Eds), *Multinational Corporations and Organization Theory: Post Millennium Perspectives*. Bingley: Emerald Group Publishing, 265–293.

Reichenbach, H. (1951). The verifiability theory of meaning. *Proceedings of the American Academy of Arts and Sciences*, 80(1): 46–60.

Siggelkow, N. (2007). Persuasion with case studies. *Academy of Management Journal*, 50(1): 20–24.

Skagestad, P. (1981). *The Road of Inquiry: Charles Peirce's Pragmatic Realism*. New York: Columbia University Press.

Strange, R. and Zucchella, A. (2017). Industry 4.0, global value chains and international business. *Multinational Business Review*, 25(3): 174–184.

The Economist (2017). The retreat of the global company (28 January). https://www.economist.com/briefing/2017/01/28/the-retreat-of-the-global-company (retrieved 2 March 2017).

Tsui, A.S. (2004). Contributing to global management knowledge: A case for high quality indigenous research. *Asia Pacific Journal of Management*, 21(4): 491–513.

Van Alstyne, M.W., Parker, G.G. and Choudary, S.P. (2016). Pipelines, platforms, and the new rules of strategy. *Harvard Business Review*, 94(4): 54–62.
Van de Ven, A.H. (1989). Nothing is quite so practical as a good theory. *Academy of Management Review*, 14(4): 486–489.
Venaik, S. and Midgley, D.F. (2019). Archetypes of marketing mix standardization-adaptation in MNC subsidiaries: Fit and equifinality as complementary explanations of performance. *European Journal of Marketing*, 53(2): 366–399.
Weick, K.E. (1995). What theory is not, theorizing is. *Administrative Science Quarterly*, 40(3): 385–390.
Welch, C., Piekkari, R., Plakoyiannaki, E. and Paavilainen-Mäntymäki, E. (2011). Theorising from case studies: Towards a pluralist future for international business research. *Journal of International Business Studies*, 42(5): 740–762.
Westney, E.D. (2019). Changing MNEs. *Japan Academy of Multinational Enterprises*, 5(2): 1–7.
Whetten, D.A. (1989). What constitutes a theoretical contribution? *Academy of Management Review*, 14(4): 490–495.
Wiltbank, R., Dew, N., Read, S. and Sarasvathy, S.D. (2006). What to do next? The case for non-predictive strategy. *Strategic Management Journal*, 27(10): 981–998.

PART V

Commentary

12. Commentary on fulfilling the future agenda in international business

Jonathan P. Doh

12.1   Introduction

International business (IB) scholars are known for self-reflection, self-criticism and self-doubt. Some surmise that this tendency emanates from the character of the field itself; namely that it is relatively new, derivative of allied behavioural and social sciences, and relies upon vague and poorly specified concepts – such as "context" – to define itself (Buckley et al., 2017). An alternative perspective is that this predisposition reflects the reality that the phenomena studied by IB scholars are in a state of constant fluctuation and change and that this change is increasingly non-ergodic (Cantwell et al., 2010) in which the future cannot be extrapolated from the past. I personally find truth in both of these interpretations, but in either case, IB scholarship naturally calls for periodic reassessment and rejuvenation. Whichever explanation is more persuasive, IB as a field has been especially evolutionary in nature as it has undergone constant reformulation in relation to the IB environment and has been subject to dynamic interactions with other fields within and outside of business.

It is in this context that Bozkurt and Geppert have assembled this impressive volume that features a range of scholars commenting upon – and contributing to – the IB research agenda. The contributions to this book reflect the diversity, breadth and wide expanse of topics, approaches and insights of the field itself. They span the full range of IB debates and controversies. Indeed, this volume offers a convenient entry into the most vigorous, controversial and pressing areas for inquiry in IB and it also outlines the most productive pathways for future research.

12.2   Comments on the chapters

In Chapter 2, Strange revisits a longstanding debate in IB regarding the core purpose and role of the multinational enterprise and the concept of "internalisation" as a theoretical explanation for the existence of the multinational enterprises (MNEs) (Buckley and Casson, 1991). Recognising the advent of factoryless goods producers and the challenges of governance over globally dispersed activities within what have been called global value chains, Strange proposes a new theory of externalisation as a counterpoint to internalisation that has guided IB for decades. He uses the examples of companies such as Apple in the smartphone sector, Nike and Adidas in the footwear industry, and a number of others that operate more as design, marketing and distribution companies that outsource their production to contract manufacturers. He emphasises "isolating mechanisms" and the governance and control vehicle for exerting influence in this loosely structured environment and determining how value additions are distributed among the various participants in global value chains (GVCs). This contribution nicely integrates literature on internalisation, outsourcing, and GVCs to generate a novel and thought-provoking addition to the IB theory toolkit.

Behavioural perspectives have gained considerable traction in a range of disciplines, especially economics. In IB, scholars are increasingly interested in the micro-level cognitive influences on IB decision-making. In their contribution to the volume, Nardella, Narula and Surdu argue that most IB theorising does not account for these factors and influences. In particular, they argue that firm-specific heterogeneity cannot be fully incorporated into empirical models without considering the realities of behavioural perspectives, in particular "cognitive limitations, availability biases and heuristics". Indeed, they suggest that these perspectives are especially important in decisions involving considerable risk, uncertainty and therefore highly consequential outcomes. Observing the wide range of both public policy and international business responses to the COVID-19 pandemic and its social and economic reverberations underscores this viewpoint. Indeed, scholars' suggestion that we are in a period of "non-ergodic" change in which executives and managers face true "Knightian" uncertainty serves to reinforce this basic thesis. Under such conditions, it would seem folly not to recognise the behavioural influences on IB decision-making.

When I assumed the role of Editor in Chief of the *Journal of World Business* in 2014, I wrote my first editorial on the topic of "Why we need phenomenon-based research in international business" (Doh, 2015). In 2017, Delios made a similar pitch, but couched in a more critical tone. It is in this spirit that Zettinig and Nummela offer a perspective on IB scholarship that emphasises connection to real-world phenomena, derived from real-world observation, and situated in the realities of complex and evolving global systems. They aptly focus on "futures-oriented IB research" that stresses curiosity, openness and inclusivity and rejects simplistic, reductionist and statistically driven explanations that have little connection to reality. They also suggest widening the lens of IB research to incorporate important global phenomena that transcend "business" but nonetheless have great relevance to the interactions of business and society. These include modern slavery, global structural violence, international money laundering, organised crime, corruption and other "neglected crises".

There is increasing interest in the influence of "the home country" in the process of internationalisation. Historically, IB scholarship has focused on firms engaging in internationalisation processes that originate in a developed country and "move" to developed or developing countries. A recent special issue on the various ways home countries influence internationalisation has highlighted this perspective (Cuervo-Cazurra et al., 2018). In this regard, the chapter by Becker-Ritterspach and Fourati continues this direction by exploring this phenomenon, with an emphasis on the *constraining or enabling* role of home country conditions. This chapter offers a nice synthesis of this literature, the important phenomena that it has explored, and importantly, links this research agenda to established theoretical perspectives in IB, showing how home country perspectives and influence may call for modification or alteration of existing IB theory.

IB scholars have become increasingly interested in critical perspectives on international business. There is a longstanding tradition in management of "critical management studies" scholars who take a more challenging and questioning perspective about core assumptions in conventional business management scholarship. The journal *Critical Perspectives on International Business* has gained traction and published a number of high impact articles, special issues and commentaries. It is in this tradition that the chapter by Dörrenbächer and Ellermann takes as a starting point the provocative contribution to the *Academy of Management Review* by Andrew Crane's (2013) on modern slavery. They first review a range of conceptual and theoretical frameworks and perspectives that have sought to understand the conditions that may lead to higher incidence of modern slavery as well as those contexts that result in lower instances. They then seek to operationalise some of the dimensions Crane outlined, which include the regulatory, socioeconomic, industry, geographical and cultural context. They pay particular attention to the cultural context, concluding that a high power distance context is associated with modern slavery and high individualism (versus collectivism) is associated with lower incidence of modern slavery. Although this analysis is largely undertaken through simple correlations, it is a helpful, preliminary analysis that provides some empirical support for Crane's theoretical intuitions regarding this important – and troubling – modern phenomenon.

The rise of emerging economy multinational corporations (EMNCs) has attracted significant interest among management scholars (for a review, see Luo and Zhang, 2016). In particular, scholars have proposed that emerging market firms may have different motivations and approaches to internationalisation when compared to traditional developed country companies. In line with this reasoning, Luo and Tung (2007) introduced the notion of highly rapid internationalisation of emerging market multinationals, a paradox given that such emerging markets are thought to lack the institutional infrastructure necessary for successful internationalisation. This "springboard" perspective suggests that emerging market firms may, in fact, internationalise rapidly to *overcome* their inherently inferior firm-specific resource base, due to weak home-country institutional and market conditions. Indeed, overcoming these obstacles may equip EMNCs with the knowledge and experience to effectively deploy those same resources in their target destination, often a developed country (Gubbi et al., 2010). Ursula Mense-Petermann makes the case that this phenomenon deserves greater attention and analysis, especially EMNCs from China. She argues, however, that the literature to date has focused primarily on the antecedents and patterns of EMNC internationalisation but that the internal workings of EMNCs, that is the actual HQ–subsidiary relations EMNCs establish, subsidiary roles and mandates, post-merger integration (PMI) processes, and knowledge transfer – all well researched topics for mature MNCs headquartered in advanced economies – have not yet been scrutinised in IB studies, and research that sheds light into the "black box" of EMNCs is virtually non-existent. She also makes the case that although the intentions of EMNCs – again especially those from China – have been scrutinised from a geopolitical perspective, these analyses have not included explicit attention to the impact of EMNCs' internationalisation on the host country and that the literature has not fully considered the embeddedness of EMNCs in a wider geopolitical context.

International economic diplomacy (IED) is a topic of longstanding interest to scholars of international political economy (IPE) and, to some extent, international business (IB). Given high-profile recent developments in the global context that involve both governments and MNEs (Brexit, US withdrawal from the Trans-Pacific Partnership Agreement and Paris Climate Accord) and the rise of new forms of global private regulation, there is renewed interest in the role of MNEs as diplomatic agents in the global political economic arena. It is in this context that Brent Burmester urges us to reconsider and rediscover the global role of MNEs as diplomatic actors. In this regard, he builds on the literature on economic and corporate diplomacy. He notes that early IB scholars such as Vernon and others focused on the role of MNEs as international diplomatic agents and urges that this perspective be reintegrated into IB theorising. He suggests that MNEs should be seen as actors with a complex international global-economic system rather than as autonomous agents seeking to navigate and respond to various country and international pressures. He uses recent anecdotal and popular examples to underscore the active role that MNEs have in global diplomatic interactions, especially in the COVID-19 environment. He draws from political science and international relations to consider the MNE's credentials as an *international actor*.

Suma Athreye returns to the issue of context to explore outward investment from emerging markets. She examines this phenomenon through the lens of context and interdisciplinarity in IB research. She traces the evolution of emerging markets outward investment with reference to the various IB theories that have been used to explain it, namely the FSA/CSA framework as developed by Rugman and colleagues. After reviewing this perspective, she then widens the lens to detail the practical phenomenological forces that are not fully incorporated in the historical theoretical traditions, namely the pressures from global financial markets, the role of wealthy migrants and their resources, and other practice factors that facilitate and constrain outward investment by emerging market firms. She proposes that a real options approach is a more suitable and flexible way to think about outward investment by emerging market MNEs.

12.3 Concluding thoughts

The field of international business has much to offer in understanding global economic and business history, charting the emergence, impact and strategy of multinational enterprises, and making sense of contemporary global phenomena. This volume adds to the collection of critiques regarding the shortcomings of IB and the qualities that it was founded upon and may need to rediscover. These include a broad, integrative perspective that calls for consideration of the range of stakeholders – business, government, civil society – an interdisciplinary approach that leverages theory and frameworks from allied social sciences, and a clear emphasis on important contemporary phenomena. This volume provides a strong foundation in these imperatives, and provides productive directions for future research.

The COVID-19 pandemic and its social and economic ramifications challenge many long-held assumptions in politics, economics, and management, and IB is no exception. Although it is a catastrophic and heart-breaking development, it also provides a sort of natural experiment for IB scholars to take a close and critical look on what we do and how we do it. This volume offers a strong basis for restoring, revitalising and reimagining the field of international business in light of challenging global phenomena such as COVID-19 and others yet to come.

References

Buckley, P.J. and Casson, M. (1991). *The Future of the Multinational Enterprise*, 2nd edition. Basingstoke: Macmillan.

Buckley, P., Doh, J.P. and Benischke, M.H. (2017). Towards a renaissance in international business research? Big questions, grand challenges, and the future of IB scholarship. *Journal of International Business Studies*, 48(9): 1045–1064.

Cantwell, J., Dunning, J.H. and Lundan, S.M. (2010). An evolutionary approach to understanding international business activity: The co-evolution of MNEs and the institutional environment. *Journal of International Business Studies*, 41(4): 567–586.

Crane, A. (2013). Modern slavery as a management practice: Exploring the conditions and capabilities for human exploitation. *Academy of Management Review*, 38(1): 49–69.

Cuervo-Cazurra, A., Ciravegna, L., Melgarejo, M. and Lopez, L. (2018). Home country uncertainty and the internationalization-performance relationship: Building an uncertainty management capability. *Journal of World Business*, 53(2): 209–221.

Delios, A. (2017). The death and rebirth (?) of international business research. *Journal of Management Studies*, 54(3): 391–397.

Doh, J.P. (2015). From the editor: Why we need phenomenon-based research in international business. *Journal of World Business*, 50(4): 609–611.

Gubbi, S., Aulakh, P., Ray, S., Sarkar, M.B. and Chittoor, R. (2010). Do international acquisitions by emerging economy firms create shareholder value? The case of Indian firms. *Journal of International Business Studies*, 41(3): 397–418.

Luo, Y. and Tung, R.L. (2007). International expansion of emerging market enterprises: A springboard perspective. *Journal of International Business Studies*, 38(4): 481–498.

Luo, Y. and Zhang, H. (2016). Emerging market MNEs: Qualitative review and theoretical directions. *Journal of International Management*, 22(4): 333–350.

Index

Printed and bound by CPI Group (UK) Ltd, Croydon, CR0 4YY

16/04/2025

14658485-0003